GEORGE W. BUSH'S HEALTHY FORESTS
Reframing the Environmental Debate

Jacqueline Vaughn and Hanna J. Cortner

GEORGE W. BUSH'S HEALTHY FORESTS
Reframing the Environmental Debate

university press of colorado

Published by the University Press of Colorado
5589 Arapahoe Avenue, Suite 206C
Boulder, Colorado 80303

AAUP All rights reserved
Printed in the United States of America

The University Press of Colorado is a proud member of
the Association of American University Presses.

The University Press of Colorado is a cooperative publishing enterprise supported, in part, by
Adams State College, Colorado State University, Fort Lewis College, Mesa State College,
Metropolitan State College of Denver, University of Colorado, University of Northern Colorado,
and Western State College of Colorado.

∞ The paper used in this publication meets the minimum requirements of the American
National Standard for Information Sciences—Permanence of Paper for Printed Library Materials.
ANSI Z39.48-1992

Library of Congress Cataloging-in-Publication Data

Switzer, Jacqueline Vaughn.
  George W. Bush's healthy forests : reframing the environmental debate / Jacqueline Vaughn and
Hanna J. Cortner.
    p. cm.
  Includes bibliographical references.
  ISBN 0-87081-817-1 (hardcover : alk. paper) — ISBN 0-87081-820-1 (pbk. : alk. paper)
1. Forest policy—United States. 2. Forest management—United States. 3. Forest management—
Environmental aspects—United States. I. Cortner, H. (Hanna), 1945– II. Title.
  SD565.S85 2005
  333.75'0973—dc22
                                                                            2005011173

Design by Daniel Pratt

14 13 12 11 10 09 08 07 06 05   10 9 8 7 6 5 4 3 2 1

In memory of Warren "Bud" Day
—JV

To Richard and Barbara, again
—HC

THIS PROJECT ORIGINALLY DEVELOPED AS A RESULT OF RESEARCH AND SEMINARS WE CONDUCTED with graduate students at Northern Arizona University and their interest in administrative rulemaking within the U.S.D.A. Forest Service. The authors wish especially to thank Gretchen Teich and Jim Buthman, who helped develop and maintain the database for the study. Other students who assisted in researching case studies include Jonathan D. Bakker, T. C. Eberly, Kristina Fernandez, Jason Kirchner, Andrew J. Meador, Rod Parish, Franklin Pemberton, Chris Seck, and Tara Tribuna.

Our thanks also go to Mike Anderson of The Wilderness Society and the anonymous reviewers who made comments on the manuscript. At the University Press of Colorado, we appreciate the continuing support of acquisitions editor Sandy Crooms, who initially expressed interest in the book proposal.

We would also like to thank the Ecological Restoration Institute at Northern Arizona University for its financial support of portions of the research. The assistance and support of these individuals and institutions was critical and appreciated, but we alone accept responsibility for any conclusions or errors of omission or commission.

ANILCA	Alaska National Interest Lands Conservation Act
APA	Administrative Procedure Act
ARA	Appeals Reform Act
AWR	Alliance for the Wild Rockies
BLM	Bureau of Land Management
BRC	Blue Ribbon Coalition
CBD	Center for Biological Diversity
CE	categorical exclusion
CEQ	Council on Environmental Quality
CFR	*Code of Federal Regulations*
CRS	Congressional Research Service
CTFHP	Crimson Tide Forest Health Project
EA	Environmental Assessment
ECL	End Commercial Lobbying Campaign
EFF	Electronic Frontier Foundation
EIS	environmental impact statements
EPA	Environmental Protection Agency
FLPMA	Federal Land Policy and Management Act

FOIA	Freedom of Information Act
FONSI	Finding of No Significant Impact
GAO	General Accounting Office (now Government Accountability Office)
HFRA	Healthy Forests Restoration Act
IBLA	Interior Board of Land Appeals
IFA	Intermountain Forest Association
LCV	League of Conservation Voters
LRMP	land and resource management plan
MOA	Memorandum of Agreement
MSLF	Mountain States Legal Foundation
NAPA	National Academy of Public Administration
NEPA	National Environmental Policy Act
NFMA	National Forest Management Act
NFP	National Fire Plan
NFPA	National Forest Protection Alliance
NLAA	not likely to adversely affect
NOAA	National Oceanic and Atmospheric Administration
NRDC	Natural Resources Defense Council
NWFP	Northwest Forest Plan
OHA	Office of Hearings and Appeals
OHV	off highway vehicle
OIRA	Office of Information and Regulatory Affairs
OMB	Office of Management and Budget
OSHA	Occupational Safety and Health Administration
OTA	Office of Technology Assessment
PMA	President's Management Agenda
RPA	Forest and Rangeland Renewable Resources Planning Act
TFANG	House Task Force for Affordable Natural Gas

GEORGE W. BUSH'S HEALTHY FORESTS

Reframing the Environmental Debate

A REVERSAL OF FORTUNES
Reframing the Environmental Debate

ON OCTOBER 21, 2003, A SERIES OF FOURTEEN FIRES ERUPTED IN SOUTHERN CALIFORNIA. The following week, President George W. Bush declared Los Angeles, San Bernardino, San Diego, and Ventura Counties major disaster areas. On November 4, with Governor Gray Davis on his left and Governor-elect Arnold Schwarzenegger on his right,[1] the president appeared in El Cajon, California, an area affected by the Cedar Fire, the largest in the state's history, to thank fire fighters and volunteers. The California fires burned 750,000 acres, killed 24 people, resulted in 237 serious injuries, destroyed 3,719 homes, and cost roughly $123 million to suppress.[2] Although making precise estimates of fire costs is an inexact process, state agencies and local governments emerged from the fire facing whopping bills for their allotted share of fire costs. By the end of the year San Diego County's costs alone had already reached an estimated $38 million—and were projected to grow.[3]

Many credit the California fires with speeding passage of the Healthy Forests Restoration Act (HFRA), a legislative response to President Bush's Healthy Forests Initiative.[4] The initiative, which Bush announced in Oregon in August 2002 after visiting the sites of the state's Biscuit and Squire Fires,[5] sought to change the direction of forest policy and step up forest thinning to reduce the massive buildup of flammable fuels that had accumulated in the nation's forests. The principal mechanism for policy change would be through regulatory reform. Although Bush declared that he remained committed to allowing citizens to have a voice, his Healthy Forests Initiative limited the use of environmental analysis, administrative appeals, and litigation. The president portrayed Forest Service administrative appeals (procedures available by law to those questioning activities proposed by the agency) and litigation as regulatory hurdles and red tape that kept forest managers from implementing high priority fuel reduction projects. Striking at the heart of administrative and legal mechanisms that had been effectively used for many years by citizens and environmental groups to press forward their environmental goals and objectives, the initiative would prove to be highly controversial.

In the time between the announcement of the initiative and passage of the legislation, Bush had made several visits to fire areas throughout the West and had devoted his weekly radio address to the subject of forest health. Even though it is questionable whether the healthy forests legislation or landscape-scale fuels reduction in the backcountry would have done anything to stop or prevent California's wind-driven fires from rushing through fire-prone chaparral vegetation,[6] the fires provided a critical push. There is no doubt that Bush exerted considerable leadership to gather political support and media attention in support of forest thinning, the Healthy Forests Initiative, and the Healthy Forests Restoration Act. Forest health became one of the most visible of the president's initiatives related to environmental and natural resource issues. And because, for the first time since the age of environmentalism began in the late 1960s and early 1970s, Republicans controlled the White House, both houses of Congress, and, with the election of Governor Schwarzenegger, twenty-eight of the fifty state governorships, the issue offered an opportunity for Bush and the Republicans to not only redirect the nation's forest policy but also reframe more generally the entire environmental policy agenda. This book tells the story of how administrative appeals and wildfires were strategically joined in the forest health issue, which facilitated the passage of the Healthy Forests Restoration Act and the changing of a multitude of administrative regulations related to the National Environmental Policy Act (NEPA), wildfire, and forest policy.

ISSUE DEFINITION, AGENDA SETTING, AND POLICY ADOPTION

Scholars traditionally have focused on two approaches to understanding the intricacies of the public policymaking process. One approach views policymaking as a series of rational, component steps that begin with the identification of a problem, followed by its appearance on the political agenda where alternatives for addressing the problem are offered and policy formulated. Policy is then adopted, implemented, and evaluated.[7] A second approach describes the policymaking process as illogical, disorderly, and unstructured—a "primeval soup" where conflicts exist over the nature and extent of problems, and where policy is often based on compromise and limited information rather than the "best" solution.[8] We rely on both approaches, focusing particularly on how problems are identified and redefined by various stakeholders as they emerge on the political agenda and work themselves through various steps of the policy process.

Much has been written about the agenda setting process. Not all problems present in society receive governmental attention, and agenda setting can be thought of as the process by which selected problems rise to prominence in the political arena and are deemed worthy of governmental consideration and action. Several theoretical frameworks related to agenda setting are appropriate to a discussion of wildfires and forest policy.

The first framework used to understand agenda setting is the concept of ownership and the ways in which issues are framed. It is important that issues be framed in such a way that they are considered legitimate for governmental attention. How a particular issue is framed may also determine which particular institutional structures or groups of individuals are considered legitimate for addressing it.[9] Ownership establishes the boundaries of debate and conditions political relationships.

Social images that are expressed in symbols, linguistic forms, stereotypical metaphors, models, and myths are important components of framing, as is an appeal to public values.[10] Rhetoric, the use of words by human agents to form attitudes or to induce actions in other human agents, is "rooted in the use of language as a symbolic means of inducing cooperation in beings that by nature respond to symbols."[11] Specific terms that relate to emotional appeals, allusions, metaphorical substitutions, and repetitions are used to frame and define problems. How the targets of proposed policy actions are socially constructed is also a powerful factor.[12] Reductions in welfare programs, for example, become more palatable when targets of the policy are socially portrayed as "welfare queens" and not the deserving poor; and protection of old-growth forests becomes more desirable when those forests are defined as virgin forests rather than "biological deserts." Policy reversals are facilitated when the good guys become the bad guys (an event common in foreign affairs as dictators fall in and out of favor depending on diplomatic objectives), or when groups of people (for example, gays) are reclassified as individuals deserving of rights rather than as deviants.

A second pertinent framework is what several theorists call the mobilization model of agenda setting. This takes place when political leaders formulate a policy change, then seek support for the change by appealing to public biases.[13] Mobilization of bias inherently involves conflict, which causes different leaders seeking different policy outcomes to struggle against one another. "Advocates for change work to convince more people that they will be positively affected by the new policy. Defenders of the status quo will fight to narrow the scope of the issue."[14] As an issue becomes more controversial, stakeholders compete for a role in the policy venue. "The implication here is that the public believes that the status quo is not adequate. Policy changes are needed. Responding to public demands, new agents struggle for a policymaking role."[15] Congress, for example, has become increasingly and more frequently involved in Forest Service activities and decision making, as evidenced by the growing number of requests for agency testimony in hearings and Forest Service–related bills and amendments introduced and enacted.[16] Sometimes, agenda setting is paired with agenda denial as opponents of change use cultural strategies such as avoidance, attack, and redefinition to impede and defeat policy initiatives.[17]

Much of agenda setting, policy formulation, and policy adoption is about issue definition and redefinition and involves elements of both frameworks. Those supporting smoking bans define the issue as a health concern, while opponents attempt to define the issue as one of individual rights. How an issue is defined may even determine if it is a problem worthy of serious governmental attention. Obesity may be recognized as a growing national health problem by many experts, but it is not one that policymakers have addressed broadly by laws or regulations yet. The targets for any policy action are too numerous, most options offered to date require a change in individual behavior and are likely to be perceived as punitive, and powerful interests, such as the fast-food industry, are hard at work to ensure agenda denial.

How problems are framed affects the kinds of solutions offered.[18] For example, defining Arizona's water problems as a lack of adequate supply favors solutions aimed at finding additional water sources. When the problems are defined as a matter of allocation, solutions center around water conservation or moving water from farming to industrial and municipal uses. The fate of proposed solutions also depends on the way problems and causes are framed.[19] Solutions to pollution problems, for instance, can deal with immediate or proximate causes, such as visible smokestack emissions, or with societal conditions far removed from actual pollution, such as population growth rates or affluence and consumption. Solutions related to societal conditions are more difficult to achieve and less comprehensible to the average citizen.[20]

Many times solutions lie dormant, waiting for an opportunity to attach themselves to a problem—a focusing event.[21] For example, reducing speed limits may not be feasible as a safety issue, but a crisis in energy supply may prompt decision makers to adopt the solution once it is defined as energy conservation. If issues can be reframed, once-favored solutions to problems may become defined as problems, and solutions thought infeasible may gain favor. For example, dams, once seen as multipurpose solutions for controlling floods, providing secure water supplies, furnishing cheap electric power, and providing recreational opportunities, are now seen as major environmental problems. Dam removal—once unthinkable— is now a feasible policy action.[22] Some problems continually alternate between being problems or solutions, as is the case with deficit spending.

Once a precedent is set in one area, it has spillover effects and can be used as a template to foster changes in another similar area.[23] Succeeding increments of policy build upon the established principle. After deregulation of the airline industry set a precedent, for example, deregulation was able to spread from airlines to other transportation modes and then to communications. The potential for spillover effects increases to the extent that widely varying problems, such as passenger screening and prisoner detention, can be lumped into the same category and perceived as parts of an overall policy, such as the war on terrorism.

REDIRECTING FOREST POLICY: REDEFINING PROCESSES, PARTICIPANTS, PROBLEMS, AND PRODUCTS

President Bush's redirection of forest policy involved a redefinition of processes, participants, problems, and products. First, this redefinition involved reframing traditionally important public participation processes, such as administrative appeals, not as opportunities for citizen involvement but as obstacles to needed action. Much of the environmental movement had been built upon the assumption that more participation meant better environmental decisions. NEPA, for example, broke apart the traditional iron triangles of agencies, user groups, and their allies in Congress, who promoted environmentally damaging timber, mining, grazing, and water development projects, and made it law that agencies examine and publicly disclose the environmental consequences of their actions. Administrative appeals evolved from their origins as largely vehicles for resolving business claims to broad mechanisms for providing additional points of access for a wide variety of individuals or groups displeased with agency plans and projects. Increased access to courts provided a venue for individuals and groups who felt disadvantaged because their access to legislative and bureaucratic arenas and their influence paled in comparison to that of business and commodity interests. NEPA can indeed be criticized for formalizing participation, focusing participation on process rather than substance, and inhibiting agency capacities to work in more informal and collaborative relationships.[24] Nonetheless, NEPA, appeals, and lawsuits have been major forces in stopping or delaying questionable projects—from massive coal-fired power plants on the Colorado Plateau to economically and environmentally questionable dams to rapid conversion of old-growth forests to meet ecologically unsustainable timber targets. In the healthy forests debate, the benefits of these processes would now be seriously questioned.

Second, redefinition of problems occurred. Following World War II the level of federal timber harvests dramatically increased. By the late 1970s and early 1980s, however, it became increasingly apparent that such levels of cutting were not sustainable, and forest policy began to focus on ameliorating the negative impact of timber harvesting on biodiversity, old-growth resources, and wilderness values. New ecological approaches such as ecosystem management emerged and emphasized the need to repair damaged ecosystems resulting from well-intentioned, but misguided nevertheless, forest policies.[25] But the forest health issue reversed the process. Failure to harvest trees was a problem and increased cutting a solution. Logging became linked to beneficial processes of fuels reduction and forest restoration.

Third, a redefinition of participants occurred. This involved a new social construction of environmental groups, not as trustees of valuable resources but as threats to those resources as well as to public safety. For years, many Americans have counted themselves environmentalists and have favored governmental intervention to protect environmental values. Traditional economic interests, such as energy companies, ranchers, and developers, had long viewed environmentalists as a threat to their economic interests, but the public generally saw environmentalists as the protectors of environmental health, fighting industry over issues of toxic waste, pollution, occupational health and safety, and damaging land and water developments. The wildfire issue provided the opportunity to recast environmentalists as threats to the public interest and whose actions damaged environmental health, compromised occupational health and safety, and destroyed natural resources.

Finally, the desired outcome (product) of the policy process was strategically defined as forest restoration rather than regulatory rollback, which had several advantages. It enabled policymakers with strong environmental records to join the coalition in favor of policy action because outcomes were portrayed in positive environmental terms, namely, forest health and forest restoration. Using the terms "health" and "restoration" offered hope to land managers and scientists who had long argued that past forest management actions had created crisis conditions necessitating a strong, proactive program of forest restoration. It also disarmed critics, since no one wants to appear to be against healthy forests. Opponents of the Bush approach argued that the Healthy Forests Initiative was more about regulatory rollback than fire policy and forest restoration, but those who wondered if the solution matched the problem went largely unheeded.

These redefinitions of processes, participants, problems, and products, are having significant spillover effects on other areas of environmental policy.

WHAT FOLLOWS

Chapter 1 places the redirection of forest policy, as exemplified by the healthy forests debate, in the social and political context of the development of U.S. environmental policy during the past forty years, up to and through the first term of President George W. Bush. It demonstrates Bush's approach to environmental policy through his executive and judicial appointments, policy actions he has taken and not taken, and strategies of timing and rhetoric used by his administration to advance his environmental agenda. It also shows how the Healthy Forests Initiative would inevitably become entwined in 2004's election-year politics.

Chapters 2 and 3 focus more specifically on Forest Service administrative appeals. Chapter 2 places Forest Service administrative appeals within the context of the growth of public involvement processes generally. It details the historical development of appeals, showing how they increasingly grew to be politically valued as an opportunity for achieving access to agency decision processes. It also demonstrates that the Forest Service has long viewed the appeals process as an impediment to achieving its management objectives—a perspective or issue definition that did not gain broad support and was specifically rejected by congressional policymakers until just recently. Building upon a database of appeal records that we created, this chapter also provides background information on just how many appeals are filed, who files appeals, what types of projects are appealed, and the types of decisions the Forest Service renders.

Chapter 3 continues to focus on Forest Service administrative appeals and provides a more in-depth examination of appellants. Although environmentalists as participants in the appeals process have been the principal target of policy change, our study found diverse groups and individuals use the appeals process. Their motivations, strategies and tactics, and expectations vary widely. This chapter also suggests that many issues surrounding the impact of appeals—such as harmful delays—are far more complex than the healthy forests debate has yet to fully acknowledge.

Chapter 4 then turns to examine how appeals and wildfires became conjoined, zeroing in on the agenda setting process as part of policy change. After providing a brief overview of the evolution of fire policy, this chapter illustrates how the

2000 and 2002 wildfires provided focusing events that propelled the issue of fire and appeals to the forefront of public consciousness. Forest ecologists have long warned that decades of fire exclusion, high-grade logging, domestic livestock grazing, and some forms of recreation have had detrimental environmental consequences, creating conditions ripe for catastrophic crown fires. Likewise, scientists and managers increasingly worry about the dangers of mixing people and flammable vegetation as people continue to build and live in areas within, or adjacent to, forested areas (the wildland-urban interface). It was not until the occurrence of several large and spectacular wildfires within a relatively short period of time, however, that widespread public concern about a nationwide problem of forest health emerged, enhancing opportunities for new policies to be formulated and adopted. This chapter examines the role of two critical factors in framing and defining the problem: the role of rhetoric and the use, misuse, and non-use of empirical data for influencing the agenda setting process. These two factors enabled environmentalists to be recast from the role of trustees to the role of threats and also paved the way for the agency's characterization of appeals as obstacles rather than opportunities to be politically accepted. The agency's long sought after solution—reducing the role of administrative appeals in agency decision making—effectively became attached to the wildfire problem.

Chapters 5 and 6 focus on the process of policy adoption. These two chapters examine the Bush administration's successful strategy of simultaneously pursuing policy change in both legislative and administrative venues. Chapter 5 documents the legislative history of the 2003 Healthy Forests Restoration Act, which put into law significant portions of the president's Healthy Forests Initiative and gave Bush a significant legislative victory just before the 2004 election year. The legislation authorizes an additional $760 million per year for fuels reduction projects on twenty million acres of federal lands managed by the Forest Service and the Bureau of Land Management. For qualifying hazardous fuels reduction projects, the act limits the number of alternatives that needed to be considered under NEPA, replaces post-decisional appeals with a pre-decisional appeals process, and places limits upon judicial review.

Legislative history shows how framing issues as forest health and restoration provided cover for politicians who might otherwise have rejected legislation that appeared environmentally hostile and also provided opportunities for areas of the country not as concerned about fires on public lands to attach their concerns about forest insects and disease in exchange for their political support. As debate over the proposed legislation proceeded, environmentalists found themselves in a quandary. They could not be against restoration, which they of course support. Cast as villains in delaying fuels reduction projects and increasing the prospects of catastrophic wildfires, they had a hard time advancing the case about how NEPA analysis, appeals, and litigation were core tools in the kit of public involvement and important as instruments for ensuring public accountability. Public safety trumped public involvement. Framing the issue as forest health blurred distinctions among the goals, objectives, and outcomes of restoration versus those of traditional timber and fire management.

Receiving far less public attention, however, but moving in tandem with the legislative proposals were a series of regulatory changes that clearly show how prominently regulatory rollback figured into the Healthy Forests Initiative and the president's environmental agenda. Chapter 6 examines four rulemakings that involve significant changes in agency decision making processes: (1) revisions of regulations guiding Forest Service land management planning that delete the use of administrative appeals in the planning process; (2) revisions of regulations governing Forest Service appeals related to NEPA project decisions that place additional limits on the use of appeals; (3) administrative guidance applied to both the Forest Service and Department of the Interior agencies that expand the types of projects that can be categorically excluded from NEPA's environmental impact statement procedures; and (4) new appeals regulations that add limits to the appeals process of the Bureau of Land Management. This chapter also discusses three other administrative actions that the administration linked to the fire problem and that demonstrate its commitment to increased timber harvests as a solution: (1) new consultation rules under the Endangered Species Act for actions related to the National Fire Plan; (2) changes to the Northwest Forest Plan; and (3) revision of the Sierra Nevada Framework.

The concluding chapter focuses on the spillover effect, viewing Bush's Healthy Forests Initiative as a template for broader environmental change. To illustrate this spillover, it examines the administration's initiatives in two other areas of environmental policy—energy and mining policy, and grazing—that also modify appeals and litigation, limit the role of the public in environmental policymaking, reduce the power and influence of environmental groups, and develop policies favoring the development and use of natural resources.

As a template for change, the success of President Bush's forest policy and its redefinition of process, participants, problems, and products delivered a severe blow to the environmental movement. Redirection of forest policy, as well as other areas of environmental policy, is being controlled and expedited through the use of certain tools and strategies that have confounded efforts of environmental organizations and advocates to stop or slow down the outcomes. The legacy of the first four years of George W. Bush's presidency will be remembered for its aggressive pursuit of a conservative, pro-industry, and pro-business policy agenda more in line with traditional political approaches for managing the nation's public lands.

NOTES

1. Austrian-born body builder, movie actor, and political novice, Republican Arnold Schwarzenegger had defeated Democratic governor Gray Davis in a high-profile California recall election amid continuing voter disapproval of Davis's handling of the state's budget problems. The election occurred two weeks prior to the outbreak of the fires.

2. For a detailed description of the 2003 Southern California fires see Jake A. Blackwell and Andrea Tuttle, *California Fire Siege 2003: The Story* (Sacramento, CA: California Department of Forestry and Fire Protection, and Washington, DC: USDA Forest Service, 2003).

3. Jeff McDonald, "Recovery Likely to Cost Billions; Agencies Face Huge Bills," *San Diego Union* (December 28, 2003) at www.signonsandiego.com/news/fires accessed February 9, 2004.

4. President George W. Bush, *Healthy Forests: An Initiative for Wildfire Prevention and Stronger Communities* (Washington, DC: White House, 2002); Healthy Forests Restoration Act of 2003, Public Law 108–148, December 12, 2003.

5. The White House, "President Announces Healthy Forest Initiative. Remarks of the President on Forest Health and Preservation," news release (August 22, 2002); and "President Thanks Work Crews and Firefighters," news release (August 22, 2002) at www.whitehouse.gov/news/releases/2002 accessed August 23, 2002.

6. Letter from the San Diego Fire Recovery Network to Walter Ekard, Chief Administrative Officer of the County of San Diego, February 5, 2004; also, letter from Jon E. Keeley, Station Leader, Western Ecological Research Center, U.S. Geological Survey, to the San Diego Fire Recovery Network, January 17, 2004. The Steering Committee of the San Diego Fire Recovery Network is chaired by the forest supervisor of the Cleveland National Forest. Members include professionals, scientists, and citizen representatives from both governmental and nongovernmental organizations. See also "Age-Patch Mosaics May Not Reduce Fire Risk, Intensity in California Shrublands," *The Forestry Source* (May 2004): 11; and Jon E. Keeley, C. J. Fotheringham, and Max A. Moritz, "Lessons from the October 2003 Wildfires in Southern California," *Journal of Forestry* 102:7 (2004): 26–33.

7. See, for example, James Anderson, *Public Policymaking: An Introduction*, Fourth Edition (Boston, MA: Houghton Mifflin, 2000).

8. See, for example, John W. Kingdon, *Agendas, Alternatives, and Public Policy*, Second Edition (New York: NY: Longman, 2003).

9. David A. Rochefort and Roger W. Cobb, *The Politics of Problem Definition: Shaping the Policy Agenda* (Lawrence, KS: University Press of Kansas, 1994); and Roger W. Cobb and Charles D. Elder, *Participation in American Politics: The Dynamics of Agenda-Building* (Baltimore, MD: Johns Hopkins University Press, 1983).

10. Larry D. Spence, *The Politics of Social Knowledge* (University Park, PA: Pennsylvania State University Press, 1978); Frank R. Baumgartner and Bryan D. Jones, *Agendas and Instability in American Politics* (Chicago, IL: University of Chicago Press, 1994).

11. Kenneth Burke, *A Rhetoric of Motives* (Berkeley, CA: University of California Press, 1969). On the role of language see also Murray Edelman, *Political Language: Words that Succeed and Policies that Fail* (New York, NY: Academic Press, 1977); and Mark P. Petracca, "Issue Definitions, Agenda-building, and Policymaking," *Policy Currents* 2:3 (1992): 1, 4.

12. On the social construction of policy targets, see Anne Larason Schneider and Helen Ingram, *Policy Design for Democracy* (Lawrence, KS: University Press of Kansas, 1997).

13. Roger W. Cobb, J. Ross, and M. H. Ross, "Agenda-Building as a Comparative Political Process," *American Political Science Review* 70:1 (1976): 126–138; E. E. Schattschneider, *The Semisovereign People* (Fort Worth, TX: Holt, Rinehart and Winston, 1983). See also Edward G. Carmines and James Stimson, "On the Structure and Sequence of Issue Evolution," *American Political Science Review* 80:3 (1986): 901–920.

14. Michael A. Smith, "The Interpretative Process of Agenda-Building: A Research Design for Public Policy," *Politics & Policy* 30:1 (2002): 9–31, at 16.

15. Ibid.

16. Elise S. Jones and Will Callaway, "Neutral Bystander, Intrusive Micromanager, or Useful Catalyst? The Role of Congress in Effecting Change Within the Forest Service," *Policy Studies Journal* 23:2 (1995): 337–350.

17. Roger W. Cobb and Marc Howard, eds., *Cultural Strategies of Agenda Denial: Avoidance, Attack, and Redefinition* (Lawrence, KS: University Press of Kansas, 1997).

18. Roy J. Lewicki, Barbara Gray, and Michael Elliott, eds., *Making Sense of Intractable Environmental Conflicts: Concepts and Cases* (Washington, DC: Island Press, 2002).

19. Petracca, "Issue Definitions, Agenda-building, and Policymaking."

20. Lettie McSpadden Wenner, *One Environment Under Law: A Public-Policy Dilemma* (Pacific Palisades, CA: Goodyear Publishing, 1975), 114.

21. Tom A. Birkland, *After Disaster: Agenda Setting, Public Policy and Focusing Events* (Washington, DC: Georgetown University Press, 1997).

22. See Brad T. Clark, "Agenda Setting and Issue Dynamics: Dam Building on the Lower Snake River," *Society and Natural Resources* 17 (2004): 599–609; and William R. Lowry, *Dam Politics: Restoring America's Rivers* (Washington, DC: Georgetown University Press, 2003).

23. Kingdon, *Agendas, Alternatives, and Public Policy.*

24. William E. Shands, "Public Involvement, Forest Planning, and Leadership in a Community of Interests," in *American Forestry: An Evolving Tradition. Proceedings of the 1992 Society of American Foresters National Convention* (Bethesda, MD: Society of American Foresters, 1992), 364–369. On NEPA more generally, see Matthew J. Lindstrom and Zachary A. Smith, *National Environmental Policy Act: Judicial Misconstruction, Legislative Indifference, and Executive Neglect* (College Station, TX: Texas A&M University Press, 2001).

25. Hanna J. Cortner and Margaret A. Moote, *The Politics of Ecosystem Management* (Washington, DC: Island Press, 1999).

FROM *SILENT SPRING* TO LUNTZSPEAK
Environmental Policy and George W. Bush

A RICH HISTORY OF U.S. ENVIRONMENTAL POLICY AND POLITICS CAN BE TRACED BACK TO colonial times,[1] but publication of Rachel Carson's *Silent Spring* in 1962 is generally credited as the triggering event of the modern environmental movement.[2] Carson wrote about indiscriminate pesticide use and its effects on wildlife: where mornings once witnessed a chorus of bird calls, now only silence lay over the land. Carson's eloquent statement began to fracture the technical optimism of a society that accepted as a matter of faith the industrial slogan of "Better Living Through Chemistry." From this point on, scientists, government, and the public examined technology and human relationships with nature in a different way. To understand the reframing of the environmental agenda is it critical to review the evolution of environmental policy since the early 1960s.

ENVIRONMENTALISM ON ALL FRONTS

A year after *Silent Spring*'s publication President John F. Kennedy's Secretary of the Interior, Stewart Udall, published *The Quiet Crisis*—which focused on the crisis that was turning a beautiful nation into an ugly one—and called for more attention "to the inner space that is our home."[3] Not only could Udall write about the environment, he could also take policy action in support of it. With presidents John F. Kennedy and Lyndon B. Johnson, both Democrats, Udall had supportive bosses. He also had another significant ally, Lady Bird Johnson, the First Lady, who made scenic beauty and the environment her issues. During the Johnson administration some 278 conservation and beautification measures were enacted. They included adding one hundred million more acres to the National Park System, creating 200 miles of national seashore, and creating a national system of rural and urban trails.[4] During this time, Congress passed the Wilderness Act (1964), the Land and Water Conservation Fund Act (1964), the Wild and Scenic Rivers Act (1968), the National Historic Preservation Act (1966), and one of Lady Bird's legacies, the Highway Beautification Act (1965).

Cleaning up pollution and protecting natural beauty were part of Johnson's Great Society. In addition to an activist government setting aside protected areas, Johnson's vision of a Great Society also meant addressing adverse aspects of a growing technological and urban America, confronting the paradox of poverty in the midst of plenty, and advancing the morality of racial equality. His program of social reform reached to welfare, education, health care, civil rights, and the environment. The Vietnam War, however, was his undoing. A black hole, it sapped the country's vitality as well as Johnson's health. He chose not to run for another term, and Republican Richard Nixon won the presidency.

Although Nixon had never embraced environmental issues, he was ever the political pragmatist and acquiesced to the potency of the nascent environmental movement. Moreover, the space program and the landing of the first human, Neil Armstrong, on the moon in July 1969 had a significant, if unintended, effect. The Apollo space program was, in reality, more about ideological conflict with the Soviet Union and national ego than it was about science,[5] but the photographs taken by the astronauts on their voyage vividly reminded Americans of the relative smallness and fragility of "spaceship Earth" and the need to protect its life-giving environment. Although Nixon had actively opposed passage of NEPA throughout the legislative process,[6] he not only chose to sign the law but did so on live television on New Year's Day 1970, declaring that the 1970s would be the "environmental decade." Nixon appointed committed environmentalists to the newly created Council on Environmental Quality (CEQ). By executive order he created the Environmental Protection Agency (EPA) and the National Oceanic and Atmospheric Administration (NOAA). As part of a blue-collar political strategy, he introduced legislation to create the Occupational Safety and Health Administration (OSHA) to deal with environmental hazards in the workplace.[7]

Nixon's actions were prescient. The 1970s was indeed the decade of the environment, producing, with bipartisan majorities, a flurry of environmental and natural resource legislation. In addition to presidential leadership, strong congressional policy entrepreneurs, such as Sens. Henry Jackson (D-WA), Edmund Muskie (D-ME), and Gaylord Nelson (D-WI) and Reps. John Dingell (D-MI) and Morris Udall (D-AZ), used their leadership positions to build a legal framework for national responsibility for environmental quality. Established interest groups such as the Audubon Society, The Wilderness Society, the Sierra Club, the Izaak Walton League, and the National Wildlife Federation became more involved in legislative activities. New interest groups such as Friends of the Earth, Greenpeace, Environmental Action, Zero Population Growth, and American Rivers organized, and new litigating groups such as the Natural Resources Defense Council emerged.[8] It was certainly a time of environmentalism on all fronts.

The legislation passed during the 1970s is an alphabet soup of laws regulating air and water pollution, toxic waste, and pesticides, including the Clean Air Act (1970 as amended in 1977), the Clean Water Act (the Federal Water Pollution Control Act Amendments of 1972 and 1977), the Resource Conservation and Recovery Act of 1972, and the Federal Environmental Pesticides Control Act of 1972. In addition to creating a massive regulatory framework for pollution control, Congress also created a legislative and regulatory framework for managing flora and fauna, including the Endangered Species Act (1973), the Marine Mammal Protection Act of 1972, and the Fishery Conservation and Management Act (1976). Additional regulations prescribed governmental responsibilities for management of public lands. In 1976 Congress passed, and President Gerald Ford signed, the National Forest Management Act (NFMA), largely in response to litigation arising from controversies over clear-cutting that originated in the Bitterroot (Montana) and Monongahela (West Virginia) National Forests. NFMA set forth prescriptive management guidelines and mandated comprehensive land management planning on all of the nation's national forests. That same year Congress also decided to settle the question of what to do with the remaining lands in the public domain. Influenced by the 1970 report of the Public Land Law Review Commission, *One Third of the Nation's Land*,[9] Congress decided in the Federal Land Policy and Management Act (FLPMA) that public domain lands should be retained in public ownership. Similar to lands under Forest Service jurisdiction, FLPMA required the Bureau of Land Management (BLM) to manage those lands for multiple use and to prepare comprehensive land management plans.

During the 1970s Congress and President Jimmy Carter, a Democrat, also moved to settle long-standing controversies about the fate of public lands in Alaska. Passed in 1980, the Alaska National Interest Lands Conservation Act (ANILCA) established ten new national parks, nine new wildlife refuges, and thirty-five new wilderness areas. The compromises in ANILCA, however, did not resolve controversies over timber management in the Tongass National Forest or oil drilling in the Arctic National Wildlife Refuge. Although President Carter was able to generate congressional support for creation of the Department of Energy and helped secure passage of the Surface Mining and Reclamation Act—twice vetoed by President Gerald Ford—many of Carter's more ambitious energy proposals ran into powerful opposition from the public as well as energy producers.

As the 1970s came to a close, inflation and unemployment plagued the economy. U.S. interests in the Persian Gulf were indirectly threatened by the Soviet invasion of Afghanistan and directly affected by the siege of the U.S. Embassy in Iran. Americans increasingly began to question the costs and competence of government in general, and the federal government in particular, and to question the wisdom of the trend toward centralizing power and authority for addressing societal problems at the national level. Public confidence in government and the bureaucracies it had established to solve those problems was eroding. The liberal, and liberated, society of the 1960s and 1970s seemed to many to have gone too far, and conservatives' advocacy of traditional values began to resonate. Movie actor and governor of California, Republican Ronald Reagan, was elected president in a landslide in 1980. The bipartisan consensus on the environment was over.

Reagan came into the presidency openly hostile to the environment. Although his efforts would be supported by a backlash movement and the attendant growth of pro-development interest groups (the wise use movement),[10] Congress was not willing to turn back the clock on other environmental issues, such as pollution control. Reagan's controversial appointments sparked increased activism by environmental interests, and membership in environmental interest groups grew dramatically.[11] Consequently, Reagan did not attempt to rewrite legislation; rather he was able to indirectly influence the environmental agenda by controlling the bureaucracy, cutting agency budgets and personnel, and using regulatory oversight to eliminate or relax regulations viewed as burdensome by industry.[12] Ironically, the conservative fiscal approach of the Reagan Republicans advanced some environmental causes, such as water policy reform. Support for measures such as increased local cost-sharing in water projects began to weed out some economically inefficient and environmentally damaging projects.

Reagan's vice-president, George H.W. Bush, succeeded Reagan as president in 1989. President Bush promised during the campaign a "no net loss" of wetlands policy and made limiting air and water pollution a priority. Probably the single most important legislative achievement of his presidency was building a bipartisan coalition to amend and strengthen the Clean Air Act—the first major amendments since 1977. Despite his success with clean air legislation, his wetlands policy floundered in debates over the administration's convoluted definition of a wetland. Bush had pledged to be "the environmental president," but his environmental image would be most defined, and damaged, by his threat to boycott the 1992 United Nations Conference on Environment and Development (Earth Summit) in Rio de Janeiro until ensured that the climate change convention would not contain any binding targets for reduction of carbon dioxide emissions. And then he refused to sign the summit's biodiversity treaty.

President George H.W. Bush served only one term and was defeated in 1992 by Bill Clinton, a Democrat from Arkansas, in an election in which the economy was a major issue. Following through on a campaign pledge, Clinton during his first term held a forest summit and produced the Northwest Forest Plan. The conference and plan attempted to bring closure to the Pacific Northwest's timber wars and end interest group gridlock over the question of how much old-growth forest needed to be protected for spotted owl habitat. Despite this promising early legislation, for the most part, however, Clinton's two terms saw only increased acrimony. He had strained relationships with the Republican-led Congress that emerged in the 1994 elections, a situation that became more pronounced during impeachment proceedings related to his sexual peccadillos. His administration will be remembered as one in which the president successfully blocked Republicans who sought major regulatory overhaul of laws covering issues such as wetlands, mining reform, and the Endangered Species Act and who tried to use the budget process to limit environmental regulations. Just as he was leaving office Clinton used his executive powers under a little-used statute, the 1906 Antiquities Act, to create several new national monuments, an act that further infuriated members of Congress and many western governors, who felt the designations had been made without appropriate consultation with political leaders or the public. As the new millennium dawned, contending interest groups appeared to be more entrenched than ever, and the public was consumed by issues other than the environment. Tired of gridlock, new community-based groups committed to working collaboratively toward both environmental stewardship and strong communities emerged at the local, tribal, and regional levels.[13] On the national political agenda, environmental protection lay dormant.

President George W. Bush entered the White House in 2001 with little national-level experience related to environmental policymaking. In order to understand his administration's approach to the environment, and specifically forest policy, it is important to look back at his previous record as governor of Texas, his statements and actions as a presidential candidate during the 2000 election cycle, his administration's stances on environmental policy during its first term, and the benchmarks of the 2004 presidential campaign, including the nomination of Massachusetts senator John Kerry as the Democratic party's nominee to challenge Bush.

GOVERNOR BUSH AND THE ENVIRONMENT IN TEXAS

George W. Bush had limited exposure to environmental issues prior to his election as governor of Texas in 1994. After receiving his bachelor's degree from Yale in 1968, serving as a fighter pilot in the Texas Air National Guard, and receiving a Master in Business Administration degree from Harvard in 1975, Bush returned to Midland, Texas, and a career in the energy industry. He ran unsuccessfully for Congress in 1978, winning 47 percent of the vote, and remained in the energy business until the industry collapsed in 1986. He began working on his father's 1988 presidential campaign and assembled a group of partners that purchased the Texas Rangers baseball franchise in 1989. He served as managing general partner of the baseball team until his campaign for governor of Texas in 1994. Bush defeated incumbent governor Ann Richards 53 percent to 46 percent, re-launching his political career.

According to his official White House biography, during the six years that George W. Bush served as governor "he earned a reputation as a compassionate conservative who shaped public policy based on the principles of limited government, personal responsibility, strong families, and local control."[14] When he was elected as governor, Bush took over responsibility for environmental policy in a state that was considered one of the country's most polluted. Texas led the nation in emissions of toxic and ozone-causing chemicals from manufacturing plants and in the discharge of developmental carcinogens known to harm children's brains and central nervous systems. Nearly two-thirds of Texas residents lived in areas with pollution levels exceeding federal clean air standards.

Not unexpectedly, assessments of Governor Bush's environmental record vary considerably, depending upon the source. Among the environmental policy benchmarks of his two-term administration, the governor

- established a voluntary emissions reduction plan affecting more than 750 manufacturing plants, oil and gas producers, and chemical plants, providing no substantial penalties for not "volunteering" to comply and altering the requirements of the Texas Natural Resources Conservation Council;
- supported cancellation of the state's auto emissions testing program;
- loosened regulations on large hog- and chicken-growing facilities and encouraged expansion of these industries despite their potential capacity to pollute surface and groundwater; and

- established a Lone Star Legacy Campaign to provide a permanent endowment for every state park, fish hatchery, and wildlife management area.

Much criticism of Bush's gubernatorial environmental record focuses on what the governor chose *not* to do. During his tenure, the state's water supply showed dangerous levels of industrial toxins, and fish taken from some waterways showed levels of contamination eleven times higher than the EPA's edible tissue criterion. The state, however, virtually stopped monitoring stream water quality and largely abandoned its pesticide-monitoring program. And no land was purchased by the Texas Parks and Wildlife Department to expand its programs.

Because state and federal lands comprise so little of Texas, the governor faced fewer land management issues than most of his western state counterparts and dealt considerably less with national forests. Only about 3 percent of the state is federally owned (87 percent is privately owned). Six percent of the state is forested with about 755,000 acres within the state's four national forests. Oregon, in comparison, has about 15,658,000 acres of national forest lands; Wyoming, 9,238,000 acres; and Washington, 9,214,000 acres.[15] Although grazing interests play a big role in the state's economy and political sphere, as do energy companies, Bush had limited contact with timber and logging representatives.

PRESIDENTIAL CANDIDATE GEORGE W. BUSH (2000)

Environmental group leaders and activists expected that Tennessee senator Al Gore as the Democratic party's presidential candidate would signal the return of environmental issues to the campaign agenda. First elected to the House of Representatives in 1976 and to the U.S. Senate in 1984, Gore had established a strong environmental record in Congress. In his best-selling 1992 book, *Earth in the Balance: Ecology and the Human Spirit*,[16] Gore argued that only a radical rethinking of human relationships with nature could save the earth's ecology for future generations. Some believed that Gore's "green" policy preferences had been muffled during the Clinton administration and that once the vice-president was running on his own credentials in 2000, there would be a national debate on natural resources and wilderness protection, along with global issues such as climate change, deforestation, pollution, and hazardous waste. There was little expectation that Governor Bush would initiate the debate, except perhaps in a discussion of energy interests crucial to his home state's economy, but the conventional wisdom was that Gore's background and interests would draw Bush into a dialogue. When Ralph Nader entered the campaign as the Green Party's presidential candidate, hopes rose even further.

These expectations were based on wishful thinking rather than the realities of political strategy. Nationwide surveys taken both before and during the 2000 campaign showed that despite overwhelming support for environmental issues in the broad sense, specific issues rank well below other concerns, such as the economy, violence and public safety, health care, and, more recently, terrorism. In an early 2000 Gallup Poll, for instance, 83 percent of respondents said they agreed with the broad goals of the environmental movement, but only 16 percent identified themselves as "active participants."[17]

This trend has been reported consistently in national studies. Both Gallup and Harris polls conducted between the mid-1960s and early 1970s, as well as the Michigan National Election Survey, found that majorities expressed pro-environment opinions, suggesting that public concern for environmental quality escalated rapidly in the sixties. However, despite relatively strong consensus in support of environmental protection and the increased salience of environmental problems during the 1970s, only a minority of the public viewed the environment as one of the nation's most important problems.[18]

Between 1978 and 1983, four national polls found between 7 and 13 percent of Americans claiming to be active in the environmental movement, and 47 to 55 percent sympathetic toward it. In another 2000 survey, the Gallup Organization found that 16 percent said they were active in the environmental movement, and 55 percent were sympathetic toward it.[19] Similar findings have been reported by the Roper polling organization, which in 1974 began asking Americans about the problems that most concerned them. In 1996, 12 percent of the respondents said pollution of air and water was one of their most troubling problems, a finding very much in line with responses throughout the 1990s. Nearly four times as many (47 percent) said they were concerned about crime and lawlessness. A Princeton Survey Research study conducted about the same time asking those polled to choose the most important issue among a list of fifteen ranked the environment as fourteenth.[20]

The difficulty, one observer has noted, is in motivating and sustaining the political activism of average Americans, which "has been an uphill battle for the environmental movement from the start. Communicating the complex nature of environmental destruction to a lay public that is not expert in science and technology" is a difficult challenge.[21] Americans do not generally cast their votes on the basis of environmental issues, limiting the extent to which the campaigns and their support organizations seek to bring environmental problems to the political debate. In the 1984 presidential election, for instance, surveys showed the percentage of those who believed Democrat Walter Mondale could do a better job of protecting the environment than Ronald Reagan ranged from 50 to 59.

After Mondale lost in a landslide, a 1985 Harris survey found two-thirds of the respondents believed that in his second term, Reagan's handling of environmental cleanup matters would be about the same (60 percent) or worse (7 percent) than in his first four years, while only 30 percent felt it would be better. One author concluded, "Apparently, the president's poor record on environmental protection had little effect on voters."[22]

Similarly, some researchers have characterized Americans as "Lite Greens," meaning that although they may engage in environmental activities like recycling, they are wary of making major lifestyle changes (such as not buying gas-guzzling vehicles) in the name of the environment. No solid green bloc of voters has materialized that is comparable to the anti-abortion or pro-gun activists. Local constituencies are likely to side with their economic interests and strong general support for the environment does not necessarily stop the public from voting for candidates with weak environmental records.[23] Candidates do not want to be vulnerable on the environment and must be sensitive to the public's environmental proclivities, but it is simply not an issue that dominates elections.

In the 2000 election, public opinion became the driving force behind the candidates' speeches and proposals, and issues like wildfires and forests rarely appeared on the campaign agenda. On the rare occasions when environmental issues were mentioned, both candidates spoke in generalizations (usually about local problems in the communities where they were visiting) and their ideas lacked specifics on funding and implementation.

Prior to the campaign, fifteen conservative environmental policy experts reportedly provided Governor Bush with a three-hour tutorial on environmental issues at the Texas governor's mansion in May 1999. Two of those who attended the meeting said that Bush opened the session by saying, "I am going to be the next president of the United States. And when I leave office, the air will be cleaner, the water will be cleaner and the environment will be better. Tell me how I'm going to make this happen." The assembled experts convinced the candidate that this could be accomplished by embracing what would later be called "a philosophy of environmental federalism" that would replace governmental regulation with market mechanisms.[24]

Candidate Bush, however, produced a laundry list of ideas that were neither new nor particularly noteworthy. Like his predecessors, he called for full funding of the Land and Water Conservation Fund and supported funding the substantial maintenance- and infrastructure-repair backlog in national parks, wildlife refuges, and other public landholdings. He promised that all federal agencies would be required to comply with environmental laws and initially called for a temporary moratorium on oil drilling off the Florida and California coasts, a way of politically helping his brother Jeb Bush, governor of Florida. Although he opposed the Kyoto Protocol on global warming that the Clinton administration had supported, Bush called for continued research into the causes and impact of global warming, the Republicans' preferred alternative to additional limitations on greenhouse gas emissions.

After the U.S. Supreme Court's controversial decision in December 2000 declaring Bush the winner of the election, the incoming president began to move forward on his policy initiatives and prioritize the changes he wanted to implement when he took office in January 2001. Because of the close popular vote and Bush's background in the energy sector, there was considerable analysis of the contributions made to the Bush campaign and the Republican National Party in comparison to what Gore had raised. Bush collected more funding from every sector of the U.S. economy, with the exception of organized labor, than Gore. Of the $314 million raised in the 2000 presidential campaign, 80 percent came from corporations or individuals employed by them. Bush's Pioneer Fundraisers, who each pledged to raise at least $100,000 for the campaign, included Kenneth Lay (Enron), Steve Ledbetter (Reliant Energy), Robert B. Holland III (Triton Energy), Richard and Nancy Kinder (Kinder Morgan Energy Partners), and Robert Madison Murphy (Murphy Oil).[25] This connection raised red flags for leaders within the environmental community, who were concerned about what the payback for these contributions might be once the Bush administration took over.

THE ENVIRONMENTAL PRESIDENCY OF GEORGE W. BUSH

The president's environmental priorities are best explained by examining three types of actions: (1) judicial appointments and key appointments to his cabinet and federal agencies; (2) major initiatives; and (3) strategies used to shape public awareness and perceptions.

EXECUTIVE AND JUDICIAL APPOINTMENTS

As usually happens when there is a partisan change of White House control, Clinton appointees were already sending out resumes when the final results of the election were certified. Bush turned to several trusted friends and advisors during the short transition period to assist him in identifying individuals who shared his ideological goals. Potential appointees to some positions, such as Secretary of the Department of Energy, were not difficult to find, given the president's familiarity with the energy industry. Others brought with them strong connections to conservative politicians, corporate interests, and major industry trade organizations as seen by the following examples.

- Interior Secretary Gale Norton spent four years working at the Mountain States Legal Foundation (MSLF), a conservative legal group known for defending property rights activists and organizations. The MSLF was co-founded by Ronald Reagan's controversial Interior Secretary James Watt, who had a reputation for opposing major environmental initiatives and supporting wise-use groups that advocated more development and fewer environmental regulations on federal lands. Norton had also been a lobbyist for NL Industries, a company that has been involved in legal battles over its mining facilities and disposal sites, and as Colorado Attorney General, had failed to take action against the mine's environmental violations.

- Ann M. Veneman, Secretary of Agriculture, had worked at the Department of Agriculture under George H.W. Bush and then became head of California's Department of Food and Agriculture. In between, she served on the board of directors for Calgene, Inc., the first company to bring genetically engineered food to supermarket consumers. Calgene was purchased by Monsanto, the nation's largest biotech company, in 1997, and in 2000 Monsanto became part of the pharmaceutical company, Pharmacia. Veneman also served on the International Policy Council on Agriculture, Food, and Trade, a group funded by industry giants Cargill, Nestle, Kraft, and Archer Daniels Midland.

- Spencer Abraham, Secretary of Energy, served one term as a Republican senator from Michigan before joining the Bush administration. He was the number-one recipient of campaign contributions from the automotive industry in his unsuccessful 2000 bid for re-election, with major contributions from General Motors, Ford, and Lear Corporation. The Coalition for Vehicle Choice, a lobbying group that opposes setting fuel economy standards, gave Abraham $178,674 in the 1999–2000 election cycle.

- William G. Myers, Solicitor for the Department of the Interior, had previously worked for the Public Lands Council, the National Cattlemen's Beef Association, and Kennecott Energy, one of the world's largest coal producers and a wholly owned subsidiary of Rio Tinto, a massive multinational mining conglomerate.

- Stephen Griles, Deputy Secretary of the Interior, was a former lobbyist for the National Mining Association, numerous coal companies, Pennsylvania Power & Light, the Edison Electric Institute, Kennecott Energy Company, and other oil and gas companies.

- Jeffrey Holmstead, EPA's Assistant Administrator for the Office of Air and Radiation, had previously represented the Alliance for Constructive Air Policy, a sixteen-member industry coalition that includes Allegheny Power, American Electric Power, the Virginia Power Company, and Wisconsin Electric Company.

- John Graham, director of the Office of Information and Regulatory Affairs in the Office of Management and Budget, previously ran an industry-funded center at Harvard that promoted economic and policy grounds for weakening environmental and public health safeguards.

- Marianne Lamont Horinko, Assistant Administrator for EPA's Office of Solid Waste, which also is responsible for enforcement of Superfund legislation, was previously with Don Clay Associates, a national environmental policy consulting firm. The company's clients have included the Chemical Manufacturers Association, the Aluminum Company of America, and the Koch Petroleum Group.[26]

The president's forest agency appointees were applauded by logging interests and generally ridiculed by environmental groups. Mark Rey, appointed as Under Secretary of Agriculture for Natural Resources and Environment, would oversee the Forest Service. Rey had been a timber industry lobbyist for twenty years and had actively lobbied to eliminate the administrative appeals process. During those twenty years he had served as Vice-President of Forest Resources for the American Forest and Paper Association, Executive Director of the American Forest Resource Alliance (a coalition of 350 timber corporations), and Vice-President of Public Forestry Programs for the National Forest Products Association. Most recently he had served as a staff member with the Senate Committee on Energy and Natural Resources, where he spearheaded Senator Larry Craig's (R-ID) unsuccessful and controversial effort to rewrite national forest legislation.[27] He was also instrumental in crafting the highly contentious 1995 Salvage Rider as an attachment to an appropriations bill, a provision that allowed the Forest Service to bypass environmental laws in designated salvage logging areas.

In August 2002 Interior Secretary Norton appointed Allan K. Fitzsimmons as the department's Fuel Coordinator, a new position charged with coordinating fuels treatment on public lands as part of the implementation of the president's Healthy Forest Initiative announced earlier that month. An environmental consultant in both the Reagan and George H.W. Bush administrations, Fitzsimmons, as president of his consulting firm Balanced Resource Solutions, was well known for his controversial stand on ecosystems. In his 2000 paper "Ecological Confusion Among the Clergy," Fitzsimmons criticized Roman Catholic bishops who he said legitimized "the effort by radical environmentalists to quarantine additional lands from human use and to prevent the legitimate use of natural resources to enhance human well-being."[28] He criticized ecosystem management, an approach to resource management that places more emphasis on sustainability than on commodity outputs, as a "train wreck in the making."[29]

Forest Service Chief Mike Dombeck, a career senior executive who had served under the Clinton administration, was protected from involuntary reassignment or removal during Veneman's first 120 days in office. Early on, it was apparent that his strong support of Clinton-era environmental initiatives, such as the rule banning new road-building and logging in 58.5 million acres of unroaded forest land, would conflict with the Bush administration's goal of increasing timber production. He chose to retire from the Forest Service in March 2001. The president chose as his successor Dale Bosworth, a respected career forester with thirty-five years experience with the agency and who was considered more of an agency insider as well as more moderate than Dombeck. Western Republicans lauded the appointment, praising Bosworth's respect for a balanced approach. Although generally supportive of the appointment, environmental groups nonetheless predicted that Bosworth would willingly go along with Mark Rey and the president's forest policies.

Another of the president's key appointments, administrator of the Environmental Protection Agency, went to Christine Todd Whitman, who had previously served as governor of New Jersey and as head of the New Jersey Board of Public Utilities. The White House portrayed Whitman "as a preservationist," lauding her efforts to improve the state's air quality, establish a comprehensive beach monitoring system, and promote smart growth.[30] But there were many observers who wondered why Whitman had been selected, given her overall lack of environmental experience. During her two-year tenure as head of the EPA, she was heavily criticized for downplaying potential air quality hazards for workers and residents near the former site of New York's World Trade Center. Others believed she was constantly being undercut by White House officials. "Time and again Whitman listened to the career bureaucracy at EPA rather than Bush-administration appointees," wrote one observer. "As a result, she was regularly off-message, pushing policies and ideas without White House blessing."[31] More specifically, she ran up against the administration's global warming policies after Bush reneged on a campaign promise to regulate greenhouse gases. When Whitman resigned from the EPA in late May 2003, she said her decision to step down was based on a conflict between work and family rather than her inability to get along with the president's staff and supporters. Bush moved quickly to find a replacement who was clearly headed in the same direction as his administration.

As part of his summer-long public relations campaign, the president traveled to Colorado in August where he named Utah governor Mike Leavitt (R) as his choice to head the EPA, but he still needed his appointee to be confirmed by the Senate. Leavitt described his environmental views as being in the "productive middle," not on the extremes. "That is where the vast majority of American people are," he said, although he had recently referred to his numerous environmental critics as "extremists."[32] Others noted that Leavitt was a moderate who had been instrumental in promoting the ten-year fire strategy developed by the Western Governors' Association, a plan that had received an award for providing "exemplary leadership" in coordinating and successfully engaging a diverse set of interests. But several environmental groups were quick to criticize the selection. The director of the Utah Environmental Congress said that "Leavitt talks a good game but doesn't deliver on environmental issues." She cited a land swap the governor negotiated with Interior Secretary Gale Norton that lifted wilderness protection from about six million acres of federal land in Utah. A Sierra Club representative accused Leavitt as being too willing to cut deals on issues like road building and oil and gas drilling on federal lands. "He patterns himself as a guy in the middle, when in fact he has an agenda that is all too often against protecting the environment."[33]

New York senator and former First Lady Hillary Clinton announced that she would place a hold on Leavitt's nomination, a procedural move that did not stop committee hearings but would prevent the full Senate from voting on his confirmation. Clinton said she would lift the hold only if the White House addressed concerns raised in an internal EPA report that said the agency had misled the public about health risks resulting from the September 11 terrorist attack on the World Trade Center. During Senate confirmation hearings, Leavitt emphasized his strengths in environmental management, his commitment to air and water quality and land conservation, and his dedication to ensuring effective stewardship of natural resources. Clinton eventually lifted her block of Leavitt's nomination, and the Senate confirmed his appointment on October 28 by a vote of 88 to 8. Leavitt decided to forgo the traditional appointment bash in favor of a subdued ceremony in which he was sworn in by Acting EPA Administrator Marianne Horinko. In his first message to the agency, Leavitt explained that his approach to environmental management could be summed up in one word: balance. "We need to balance the needs of the environment and the needs of humanity . . . balance the needs of this generation and the next."[34]

Perhaps even more important than appointments within the executive branch, which "expire" when the president leaves office, are appointments to the judicial branch. Given that all federal judges appointed under Article III of the Constitution serve for life, a president's impact on policy can endure long after he has left office. President Reagan, for example, appointed 358 conservative-leaning federal judges, more than any other president up to then. Federal judicial appointments by Reagan's successor, George H.W. Bush, continued the pattern; almost all of the 187 lifetime appointees from his administration are still deciding cases today.

25

Although Bill Clinton made 367 federal judicial appointments during his two terms in office, the ideological tenor of his appointees was much more moderate because of the need for confirmation approval from the Republican-controlled Senate Judiciary Committee.[35] The effect of these conservative judicial appointments will make it increasingly difficult for environmental groups to find sympathetic judges for cases they bring to the judicial arena.

George W. Bush has continued the trend of appointing conservative judges, and several of his federal judicial appointees have had an obvious anti-environmental tilt. Victor Wolski, who previously served with the Pacific Legal Foundation filing suit against land-use planning and other environmental measures, was appointed by Bush to the U.S. Court of Federal Claims, whose jurisdiction includes property rights and takings cases. Other justices appointed by Bush with a similar ideological bent include Lawrence Block, a supporter of takings cases; Sam Cassell, a former aide to conservative Utah senator Orrin Hatch (R); a district judge in Utah who had served as a consultant to a nuclear waste company; and Sam Haddon, Bush's first judicial appointment in the West in 2001. Haddon's cases thus far have included one in which he ruled that salty groundwater discharged from coalbed methane wells is not a pollutant under the Clean Water Act and another in which he prohibited the State of Montana from billing a mining company for environmental restoration on a Superfund site.[36]

Although conventional wisdom argues that once a judge is appointed to the bench, all ideological and political biases are discarded, there is little doubt that federal judges appointed by Republican presidents have made a difference in environmental policy. A study by the Defenders of Wildlife and the Vermont Law School's Clinic on Environmental Law and Policy has argued that the partisan gap in the composition of the federal appellate court panel has made a difference in the outcome of court challenges. When the three-judge panel was composed of a majority of Republican-appointed judges, the success rate of NEPA-hostile arguments was 60 percent, compared to an 11 percent success rate when panels had a majority of Democrat-appointed judges.[37] This pattern is also seen in two other academic studies involving the makeup of judicial panels and environmental policy. One survey found that Republican-appointed judges voted to deny standing to environmental plaintiffs in 79 percent of cases, but Democrat-appointed judges voted to deny standing to environmental plaintiffs in only 18 percent of cases.[38] Another researcher found that between 1987 and 1994, panels consisting of two Democrat-appointed judges and one Republican-appointee reversed the EPA on procedural grounds raised by industry in between 2 and 13 percent of cases. Panels consisting of two Republican appointees and one Democratic appointee, in contrast, reversed the EPA in 54 to 89 percent of cases decided.[39] Moreover,

Republicans have proposed splitting the San Francisco–based Ninth Circuit Court of Appeals, which is seen by conservatives—particularly those in the highly Republican Intermountain West—as too often ruling against "ranchers, miners and our timber industry."[40] One analyst concludes there is a clear pattern of anti-environmental decision making. "Future appointments by the Bush administration seem likely to make the situation worse and the long-term impact of an actively anti-environmental judiciary is potentially incalculable."[41]

ACTIONS TAKEN AND NOT TAKEN

Just as his appointments reflect his political stance on environmental issues, Bush's policy initiatives have made clear the direction he has chosen for his administration. Almost immediately upon taking office, environmental groups accused Bush of an "assault on the environment [that] has been so blatant and relentless that even American television now reports it as a simple fact, like gravity."[42] A brief glance at his first term shows a president acting on several environmental fronts almost simultaneously. Actions seen as generally hostile to the environment include the following examples:

- announcing that the United States would abandon its pledge to reduce carbon dioxide emissions;
- rejecting the Kyoto Protocol;
- proposing to open up the Arctic National Wildlife Refuge to oil and gas drilling;
- reducing funding for greenhouse gas reductions in developing countries;
- weakening the acceptable level standards for arsenic in drinking water;
- supporting Yucca Mountain, Nevada, as a long-term nuclear waste depository;
- failing to meet the deadline for increasing automobile fuel efficiency;
- allowing mining in the Florida Everglades;
- ending corporate taxes on polluters that fund the cleanup of toxic waste sites;
- calling for increased logging to reduce the threat of wildfires;
- refusing to attend the United Nations Summit on Sustainable Development (the only major world leader to do so);
- reversing a phase-out of polluting snowmobiles in Yellowstone National Park;
- issuing a new regulation that weakens pollution controls on factory farms;

- announcing plans to allow companies to purchase pollution credits rather than cleaning up their own discharges into waterways;
- supporting an EPA proposal that would give municipalities flexibility in determining how to meet federal air quality standards;
- making it easier for oil and gas projects to move forward on BLM lands;
- revising grazing regulations to give ranchers more rights and reduce public input on grazing decisions;
- allowing states to seek exemptions from Forest Service Roadless Area Conservation rules; and
- opening three hundred thousand acres of Tongass National Forest in southeast Alaska to logging and development.

His shorter list of actions generally seen as pro-environment include the following examples:

- signing the reauthorization of the North American Wetlands Conservation Act;
- approving legislation that added more than five hundred thousand acres to the National Wilderness Preservation System; and
- supporting an EPA proposal requiring cleaner fuel and engines for non-road diesel engines.

Bush seized upon the strategy of blaming environmentalists for nearly every problem his administration encountered—a tactic that would become the cornerstone of his plans for forest policy reform. California's energy crisis, soaring utility prices, and rolling brownouts were the result of air quality regulations pushed by environmental groups that kept the state from building needed power plants, Bush said. His answer was to open up the Arctic National Wildlife Refuge to oil and gas exploration to provide a more stable energy supply. When that proposal met with fierce opposition, it was placed on political hold while the administration made plans to begin drilling in the western Rocky Mountains.

Bush also pinpointed the regulatory process as a barrier to improving the nation's economic and environmental health. Declines in the economy were tied to burdensome regulations under the Clean Air Act, which ironically had been signed in 1990 by his father when president. Environmentalists had worked closely with the first Bush administration to enact the air pollution legislation. But under George W. Bush, the statute's New Source Review provisions were criticized as discouraging modernization of old power plants, and thus the rules became voluntary rather than mandatory—just as he had done in Texas when governor.

Although the Bush administration seems to rely primarily on the legislative and regulatory process to advance its environmental agenda, the judicial arena has also been a venue for pursuing substantial change. And in this case, not taking action has been as important as new initiatives. The Bush administration has repeatedly used the federal courts to try and undermine NEPA and its provisions requiring federal agencies to prepare environmental impact statements (EIS) on proposed projects that significantly affect the environment. The Defenders of Wildlife and Vermont Law School study examined all 172 cases involving substantive NEPA issues decided by federal courts in the first two years of the administration. Government arguments were categorized by the study as "NEPA consistent" where evidence indicates the government advocated a position not tending to erode NEPA law or accepted precedent. "NEPA-hostile" arguments were defined as those where substantial evidence shows that the government advocated a position avoiding or eroding NEPA law and accepted precedent. In cases where the government's arguments were consistent with NEPA, the Bush administration won 75 of 78 cases—or 96 percent.[43] In ninety-four of the cases (the majority), federal litigators presented arguments to weaken the application of the statute; federal judges rejected the arguments in 78 percent of the cases. Just over one-third of the losing NEPA-hostile arguments were presented by the Forest Service, with about one-fifth originating in the Department of the Interior and the remainder coming primarily from the Department of Transportation (15 percent), Army Corps of Engineers (8 percent), and the National Marine Fisheries Service (8 percent).[44]

Another way to view the Bush administration's legal record on NEPA is to compare it with that of former president Bill Clinton. A study found that although the Bush administration's executive branch agencies were active in at least 172 decided court cases between January 2001 and January 2003, during the first two years of the Clinton administration, 105 cases were decided. In these cases, the Bush administration was found to have a 55 percent "win rate," but the Clinton administration's rate was 74 percent of its total NEPA arguments.[45]

The Forest Service cases are of particular interest because they represent the type of approach the Bush administration has used to promote its reform agenda. In *Wilderness Society v. Rey*[46] the Forest Service was attempting to develop a salvage project for areas burned after the 2000 fires in the Bitterroot National Forest. After the Forest Service released a final EIS, USDA Undersecretary Mark Rey signed a record of decision in an effort to speed up implementation of the project by avoiding the normal administrative appeal process. The district court criticized the agency's "extra legal effort to circumvent the law" and rejected the approach, enjoining the salvage operations until the government complied with NEPA rules.

In another Montana District Court case, the Forest Service issued an Environmental Assessment (EA) and a Finding of No Significant Impact (FONSI) for a proposed timber sale involving three million board feet on 3,340 acres of forest. But the agency subsequently solicited salvage bids for a much different timber sale—9.5 million board feet from eight hundred acres. The Forest Service was sued by environmental organizations, and the court found that the agency had planned to authorize the larger sale all along while intentionally misleading the public. The court stated, "The bait and switch tactic the Forest Service employed defeats the purpose and intent of NEPA to allow the public opportunity to participate in the decision-making process."[47] The court then ordered the Forest Service to prepare an EA for the amended sale.

Timing, "Freaky Fridays," and Language Neutralizing the Problem

One of the ways in which policymakers can affect policy outcomes is by strategically timing the release of proposals, information, and responses. The Bush administration's environmental agenda has frequently taken advantage of congressional recesses, holidays, and what conservation groups like the Natural Resources Defense Council (NRDC) began to call "Freaky Fridays" as a way of limiting the visibility and debate over contentious legislative initiatives and regulatory proposals. The NRDC used the term in compiling a list of more than 100 environmental policy "rollbacks," with more than half announced on Fridays or just before holidays. "Friday is always a terrible day for coverage, and the fewest people read newspapers on Saturdays, so even if a story does get cranked out fewer people are going to see it," one NRDC leader noted. But "it's a very effective strategy, a very cynical strategy."[48]

Political life often imitates art. In an episode of the popular television drama "The West Wing," presidential press secretary C. J. Craig told staffers that controversial issues were to be "thrown out with the trash"—referring to the common practice of releasing information on Friday afternoons when media coverage would be minimal.

The NRDC cited the following examples: the EPA's relaxation of New Source Review air pollution regulations (two decisions announced on Fridays in October and November 2002, then another on New Year's Eve); the EPA's reduction of wetlands protection announced on Friday, January 10, 2003; a settlement of a lawsuit over wilderness in Utah opening the door for development announced on Friday, April 11, 2003; and at a 5:00 P.M. Friday press conference in October 2003, right before a three-day Columbus Day weekend, an announcement on the dumping of mine tailings on federal land.[49] Similarly, congressional Republicans announced they had finished a draft of the administration's proposals for a broad energy bill on a Friday afternoon even though the 1,700-page measure was still being printed.

To reduce media coverage and public attention, the White House also chose Fridays to respond to controversial or negative reports. In February 2004 the Union of Concerned Scientists issued a thirty-eight-page report, *Scientific Integrity in Policymaking: An Investigation into the Bush Administration's Misuse of Science,* that accused the administration of manipulating, suppressing, and misrepresenting science, actions the group called "unprecedented."[50] The administration's response, issued on Friday, April 2, included a point-by-point rebuttal of the February report.[51]

Strategic timing also played a part in other non-forest-related issues proposed by the administration. When EPA Administrator Whitman resigned in May 2003, observers wondered if the former New Jersey governor had been dissatisfied with the direction she had received from the White House. Some believed she felt that the president's advisors and staff were improperly "reinterpreting" legislation and policies that had been enacted under previous administrations. Because policies were not being "revised," there was no requirement for public comment, and the policy changes became effective immediately rather than going through a lengthy and visible regulatory process. This avoided potential delays in implementation and political clashes between the administration and affected stakeholders.

For example, after Whitman's departure, the EPA made what were considered "industry-friendly" revisions to the Clean Air Act, rescinded a twenty-seven-year-old policy that banned the sale of real estate contaminated with cancer-causing PCBs, and virtually abandoned programs like Superfund in favor of less restrictive policies. Jeff Ruch, director of Public Employees for Environmental Responsibility, noted that many of these actions took place in August 2003 when Congress was out of town.[52] A draft revision of the rules implementing the Clean Air Act Amendments that dealt with New Source Review called for "streamlining" requirements that older power plants and factories conform to newer air pollution laws. Thus, the administration's plans allowed companies to expand their facilities without also updating their pollution control systems. One observer noted the haste in which EPA sought to make the revisions reality. "They were under such pressure to put the rule out [in August] before Congress returned to town that they failed to clean up the internal edits in the rule."[53] Arguing that the rules would substantially increase air pollution, Earthjustice and a coalition of environmental groups joined by twelve states sued in federal court, arguing that the rule changes drafted by the EPA were a rollback from existing air quality standards. On December 24, 2003, the U.S. District Court of Appeals in Washington, D.C., temporarily blocked implementation of a key portion of the new rule just days before it was to go into effect. The decision was only a postponement until the court actually tried the case the next year.[54]

31

The use of specially crafted language to neutralize problems is also key to understanding the Bush administration's overall environmental record during his first term. Nationally known Republican consultant and pollster Frank Luntz was almost single-handedly directing the way in which both appointees and initiatives were presented to the media and to the public. Luntz, who had helped draft the Republicans' 1994 "Contract with America" for House Speaker Newt Gingrich, had also recommended that the party tone down its rhetoric on the environment during the 1995–1996 backlash against the party's plan. *The New York Times* had published an editorial noting that it had become clear "that the Gingrich revolution had gone too far in its attacks on environmental law."[55]

In early 2003 the Environmental Working Group obtained documents purported to be part of a briefing book prepared by Luntz Research Companies for the Republican party and its candidates. Among the documents was a memo—"The Environment: A Cleaner, Safer, Healthier America"—that started by noting, "The core of the Democrat argument depends on the belief that '*Washington regulations*' represent the best way to preserve the environment. We don't agree." It continued with a sentence that would become one of the most oft-repeated warnings the Republicans would hear from Luntz. "The environment is probably the single issue on which Republicans in general—and President Bush in particular—are most vulnerable."[56]

Luntz focused on eight strategies that could be used to "neutralize the problem and eventually bring people around to your point of view on environmental issues."

- Assure your audience that you are committed to "preserving and protecting" the environment but that "it can be done more wisely and effectively."
- Provide specific examples of federal bureaucrats failing to meet their responsibilities to protect the environment.
- Put your plan in terms of the future, not the past or present.
- Use the three words Americans are looking for in an environmental policy: "safer," "cleaner," and "healthier."
- Stay away from "risk assessment," "cost-benefit analysis," and the other traditional environmental terminology used by industry and corporations.
- Stress that you are seeking "a fair balance" between the environment and the economy if you must use the economic argument.
- Describe the limited role of Washington.
- Emphasize common sense.[57]

The memo also provided specific examples of language and phrases that could be used on issues such as arsenic in drinking water, preserving parks and open spaces, and global warming. Among the recommendations was a series of "Words that Work" and "Language that Works" with precise phrasing. The section on the environmental regulatory process notes:

> You cannot allow yourself to be labeled "anti-environment" simply because you are opposed to the current regulatory configuration. The public does not approve of the present regulatory process, and Americans certainly don't want an increased regulatory burden, but they will put a higher priority on environmental protection and public health than on cutting regulations. That is why you must explain how it is possible to pursue a *common sense* or *sensible* environmental policy that *"preserves all the gains of the past two decades"* without going to extremes.[58]

The importance of the Luntz memo is that it framed the environmental debate in terms that kept Republicans on message for the rest of Bush's first term. The National Environmental Trust created a Web site, LuntzSpeak.com, and The Luntzie Award, "given periodically to members of the Bush administration and Congress who best exemplify using LuntzSpeak to hide terrible environmental records."[59] The organization began to chronicle examples where LuntzSpeak had been used by administration officials, from Agriculture Secretary Ann Veneman to EPA Administrator Mike Leavitt. In commenting on new forest regulations in the *Washington Post*, Veneman states that the program's goal is to "streamline unnecessary, burdensome red tape" and the *New York Times* paraphrases Veneman's comments on the new regulations as "intended to streamline the bureaucratic process."[60] Many of these rhetorical devices would find their way into congressional hearings and comments on the administration's forest policies, as subsequent chapters will demonstrate.

By the midpoint of the president's first term, environmental report cards were showing up everywhere, with groups on both sides of the political continuum ranking the administration's record on major issues. The Natural Resources Defense Council claimed in its *2002 Year End Report* that "every federal agency with authority over environmental programs has been enlisted in a coordinated effort to help oil, coal, logging, mining, chemical, and auto companies and others promote their short term profits at the expense of America's public health and natural heritage."[61] Another author noted, "The irony is that Bush has compiled this odious record without having an environmental policy as such. Instead, his environmental achievements—an ever-lengthening list of regulations relaxed, actions delayed and foxes put in charge of hen houses—have come mainly as a consequence of policies pursued in other fields: economic, military, and above all, energy."[62]

Other observers argued that Bush successfully pushed his environmental agenda forward at a time when the public was focused on foreign policy. After the terrorist attacks of September 11, the president's popularity soared. The attacks fundamentally changed U.S. attitudes and politics and further removed domestic issues from the policy arena. Terrorism and homeland security captured Americans' attention, and the president was given great latitude to use his power and authority to respond to perceived and actual threats. When the United States began bombing Iraq in March 2003, public opinion was strongly on the side of the president, even as the number of casualties began to grow and it appeared the war would not end as quickly as many had predicted. Concerns about North Korea's potential for building nuclear weapons and the continuing hunt in Afghanistan for terrorist leader Osama bin Laden continued to dominate media headlines.

As a result of the foreign policy emphasis, Bush was able to promote many industry-friendly proposals. The president of the National Environmental Trust noted, "There is a quite distinct desire on the part of a number of agencies to hide under the air cover of the war in Afghanistan to roll back or weaken various environmental regulations while attention is on military developments in Afghanistan."[63] The administration responded that it was creating balance by giving business a role in environmental policies that was denied in the Clinton administration.

In 2003 the report card grades continued to fall. The League of Conservation Voters (LCV), which has published a national environmental scorecard since 1970, said the president was well on the way to compiling the worst environmental record of any president in U.S. history. The organization gave Bush an "F" for his administration's environmental performance, saying the president was waging an aggressive, but subtle, campaign to roll back environmental protection by using "deceptive rhetoric, arcane procedural methods, and funding cuts . . . [and] using the regulatory rulemaking process to slip through broad changes to land use policy and environmental protections that are difficult to explain to the American public."[64]

By summer 2003 the administration clearly focused its attention on forest policy as Congress began to show signs that they might be willing to sign off on new legislation weakening some regulations deemed burdensome to the timber industry. Anticipating another relentless wildfire season, it appeared that public support for the federal government to "do something" was sufficient to move proposals further, a process described in detail in Chapters 4 through 6.

THE 2004 PRESIDENTIAL CAMPAIGN

In most elections, candidates take their cues from public opinion polls to formulate their stance on specific issues, and the election cycle for the 2004 presidential campaign was no different. An early 2003 survey taken by the Pew Research Center found that only 2 percent of the voters contacted said they wanted to hear more about environmental issues from their elected representatives; 55 percent wanted to hear more about the economy.[65] In March 2003, 69 percent of Arizona adults surveyed in the Rocky Mountain Poll said Bush was doing a "good" or "excellent" job as president; by mid-July, the numbers had dropped to 56 percent.[66] The numbers were virtually unchanged from what they had been in the previous sixteen months, despite dozens of regulatory changes that had been promulgated but rarely covered by the media. An Andreas McKenna Research poll in July 2003 found that only 5 percent of respondents considered the environment their "most important issue,"[67] continuing the trends of previous years' results: environmental issues were almost invisible to most voters.

Despite the low salience of the environment as a political issue, political strategists said that the 2004 election could be decided by a small number of "swing" voters who generally see themselves as moderates. Democrats believed that if Bush were painted as an extreme anti-environmentalist, moderates might not support him. Republicans countered that it was possible to make the president more appealing to moderate voters to attract them on otherwise marginal issues. "They are making an effort to make him less odious in the eyes of people who might not be members of Friends of the Earth but who have a citizen's regard for the environment," said one political scientist. "It's an effort to render less toxic an issue that could be troublesome for swing voters."[68]

As the election cycle for the 2004 presidential campaign began, there were nine Democratic contenders, all of whom used the term "rollback" in their references to the Bush record. In June 2003, just as the president was about to visit California, the LCV held its first ever presidential candidate debate on the environment. Five of the contenders participated in the ninety-minute debate at the University of California, Los Angeles. The candidates used this opportunity to blast Bush's record and to show how their positions compared. The Reverend Al Sharpton seemed to gather the most sound bites by complaining that with big political contributions, oil and timber groups had been allowed to "buy their way into" policies that put Americans in environmental danger. The administration is so oil-friendly, Sharpton said, that "Washington is downright greasy. . . . We need to get the greasy people out of Washington."[69]

The president spent much of summer 2003 making public appearances with an environmental theme—shoveling dirt on a trail in California's Santa Monica Mountains, visiting a salmon preservation program in Washington, and surveying wildfire damage in Oregon. On August 11, 2003, he visited the Aspen Fire area that burned through the Summerhaven/Mt. Lemmon area of the Coronado

National Forest outside Tucson, Arizona, urging Congress to speed up tree cutting in overgrown forests to prevent more disastrous wildfires. He called past forest policies "failed" and "backward" as he promoted his Healthy Forests Initiative.[70]

Political analysts noted that although the environment had ranked as a low concern for most voters, the visit was the first half of a two-part strategy by the president to appeal to swing voters in states like Arizona where otherwise marginal issues can become central.[71] The second half of the strategy was to visit battleground states. The choice of venues was critical; Bush had narrowly lost the electoral votes in Oregon and Washington in 2000, and had won Arizona by just six percentage points. By the time that the first debates sponsored by the Democratic National Committee took place in Phoenix on October 9, all nine Democratic candidates had carved out positions on the Healthy Forests Initiative, recognizing that wildfires and forest policy were extremely salient issues in the West.

Despite the success of the forest measure, the president's energy proposal was a losing proposition. Two days after the Healthy Forests Restoration Act was passed, Senate Majority Leader Bill Frist (R-TN) announced that the energy bill did not have sufficient votes to pass during the 2003 session. The House had easily passed the measure, but in the Senate a coalition of Democrats and Republicans, joining together for different reasons, blocked further action. An attempt to shut off debate and bring the measure to a vote fell two senators short of the sixty needed. Supporters promised to revive the proposal once the session reconvened in 2004.

Despite coverage given to Democratic candidates during the primaries, President Bush was able to gain the media spotlight on several occasions, avoiding and deflecting attention from environmental issues. In his January 2004 State of the Union Address, for instance, he made a one-sentence reference to energy policy, but the word environment was not used at all during the speech. By mid-February John Kerry had emerged as the de facto Democratic nominee, and although he would not be confirmed until the party's national convention in August, he and vice-presidential running mate John Edwards began to seek support for their environmental proposals.

Kerry received the League of Conservation Voters endorsement for his "unparalleled record on environmental issues," along with the support of forty-eight Nobel Prize–winning scientists. The Democratic candidates, however, found themselves responding to the issues of terrorism and the continuing war in Iraq, driven by the president's agenda rather than their own. The Kerry-Edwards campaign did release a forest management plan called "Putting Communities First." The proposal cited their commitment "to preserving and maintaining healthy forests that generate good jobs and support productive communities," as well as support "for logging and fuel reduction activities required to support the timber industry and protect communities from devastating forest fires."[72]

Meanwhile President Bush quietly continued to move his environmental agenda forward. The Tribal Forest Protection Act of 2004 was introduced concurrently in the House and Senate on February 26, 2004, with bipartisan support. A response to the wildfires of 2003 that damaged timber on nearly twenty Indian reservations, this legislation allowed Indian tribes to submit requests or enter into an agreement or contract for projects to protect Indian forest land from wildfires, including hazardous fuels removal or thinning. Congressmembers were driven in part by criticism that the Healthy Forests Restoration Act passed the previous year lacked a quick and effective mechanism to deal with mudslides and other problems that endangered Indian communities. In hearings, members also noted that passage of the bill would help reduce the number of forest project lawsuits because tribes would play a more significant role in fuels reduction activities. These projects would also expand economic opportunities on the reservations. Moving swiftly through committees in both houses, the measure was signed by President Bush on July 22, 2004.[73]

On Earth Day, April 22, the president announced a new goal of moving beyond a policy of "no net loss" of wetlands to one that would lead to an overall increase of wetlands each year. Bush said that the administration was placing a premium on conservation efforts and would implement "cooperative conservation efforts as a better way to achieve and sustain success."[74] The term "cooperative conservation" began showing up in a series of proposals over the next few months. Interior Secretary Gale Norton announced awards of $21 million in challenge cost-share grants under President Bush's Cooperative Conservation Initiative to complete 377 conservation projects in conjunction with states, local communities, and other partners. In a May 24, 2004, press release, Norton said, "The goal of the Cooperative Conservation Initiative is to empower federal land managers to form partnerships within local communities to better care for the land and its wildlife."[75]

At the same time the Democrats were going into high gear, the president released an executive order "to ensure that the Departments of the Interior, Agriculture, Commerce, and Defense, and the Environmental Protection Agency implement laws relating to the environment and natural resources in a manner that promotes cooperative conservation, with an emphasis on appropriate inclusion of local participation in Federal decision making."[76] Carl Pope, executive director of the Sierra Club, said the executive order was "part of the 'shrinking-the-federal-safety-net' efforts by the Bush administration. "It's another signal to federal agencies that they're supposed to ignore enforcing the law and defer to local governments and landowners."[77]

With the help of conservative members of Congress, the administration was able to defeat efforts to ban snowmobiles in Yellowstone and Grant Teton National Parks in June. And a month later Department of Agriculture Secretary Ann Veneman unveiled a proposal outlining "five common sense conservation principles" that included a plan to give the state's governors eighteen months to ask the Forest Service to protect roadless areas in their states. States seeking protection would need to conduct environmental studies with public comment periods, which one conservation group leader called "foisting" the roadless controversy on the states at a time when they were already overwhelmed with financial problems.[78] "Our actions today advance the Bush administration's commitment to cooperatively conserving roadless areas," Veneman said. But as she spoke, plans were proceeding for new roads in roadless areas for oil and gas development in Colorado and Wyoming and for timber sales in Alaska and Oregon. Not unexpectedly, the proposed new roadless area rules generated a storm of controversy, and on September 8 the Forest Service announced it was extending the public comment period on the rule until November 1.[79] Final rules would therefore not be published until after the election.

The Kerry-Edwards campaign became bogged down by accusations over Kerry's Vietnam War record and allegations that Kerry had repeatedly changed his mind on his support for the war in Iraq, sidetracking any of his efforts to bring environmental issues to the campaign agenda. For the most part the Bush administration was also able to sidestep any serious questioning of the president's environmental record. During one of the three presidential debates, however, the president was asked about his environmental policies. Included in his response was reference to his forest policy successes.

> We proposed and passed a healthy forest bill which was essential to working with—particularly in Western states—to make sure that our forests were protected. What happens in those forests, because of lousy federal policy, is they grow to be—they are not—they're not harvested. They're not taken care of. And as a result, they're like tinder boxes. And over the last summers I've flown over there. And so, this is a reasonable policy to protect old stands of trees and at the same time make sure our forests aren't vulnerable to the forest fires that have destroyed acres after acres in the West. We've got a good, common sense policy.[80]

But generally, by Election Day on November 2, voters interested in environmental issues had heard little from either of the two main candidates. Bush defeated Kerry by more than three million popular votes and by thirty-four electoral college votes.

NOTES

1. For histories of the environmental movement, see Richard N.L. Andrews, *Managing the Environment, Managing Ourselves: A History of American Environmental Policy* (New Haven, CT: Yale University Press, 1999); William Cronon, *Changes in the Land: Indians, Colonists, and the Ecology of New England* (New York: Hill and Wang, 1983); Roderick Frazier Nash, *Wilderness and the American Mind,* Revised edition (New Haven, CT: Yale University Press, 1973); Jeanne Nienaber Clarke and Hanna J. Cortner, *The State and Nature: Voices Heard, Voices Unheard in America's Environmental Dialogue* (Upper Saddle River, NJ: Prentice Hall, 2002); and Michael Williams, *Americans and Their Forests: A Historical Geography* (New York, NY: Cambridge University Press, 1989).

2. Rachel Carson, *Silent Spring* (Boston, MA: Houghton Mifflin, 1962).

3. Stewart Udall, *The Quiet Crisis* (New York, NY: Avon Books, 1963), 175.

4. Lady Bird Johnson and Carlton B. Lees, *Wildflowers Across America* (New York: Abbeville Publishing, 1988), 265. See also Lewis L. Gould, *Lady Bird Johnson: Our Environmental First Lady* (Lawrence, KS: University Press of Kansas, 1999); and Lewis L. Gould, *Lady Bird Johnson and the Environment* (Lawrence, KS: University Press of Kansas, 1988).

5. Carl Sagan, *Pale Blue Dot: A Vision of the Human Future in Space* (New York, NY: Random House, 1994).

6. Daniel A. Dreyfus and Helen M. Ingram, "The National Environmental Policy Act: A View of Intent and Practice," *Natural Resources Journal* 16:2 (1976): 243–262.

7. Robert Gottlieb, *Forcing the Spring: The Transformation of the American Environmental Movement* (Washington, DC: Island Press, 1993), 282.

8. John C. Hendee and Randall C. Pitstick, "The Growth of Environmental and Conservation-Related Organizations: 1980–1991," *Renewable Resources Journal* 10:2 (1992): 6–19.

9. Public Land Law Review Commission, *One Third of the Nation's Land* (Washington, DC: Government Printing Office, 1970).

10. On the wise use movement, see Jacqueline Switzer, *Green Backlash: The History and Politics of Environmental Opposition in the U.S.* (Boulder, CO: Lynn Rienner, 1997); John Echeverria and Raymond Booth Eby, eds., *Let the People Judge: Wise Use and the Private Property Rights Movement* (Washington, DC: Island Press, 1995); Philip D. Brick and R. McGreggor Cawley, eds., *A Wolf in the Garden: The Lands Rights Movement and the New Environmental Debate* (Lanham, MD: Rowman and Littlefield, 1996); and R. McGreggor Cawley, *Western Land, Western Anger: The Sagebrush Rebellion and Environmental Politics* (Lawrence, KS: University Press of Kansas, 1993).

11. Hendee and Pitstick, "The Growth of Environmental and Conservation-Related Organizations."

12. Norman J. Vig, "Presidential Leadership and the Environment: From Reagan to Clinton," in *Environmental Policy,* Fourth edition, ed. Norman J. Vig and Michael E. Kraft (Washington, DC: CQ Press, 2003), 98–120.

13. Mark Baker and Jonathan Kusel, *Community Forestry in the United States: Learning from the Past, Crafting the Future* (Washington, DC: Island Press, 2003); and Ronald D.

Brunner, Christine H. Colburn, Christina M. Cromley, Roberta A. Klein, and Elizabeth A. Olson, *Finding Common Ground: Governance and Natural Resources in the American West* (New Haven, CT: Yale University Press, 2002).

14. "President George W. Bush," at www.whitehouse.gov/president/gwbbio accessed July 14, 2003.

15. Statistics on land ownership are compiled from www.southernregion.fs.fed.us/texas/about_us accessed July 10, 2003, and National Forest System acreage at www.roadless.fs.fed.us/documents/feis/data/sheets/acres/appendix accessed January 25, 2004.

16. Al Gore Jr., *Earth in the Balance: Ecology and the Human Spirit* (Boston, MA: Houghton Mifflin, 1992).

17. Lydia Saad and Riley E. Dunlap, "Americans Are Environmentally Friendly, But Issue Not Seen As Urgent Problem," *Gallup Poll Monthly* 415 (April 2000): 12–18.

18. Riley E. Dunlap, "Public Opinion and Environmental Policy," in *Environmental Politics and Policy*, ed. James P. Lester (Durham, NC: Duke University Press, 1989), 87–134.

19. Riley E. Dunlap, "The Environmental Movement at 30," *The Polling Report* 16:8 (April 24, 2000), 3.

20. Everett Carll Ladd and Karlyn Bowman, "Public Opinion on the Environment," *Resources* 124 (Summer 1996): 5–7.

21. Deborah Lynn Guber, *The Grassroots of a Green Revolution: Polling America on the Environment* (Cambridge, MA: MIT Press, 2003).

22. Rochelle L. Stanfield, "Ruckelshaus and Clark Seek to Blunt Environmental Lobby's Political Swords," *National Journal* 16 (June 30, 1984): 1256–1260.

23. Christopher J. Bosso, "Environmental Groups and the New Political Landscape," in *Environmental Policy*, Fourth edition, ed. Norman J. Vig and Michael E. Kraft (Washington, DC: CQ Press, 2000), 55 76.

24. Mark Hertsgaard, "Trashing the Environment: Kyoto Was Just a Start for Bush," *The Nation* (February 13, 2003): 16.

25. Margot Higgins, "Payback Time for Bush—At the Expense of Environment," *Environmental News Service* (April 24, 2001) at www.enn.com/extras accessed July 1, 2003, and "Paybacks: Policies, Patrons and Personnel: How the Bush Administration is Giving Away Our Environment to its Corporate Contributors," at www.earthjustice.org/policy/admin accessed January 15, 2004.

26. Ibid.

27. J. E. deSteiguer, "Senator Craig's Public Lands Management Improvement Act of 1997," *Journal of Forestry* 96:9 (1998): 7–10.

28. Michael Milstein, "Bush's Chief of Wildlands Kindles Worry," *The Oregonian* (August 30, 2002) at www.oregonlive.com/news/oregonian/index accessed September 1, 2002.

29. Allan K. Fitzsimmons, "Federal Ecosystem Management: A 'Train Wreck' in the Making," *Cato Institute Policy Analysis* 17 (1994); and Allan K. Fitzsimmons, "Sound Policy or Smoke and Mirrors: Does Ecosystem Management Make Sense?" *Water Resources Bulletin* 32:2 (1996): 217–227.

30. The White House, "Environmental Protection Agency, Administrator Christie Todd Whitman" (2001) at www.whitehouse.gov/government/whitman-bio accessed November 28, 2003.

31. Jonathan H. Adler, "Post-Whitman EPA," *National Review Magazine Online* (June 2, 2003) at www.nationalreview.com/adler accessed November 28, 2003.

32. Katherine Q. Seelye, "Bush Choice to Head EPA Asks Clinton Administrator for Reference," *New York Times* (August 12, 2003) at www.nytimes.com/2003/08/13/politics accessed August 13, 2003.

33. Rich Vosepka, "Enviros Unhappy to See Leavitt Head EPA," *Arizona Daily Sun* (August 12, 2003) at www.azdailysun.com accessed August 12, 2003.

34. Business and Legal Reports, "Mike Leavitt Sworn in as EPA Administrator," (November 7, 2003) at www.enviro2.blr.com accessed November 28, 2003.

35. Ray Ring, "Tipping the Scales," *High Country News* (February 16, 2004), 8–10, 13–15, 19.

36. Ibid.

37. Defenders of Wildlife Judicial Accountability Project, *Weakening the National Environmental Policy Act: How the Bush Administration Uses the Judicial System to Weaken Environmental Protections* (Washington, DC: Defenders of Wildlife, 2003) 21.

38. Richard J. Pierce Jr., "Is Standing Law or Politics?" *North Carolina Law Review* 77 (1999): 1741.

39. Richard L. Revesz, "Environmental Regulation, Ideology, and the D.C. Circuit," *Virginia Law Review* 83 (1997): 1717.

40. "Renzi Attempting to Short-Circuit 9th Circuit," *Arizona Daily Sun* (May 9, 2004), A-2.

41. Defenders of Wildlife, *Weakening the National Environmental Policy Act*.

42. Hertsgaard, "Trashing the Environment," 15.

43. Defenders of Wildlife, *Weakening the National Environmental Policy Act*, 5.

44. Ibid, 30.

45. Ibid, 5.

46. 180 F.Supp.2d 1141 (D. Mont. 2002).

47. *Friends of Clearwater v. McAllister*, 214 F.Supp.2d 1083, quotation cited at 1089.

48. Ray Ring, "Freaky Fridays with the Bush Administration," *High Country News* (November 30, 2003), 3.

49. Ibid.

50. Andrew C. Revkin, "White House Denies Distorting Science Data," *Arizona Republic* (April 3, 2004). The Union of Concerned Scientists report is available online at www.ucsusa.org accessed April 3, 2004.

51. The administration's response in available online at www.ostp.gov accessed April 3, 2004.

52. Laura Paskus, "Who's at the Helm?" *High Country News* (September 29, 2003), 3.

53. Ibid.

54. Gary Polakovic, "Bush's Exemption of Air Quality Plan Blocked by Judge," *Arizona Republic* (December 25, 2003): A4.

55. Bill Berkowitz, "Wreckreation: Paying to Play on Public Lands" (2003) at www.workingforchange.com/article accessed February 7, 2004.

56. Portions of the Luntz memo have been circulated on the Internet by a variety of organizations. The version referred to here is based on what appears to be part of a larger document called "Straight Talk," 131–143, at www.ewg.org/briefings/luntzmemo accessed January 25, 2004.

57. Ibid.

58. Ibid.

59. Environmental Media Services, "EPA Nominee Leavitt Followed Luntz Enviro Spin Word-For-Word," News release (September 29, 2003) at www.ems.org/leavitt accessed January 25, 2004.

60. Environmental Working Group, "Briefing: Luntz Memo on the Environment," at www.ewg.org/briefings/luntzmemo accessed January 25, 2004.

61. Executive Summary at www.nrdc.org/legislation/rollbacks/execsum accessed July 1, 2003.

62. Hertsgaard, "Trashing the Environment," 15.

63. Elizabeth Shogren, "Environmental Rulings Aid Congress," *Arizona Republic* (December 28, 2001): A6.

64. J. R. Pegg, "League of Conservation Voters Slams Bush Record," *Environment News Service* (June 24, 2003) at www.ens-news.com/end/jun2003 accessed June 27, 2003.

65. Margaret Kriz, "Has George W. Bush Gone Green? *Hoover Digest* 2 (2003) at www.hoover.standford.edu/publications/digest/032/kriz accessed June 27, 2003.

66. C. J. Karamargin, "04 Politics at Heart of Bush Trip," *Arizona Daily Star* (August 11, 2003) at www.azstarnet.com/star/today accessed August 11, 2003.

67. Maura Reynolds, "Bush Touching on Environment," *Arizona Republic* (August 21, 2003), A6.

68. Ibid.

69. Carla Marinucci, "Bush Attacked on Environment," (June 27, 2003) at www.sfgate.com accessed November 28, 2003.

70. Mitch Tobin, "Bush Calls for Fast Action to Fix 'Failed' Forest Policies," *Arizona Star* (August 12, 2003) at www.azstarnet.com accessed August 12, 2003.

71. Reynolds, "Bush Touching on Environment."

72. "The Kerry-Edwards Forest Plan: Putting Communities First," at www.johnkerry.com/issues/environment accessed August 13, 2004.

73. The two measures were S. 2134 and H.R. 3846; the House bill was the one ultimately signed by the president. See Erica Werner, "Tribes Seek Federal Lands Access to Keep Threat off Reservations," *San Diego Union-Tribune* (April 22, 2004) at www.signonsandiego.com accessed May 5, 2004; "Senate Passes Feinstein-Pombo Tribal Forest Protection Act," News release (June 25, 2004) at www.feinstein.senate.gov accessed August 2, 2004.

74. White House, "President Announces Wetlands Initiative on Earth Day," Fact sheet (April 22, 2004) at www.whitehouse.gov/news/releases accessed August 28, 2004.

75. "Secretary Norton Announces $21 Million in Grants to Support Conservation in 43 States," News release (May 24, 2004) at www.doi.gov/news accessed August 28, 2004.

76. "Executive Order Facilitation of Cooperative Conservation," News release (August 26, 2004) at www.whitehouse.gov/news/releases accessed August 28, 2004.

77. John Heilprin, "Bush: Consider Landowners on Environment," *Newsday* (August 27, 2004) at www.newsday.com/news/politics accessed August 28, 2004.

78. Laura Paskus, "Feds Pass Roadless Headache to States," *High Country News* (August 16, 2004): 3.

79. Chris Wood, "'Conservation' Strategy is a Wolf in Sheep's Clothing," *High Country News* (August 16, 2004), 23; "Forest Service Extends Timeframe for Public to Comment on Proposed Roadless Rule," News release (September 8, 2004) at www.roadless.fs.fed.us accessed October 28, 2004.

80. Commission on Presidential Debates, Debate Transcript, The Second Bush-Kerry Debate (October 8, 2004), Washington University, St. Louis, Missouri at www.debates.org/pages/trans2004c accessed November 16, 2004.

THE RIGHT TO OBJECT
Historic Landmarks in the
Development and Use of Appeals

THE ADMINISTRATIVE APPEALS THAT IGNITED THE DEBATE OVER WILDFIRES AND FOREST POLICIES between 2000 and 2003 are part of a somewhat arcane and poorly understood aspect of politics called administrative rulemaking. Most textbooks on U.S. politics, from elementary and secondary schools through college, ignore or gloss over this process. As a result, most people believe that Congress makes laws without giving much thought to what happens next. Policies go from the House and Senate to the president's desk for signing, and a magical stage called "implementation" begins (although it is doubtful many citizens could attach that term to what goes on; implementation is an artifice of academicians seeking to find order in a disorderly process). There is seldom any implication that the process might be political; in fact, many of those who have even an inkling of what administrative rulemaking involves consider the subject to be somewhat boring.

The process stems, in part, from the 1946 Administrative Procedure Act (APA), which was enacted to provide standardization and predictability to the ways in which government agencies make decisions. The APA divides administrative procedure into three types of actions: rulemaking, when agencies act like legislatures; adjudication, when agencies act like courts; and everything else.[1] According to one scholar of administrative law as contemplated by the

APA, "Rulemaking authority, safely ensconced in the bowels of agencies, was attended to by specialized staffs with narrow responsibilities and without the presence of constituencies holding the big stick of re-election in their hands."[2]

The APA defines a rule as "the whole or part of an agency statement of general or particular applicability and future effect designed to implement, interpret, or prescribe law or policy."[3] There is another much more apropos explanation: "Rules are products of the bureaucratic institutions to which we entrust the implementation, management, and administration of our law and public policy."[4]

Congress initiates and enacts legislation, delegating authority to implement laws to agencies within the executive branch. Laws often provide only vague definitions and direction, leaving government bureaucracies to interpret statutes, once they have been signed by the president, and then originate and develop procedures to make the laws work as Congress intended. Rules can only be derived from legislation, limiting to some extent the number and types of rules that can be developed. Thus, they are a by-product of the legislative process and part of the symbiotic relationship between Congress and agencies. Rulemaking is designed to sort through facts from multiple sources in order to select standards that can be applied generally.[5] Most procedures called "notice and comment" or "informal" rulemaking, which allow public participation, are found in section 553 of the APA, constituting what another noted administrative law scholar has called one of the "greatest inventions of modern government."[6]

Public participation in rulemaking was studied years before passage of the APA and has varied considerably since the law's enactment. In the late 1930s, a study by the Attorney General's Office found that departments were engaging stakeholders in varied ways. Some used informal and formal conferences, or advisory bodies, while others simply collected public comments on proposed rules, but few opportunities existed for other forms of involvement. There appeared to be an assumption that each agency with rulemaking responsibilities would develop procedures for public-agency interaction. In one sense, this allowed room for innovation and for departmental discretion to tailor procedures to specific circumstances. This chapter traces the evolution of public-agency interactions in the development and use of the administrative appeals process during the almost 100-year history of the Forest Service and provides a more detailed overview of public use of the appeals process from 1997 through 2003.

EARLY DISPUTE PROCEDURES: 1906–1936[7]

When the Forest Service was established within the U.S. Department of Agriculture by the Transfer Act of 1905, the agency began to develop its own internal guidelines, which eventually were formalized in the *Forest Service Manual of Procedure*. A series of early regulations dealt with livestock; until the enactment of the 1934 Taylor Grazing Act and the creation of the Bureau of Land Management (BLM) in 1946, the Forest Service supervised grazing on public lands, a controversial part of the agency's responsibilities. In *Forest Circular #36*, published in 1906, the agency implied that there had been opposition to federal regulations on grazing practices, mentioning lawsuits against the government by ranchers dissatisfied with Forest Service decisions. Subsequent regulations outlined the procedures by which citizens could access agency records and the handling of legal claims.[8] Thus, almost from the Forest Service's inception mechanisms have been in place by which those aggrieved by an agency decision could appeal,[9] although such early appeals were used mostly by interests that had a business relationship with the agency.

Appeals procedures were not codified until 1936 in a rule published in the *Federal Register*. Regulation A-10 of that rule states:

> An appeal may be taken from any administrative action or decision by filing with the officer who rendered the decision a written request for reconsideration thereof or notice of appeal. Decisions of forest officers shall be final unless appeal is taken therefrom within a reasonable time. The decision appealed shall be reviewed by the immediate superior of the officer by whom the decision was rendered; that is, in the following order: Supervisor, Regional Forester, Chief of the Forest Service, Secretary of Agriculture.[10]

The 1936 rules became part of the *Code of Federal Regulations* (CFR), Title 36, and remained in effect for nearly thirty years. (Figure 2.1 schematically summarizes the incremental development of the appeals system from 1906 through 2004.)

ENVIRONMENTAL REGULATORY PROCEDURES: 1965–1989

The appeals process was modified in 1965 by changes to the CFR that created three classes of administrative appeals for different types of decisions. Although the 1936 regulations had stated that appeals could apply to "any administrative action or decision," the 1965 regulations (36 CFR 211.20) designated certain types of decisions that were excluded from the appeals process. (The only section of Forest Service regulations addressing appeals until 1989, Part 211 would be revised several times in the ensuing years.) The changes in 1965 also established a Board of Forest Appeals, which administered the Forest Service administrative appeals process, although it was external to—and independent from—the agency. This board existed until 1974.[11] Again, the kinds of grievances covered by the

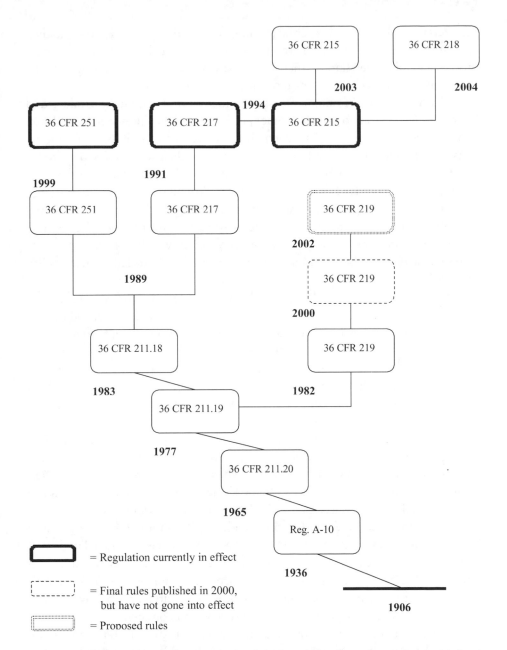

FIGURE 2.1. *Evolution of existing Forest Service administrative appeals regulations. Source: Updated from Gretchen M.R. Teich, "Analysis Paralysis? Examining Administrative Appeals of Forest Service Decisions," Masters thesis (Flagstaff, AZ: Northern Arizona University School of Forestry, 2003)*

rules promulgated during this period primarily involved issues with parties holding a permit or having another sort of business relationship with the agency. Environmental era legislation, such as the NEPA and the NFMA, as well as the concomitant public involvement movement, changed all that.

NEPA expanded requirements for consideration of the public's values and interests—factors that forced government agencies like the Forest Service to listen and respond to the growing environmental movement as well as to traditional constituents like timber, mining, and ranching industries. NEPA declared a national policy on the environment, required all agencies to prepare EISs detailing the effects of proposed federal projects on the environment, and created the CEQ. The EIS requirement, NEPA's unique "action-forcing mechanism," was inserted into NEPA specifically to compel agencies to go beyond traditional economic and technical analyses when looking at project feasibility and to consider environmental ramifications, thus ensuring agency compliance with the law's general policy goals.

NEPA was extraordinarily vague and broad in its directives to federal agencies. Originally, agencies such as the Forest Service, National Park Service, and Bureau of Outdoor Recreation (now defunct) believed they were exempt from the act because they were on the side of the environment,[12] a notion they were soon disabused of. NEPA's procedural requirements opened up a significant avenue for groups to sue recalcitrant agencies that ignored important environmental effects or did not consider a full range of alternatives to their favored projects. Courts began to play a leading role in NEPA implementation, which may be traced in large measure to their willingness to review all agency action more closely than they had in previous years and a broadening of the legal requirement of standing.[13] Courts decided such NEPA issues such as what constituted major federal issues, what kinds of actions "significantly affected" the environment, and what an EIS should contain. The courts gave NEPA and its action-forcing EIS provision meaning, substance, and vitality and made NEPA more than a vague and insignificant policy declaration. Much of NEPA's success is associated with environmental group successes in litigation, the results of which were incorporated into revised rules. These regulations direct agencies to follow specific steps with timelines and procedural requirements, including requirements for agencies to make their EISs available to the public for review and comment.

Under the administrations of President Richard Nixon and later Gerald Ford, the president took a much more active role in using the regulatory process as a way of retaining control over legislative initiatives like NEPA. These efforts coincided with a rise in social regulations and the overall expansion of the federal government during the 1970s. "Presidents came to realize that their grip on the course of domestic public policy hinged to a considerable extent on their ability to influence the thousands of rules that put programs into action."[14]

The numerous environmental statutes passed by Congress during the 1970s provided dozens of opportunities for the president to influence policy implementation. Initially, federal agencies were instructed by Nixon's Executive Order 11514 to initiate their own rules for implementing NEPA; in 1977, President Jimmy Carter's Executive Order 11991 gave the CEQ specific authority to issue regulations to agencies, thereby reversing the process. Under Title 40 of the *Code of Federal Regulations,* agencies were directed to involve the public in planning and analysis prior to making determinations, mandating the development of specific procedures for public participation. The indirect effect of CEQ's actions was to open up federal agencies and their procedures to additional scrutiny at a time when there was a considerable amount of public distrust of the government.

Other legislation, such as the 1974 Forest and Rangeland Renewable Resources Planning Act (RPA), formalized planning procedures for the Forest Service. By requiring the agency to develop a comprehensive assessment of all the nation's forests and rangelands and a national program of work specific to the agency's own activities, planning became institutionalized. Similarly, NFMA mandated public participation in the Forest Service's development of a land and resource management plan (LRMP) for each national forest although it did not specifically mention administrative appeals.

In response to NFMA, however, the Forest Service did review the administrative appeals regulations that had been in place since 1965. The 1977 revisions (36 CFR 211.19) provided "what was perhaps the most liberal voluntary administrative appeals system of any federal agency."[15] Another key element of the NFMA was the creation of an external Committee of Scientists, appointed by the Secretary of Agriculture, to provide scientific and technical advice and counsel on regulations implementing NFMA's planning mandate. Convened in May 1977, the committee addressed the issue of administrative appeals. The agency had proposed putting limits on plan appeals. Noting that such limitations would be controversial, the committee nonetheless concluded that the Forest Service's fear of planning and implementation delays must be balanced against the public's right to participate and potential litigation.[16]

Although the Committee of Scientists recommended that the Forest Service "offer a different solution" to the administrative appeals regulations, the agency balked. The planning rules adopted in September 1979 extended the provisions for appeal under 36 CFR 211.19 to decisions approving forest plans, revisions, or significant amendments, and limited appeals to those who had participated in "direct and documented involvement" in the planning process. The rules did not contain provisions for appeals of regional plans and specifically excluded decisions made during the planning process.

The focus on public participation in decision making was also being expanded beyond forest issues in the late 1970s, largely as a result of the momentum of mainstream environmental organizations who demanded a voice in the policy process. Change was facilitated by the vision of the Carter administration, which sought to broaden public input as a way of reforming government and restoring the public's trust. In March 1978, Carter signed Executive Order 12044, which applied to all rules and regulations within federal agencies. The president's initiative required government agencies to develop procedures to allow public comment in the development of all new rules and regulations and to conduct periodic reviews of their clarity, effectiveness, and efficiency. The president's action also created a regulatory council—consisting of agency directors responsible for the most substantial regulatory programs—that would coordinate rulemaking activities for the federal government. In addition to preparing a calendar of key regulatory events and activities, this council was expected to study the cumulative effects of regulations on "particularly vulnerable industries or sectors."[17]

Executive Order 12044 also created the Regulatory Analysis Review Group headed by the Council of Economic Advisors to "improve the quality of analysis supporting proposed regulations, identify and attempt to resolve common analytic problems among the agencies and assure adequate consideration of least costly alternatives."[18] Potentially, the group would be used as a vehicle for all regulatory agencies to review and comment on rules developed by a particular agency, therefore increasing available expertise and promoting rulemaking consistency. The president also had the Office of Management and Budget (OMB) report to him about regulatory activities and the performance of agencies implementing EO 12044.[19]

In that same year, congressional action in the Contract Disputes Act of 1978 gave an independent Board of Contract Appeals the authority to decide the kind of contractual appeals that had previously been handled by the Board of Forest Appeals. Still operating today, the Board of Contract Appeals handles contractual disputes for all Department of Agriculture agencies, not just the Forest Service. With regard to the Forest Service, the board primarily handles disputes between the agency and contractors over timber sale agreements. Jurisdiction applies once a timber sale contract has been awarded; in contrast, the appeals process is applicable before the agency makes the final decision to offer a sale contract, prior to bidding from a contractor. The process is entirely separate from the administrative appeals process.

The environmental movement's momentum was blocked when, shortly after taking office, President Ronald Reagan revoked Carter's EO 12044. In its place,

Reagan's Executive Order 12291, issued in February 1981, instituted a sixty-day moratorium on any new rules. The director of the OMB was given oversight authority for regulations, and the Reagan administration made it clear that rules that were "burdensome" to business were to be strictly scrutinized. Executive Order 12291 also called for a Presidential Task Force on Regulatory Relief (elevating the status of Carter's Regulatory Council) to review existing regulations, with a focus on many of the environmental rules enacted under his predecessor. In effect, Reagan used the power of the presidency to delay rules that were not congruent with his administration's environmental policies and had "a more profound effect on the rulemaking process than the entire Carter program."[20]

As part of the regulatory review mandated by the president (the task force had identified the Forest Service's planning rules as a high priority for review), the Forest Service began another round of reviews of its administrative appeals system. In summer 1982 it briefly reconvened members of the Committee of Scientists to comment on proposed changes to the planning rules. The final planning rules (adopted in 1982 and amended in part in 1983) extended the provisions of Part 211 to decisions associated with regional guides and to the forest plans themselves. (The 1977 regulations had only contained a provision to appeal the decision to approve or disapprove the forest plan.)

In March 1983, as a continuing part of the regulatory review process, the agency revised Part 211 once again. The final 1983 rule (36 CFR 211.18) provided detailed procedures for interactions between the agency and appellants. Under these rule changes, there was no formal requirement of legal standing to file an appeal, but a forty-five-day time limit was imposed and limits placed on extensions of deadlines for filing an appeal. The new rules also required appellants to provide a statement of reasons for the appeal. The Forest Service Deciding Officer was required to issue a "responsive statement" within thirty days, and appellants then had twenty days to issue a "concise reply." At that point, the appeal was to be forwarded to the Appeal Reviewing Officer.[21] The final rule also made provisions for a stay of decision, a second level of appeal, and created a status of "intervenor" that allowed individuals or groups to file separate written comments and to request oral presentations.[22]

The rule changes created a system that was much more adversarial and legalistic, requiring an extensive paper trail of documentation by the agency. This coincided with the development and expansion of public interest environmental law firms with well-trained legal staff eager to test and challenge federal environmental statutes. Groups like the Environmental Defense Fund, the Natural Resources Defense Council, and the Sierra Club Legal Defense Fund were joined in challenging agency decisions by grassroots groups that provided citizen oversight to individual national forests. In addition to filing appeals to forest plans, environmental group advocates began challenging forest projects, further adding to the Forest Service's workload. Litigation became a major tool of the environmental movement, with national organizations providing legal assistance to smaller local or regional groups that felt lawsuits were their only weapon against the Reagan administration's assault on the environment. Not surprisingly, as the rules become more legalistic and process oriented, objections focused more on procedural rather than substantive issues.

After the 1983 rule changes went into effect, the number of administrative appeals filed remained stable for three years: in fiscal year 1983, 584 appeals, followed by 439 in fiscal year 1984, and 581 in fiscal year 1985. But in fiscal year 1986, appeals nearly doubled to 1,081, followed by 874 in fiscal year 1987, 1,609 in fiscal year 1988, and 1,291 in fiscal year 1989.[23] The Congressional Research Service (CRS), the public policy research arm of Congress, theorized that the mid-1980s jump in appeals coincided with the promulgation of many of the first round of forest management plans required by NFMA. By 1990, approximately 100 of the 123 NFMA plans had been completed, "so it is possible," the CRS concluded, "that the surge in appeals may soon begin to decline. On the other hand, plans for some of the most timber-important regions are still not finalized, and there will still be many more appeals as various activities implementing the plans are challenged."[24]

The Forest Service became increasingly frustrated with the appeals process. According to one former employee, "This frustration grew as Forest Service managers recognized that appeals had changed from a tool to resolve disputes over project design and location to a means to delay or postpone projects."[25] There were concerns about the increasing number of appeals, time to resolve appeals, staff resources to process appeals, and costs of appeals.

During 1989 the agency made a series of changes to its appeals system. These revisions were based on the recommendations of the Appeals Regulation Review Team that the Chief of the Forest Service had convened in 1987 to evaluate the 1983 rule and recommend revisions. The agency separated out appeals in Part 211 that related to permits from appeals related to projects; provisions related to permits were now contained in 36 CFR 251, and provisions related to projects and plans in 36 CFR 217. The decision to bifurcate the 211 appeals system at this time "was based on the agency's view that disputes involving written instruments were 'grievances' and were 'adjudicatory' in nature . . . while disputes involving decisions contested by members of the public were merely a continuation of the 'public participation process.'"[26] This move was consistent with the principle established by the 1965 rules that there should be different types of appeals for different types of decisions. The Forest Service now had in place three separate avenues of appeals: one related to the occupancy and use of national forest lands, such as use permits and grazing allotments (36 CFR 251); a second procedure for decisions related to projects proposed under the LRMPs subject to NEPA (CFR 217); and a third pertaining to appeals of the LRMPs themselves (CFR 219).

The new rules regarding appeals for plans and projects eliminated the previous requirement that the appellant file a statement of reasons, and substituted an explanation of the issues under contention as a part of the original Notice of Appeal. There was no longer an opportunity for appellants or intervenors to make an oral presentation, and restrictions were placed on granting an appellant's request for a stay of decision while the appeal was being reviewed.[27] As a result, there were typically two levels of review, but the second level of review was largely discretionary. For LRMPs, Forest Service reviews were to be completed within 250 days; for projects, reviews were to be completed within 145 days (45 days to file and 100 days from receipt of an appeal for the agency to render an opinion). After a project appeal decision was reached, appellants had an additional 30 days from receipt of the record of the appeal for a second level review. There were no provisions for formal hearings or a hearing board, only the interaction between the agency and appellant.

Just after these CFR changes were finalized, the General Accounting Office (GAO),[28] the investigative arm of Congress charged with examining matters relating to the receipt and payment of public funds, released a report on appeals of timber sale decisions and forest plans in response to a request from Senator Max Baucus (D-MT). Examining the number of appeals between 1983 and 1988, the GAO concluded that "the increases in appeals processing times and in the backlog of unresolved appeals do not appear to be due to problems with the appeals system itself. Rather, they most often occurred because the Forest Service has experienced difficulties in resolving complex environmental issues raised in the increasing number of timber sale and forest plan appeals." The report noted that the 1989 rule changes "do not directly address the difficulties that the Forest Service has experienced in resolving environmental issues raised by appeals—the factor that is principally responsible for these time overruns."[29] The GAO report also raised the issue of delays in timber sales resulting from the fear of anticipated appeals. "The Forest Service has been avoiding timber sales in certain areas because of the likelihood of appeals; however, this problem varies by locality."

The 1989 GAO report was the first of many that would be requested by members of Congress over the next fifteen years, all intended to find a justification to further limit the administrative appeals process. Even though the report did not provide the ammunition many members of Congress wanted—placing the blame for on-the-ground delays in Forest Service projects on administrative appeals—it set into motion a pattern of decision making that became de rigueur. One or more members of Congress would request an investigation by the GAO or a report by the CRS and, once the results were in, would request follow-up congressional hearings to try to extend the blame using witness testimony and rhetoric.

On May 18, 1989, the Senate Subcommittee on Conservation and Forestry held a hearing in Washington on the increasing number of appeals and was told by the Forest Service's Associate Chief George Leonard that "appeals and litigation have resulted in delays and withdrawals of timber sales, and they have also identified the need for us to go back and rework previously prepared sales to bring the NEPA documentation up to standard."[30] His sentiments were echoed by Senator Conrad Burns (R-MT), who expressed additional concerns about the effect of administrative appeals on the economic health of industries and local communities. On the other hand, subcommittee chair Wyche Fowler (D-GA) stated, "While we want to avoid unnecessary impediments to Forest Service management activities, the solution to such problems cannot come at the expense of public participation and interest in good forest planning and management."[31]

Over the next three years, Congress made several attempts to amend NFMA because of the perception that administrative appeals were delaying preparation of forest plans. In June 1990, Rep. Les AuCoin (D-OR) introduced legislation containing two provisions that would later become key elements of Forest Service administrative appeals reform. The first provision of H.R. 5094 required appellants to show standing to sue by providing oral or written comment during preparation of the forest plan. This was an extremely contentious issue because policymakers and stakeholders believed that some appeals were being filed by "outsiders" who had never actually participated in the early planning process. By identifying themselves early on, it was thought, potential opposition might be reviewed and even mitigated without having to resort to appeals or time-consuming litigation. The second provision of the bill stated that if the Forest Service did not make a decision on the appeal during the prescribed time period, the appeal would be considered denied. The AuCoin bill never made it past the committee stage but did serve as a precedent for similar proposals in 1991.

REGULATORY AND LEGISLATIVE CHANGE: 1991–1993

Both the Forest Service and Congress moved forward on changes to the administrative appeals process as timber company officials as well as members of Congress maintained that appeals were delaying timber contracts and reducing revenue.[32] Environmental groups were also unhappy with the appeals process, arguing that they were not being given sufficient opportunities to participate in forest policymaking, line officers were biased against them, appeal decisions were unresponsive to legal arguments, and time frames did not allow enough time to make their cases.[33]

The Forest Service initiated another major regulatory change in February 1991 with changes to 36 CFR 217 (decisions related to plans and projects). The changes responded to complaints from individuals and groups who reported they were not being notified of the agency's proposed actions. Under the amended rule, the Forest Service was required to publicize proposals in newspapers readily available to a majority of the public affected by the decision. Previously, notices had been sent by mail only to "interested or potentially affected individuals or organizations." The agency also had to publish twice per year in the *Federal Register* the names of the principal newspapers used to provide Notice of Decisions, "to assure that interested or affected parties receive[d] constructive notice of a decision, to provide clear evidence of timely notice, and to improve efficiency and achieve consistency in administering the appeals process."[34]

This small but significant change in language had several effects on the administrative appeals process. First, by increasing the visibility of its actions, the Forest Service increased the potential number of groups and individuals that might become involved in an appeal and/or litigation. Second, it gave the appearance of transparency at a time when there was still considerable distrust of the agency and its relationship to the timber industry. Third, it helped to establish a paper trail that could be used to document Forest Service attempts to enhance public participation.

Just a few months after the amendments to the CFR were made, several members of Congress introduced legislation that reopened the issue of administrative appeals and delays in timber harvesting. Sen. Robert Packwood (R-OR) sponsored S. 1156, the Federal Lands and Families Protection Act, which was based on the premise that the increase in administrative appeals was contributing to "social or economic disruption in timber-dependent communities." Packwood's measure sought to establish requirements for legal standing of appellants and, like AuCoin's bill the year before, stated that failure to decide on an appeal would constitute denial. Sen. Slade Gorton (R-WA), a co-sponsor of the Packwood bill, also sought a review of the administrative appeals process and revocation of existing procedures "until a more efficient one was in place."[35]

Both senators were riding on public opinion that blamed the decline in logging jobs and delays in timber sales on the Northern spotted owl, which was being considered for designation as a threatened species under the Endangered Species

Act. In the Northwest, the spotted owl controversy was extremely volatile, and Gorton and Packwood used the opportunity to combine arguments against the administrative appeals process with threats to the region's economic health.

With what the Forest Service perceived to be congressional support, the agency published a proposed rule in March 1992 to eliminate administrative appeals of forest projects altogether, although the appeals process for final decisions, revisions, and amendments of forest plans was retained. As an alternative, the Forest Service proposed a pre-decisional public notice and comment opportunity that would reduce the time period of uncertainty resulting from the existing process.

> [A]dministrative appeals adversely affect jobs, families, and communities by delaying or withdrawing projects which support the local economy, thus creating uncertainty for communities dependent upon Forest Service goods and services. . . . The current post-decisional appeal process creates uncertainty as to the Forest Service's ability to deliver those goods and services, impeding economic growth and development. Delays in delivery of National Forest System goods and services can place the economic viability of communities at risk.[36]

In contrast to the 1989 rules, the 1992 proposal would allow the public only to comment on proposed actions in a draft EA and FONSI. The public would have thirty days to comment, and the responsible official would generally have twenty-one days after the comment period closed to respond. Comments were to be addressed in the Decision Notice, which would be mailed to all those who filed comments. Another important element of the proposed regulations allowed timber sales held in response to extraordinary circumstances, such as wildfires or insect and disease infestation, to be exempt from both public notice and comments, and thus potentially implemented without any public input or involvement.[37] This issue would also reappear in subsequent proposals.

To bolster proposed rule changes, despite a lack of confirmation that administrative appeals were, in fact, causing delays, the agency and members of Congress once again asked the CRS to report on the number and cost of administrative appeals for Forest Service timber sales. Those seeking impartial documentation in support of what had been largely anecdotal information about the detrimental impact of appeals would be disappointed by the resulting study. The CRS report noted that of the 1,386 administrative appeals filed on agency decisions in fiscal year 1991, 397 sales, representing 10.3 percent of the agency's commercial timber sales, had been appealed. But the report also found that appeals were only one reason why fiscal year 1991 timber sale targets had not been met and in fact, appeals prevented achievement of only about 5 percent of timber targets because many appeals had been resolved in a timely manner.[38]

In Senate hearings, several members had argued that the existing administrative appeals process needed to be changed because of the number of "frivolous" appeals. The existence of frivolous appeals was seldom documented, but this was a common argument used to advance the call for reform. The definition of what constituted a frivolous appeal was used broadly in the CRS report, which included those found to be without merit, as well as appeals that did not meet time deadlines, and those where relief could not be granted. But the report also noted that nearly a third of the appeals resulted in the Forest Service withdrawing or remanding the timber sale, including some sales with procedural or substantive flaws. "If the appeals process corrects flawed sales, arguably the appeals were not frivolous."[39]

On the issue of economic uncertainty caused by administrative appeals, CRS found that most timber sales were resolved in a timely manner (within four months), and although the proposed rules changes would probably reduce delays by about half, the Forest Service "has not explained how saving less than two months would greatly reduce uncertainty."[40] On the question of cost (many proponents of rules changes argued that appeals caused timber sales plans to be revised, increasing sales costs), the CRS report found that by reworking timber sales plans, the government might actually save money if appeals prevented subsequent litigation.

As if the CRS report were not damning enough, the media and public opinion came down squarely against the proposed rules changes. The lines were now clearly drawn. President George H.W. Bush's administration blamed environmental groups for abusing the process and unnecessarily delaying or halting logging and creating economic chaos in resource-dependent communities.[41] The *New York Times* reported, "The proposal is the latest political thrust by the Administration into a slashing fight between the timber industry and community environmental groups in the West and South over how much of the nation's last great stands of spruce, fir and Ponderosa pine will be cut."[42] In the midst of an election year, there were claims that Bush was seeking to loosen environmental regulations to appease wise use groups and to shore up support in western states.[43] Environmental and conservation groups that had previously expressed their own frustration with the appeals process now rallied to save it, arguing that appeals tested the soundness of decisions and encouraged responsible decision making, and was an internal mechanism for clarifying legal requirements.[44] More than thirty thousand comments were received from the public, organizations, business interests, and various government entities in response to the proposed rules changes. The majority supported the "right to object" to Forest Service decisions in opposition to the proposed rules. Even within the Forest Service there was no universal agreement about what to do about appeals. Some within the agency supported retaining the process, believing that higher-level appeal was a long tradition of the Forest Service,[45] or had previously publicly stated that appeals had positively "forced the agency to look closely at some policies, processes, and procedures it would not otherwise have reviewed."[46] The 1987 Appeals Regulation Review Team had even reported that "probably the comment the team heard most often was that we are proud to work for an Agency that has an appeals process and we should never seriously consider getting rid of it."[47]

At this point—while the proposed rules were still under consideration—members of Congress took over the debate and the reins of reform. Sen. Fowler held another hearing on appeals before the Senate Subcommittee on Conservation Forestry in May 1992, opening with the following statement:

> I'm not going to rehash the administration's unilateral decisions to gut the
> Endangered Species Act, the Clean Air Act, and the rest of the pitiful record.
> As chairman of this subcommittee, however, I intend to find out what the
> President really has in mind with respect to sales of timber on Federal lands. . . .
> The system should not be abused—we agree on that much. But closing the
> system the public relies upon is certainly not the answer. . . . The Forest
> Service claims that "the intended effort is to expand opportunities for pre-
> decisional involvement of the public in Forest Service decision-making." I
> submit, on the contrary, that—while "the intended effort" is disguised here in
> a pretty God-awful bureaucratic perversion of plain English—the actual result
> will be the exact opposite.[48]

Other witnesses at the subcommittee hearing raised different issues. Sen. Burns argued that sawmills in his state and elsewhere had been shut down because the Forest Service "has been completely snowed under in its own appeals avalanche."[49] USDA Forest Service Chief Dale Robertson testified on the "significant" cost savings that would accrue during the economic crisis and how the proposed rules would fit into President Bush's efforts to review regulations that unnecessarily affected growth and jobs.[50]

Fowler decided to continue his campaign against the agency's proposed rules by introducing his own legislation to save the appeals process in July 1992 and again in August 1992. The first bill, the Forest Service Decisionmaking and Appeals Reform Act, never made it out of the Senate Committee on Agriculture, Nutrition, and Forestry, where it had been referred. Fowler re-introduced the measure, but in the second instance he proposed it as an amendment to the Interior and Related Agencies Appropriations Act for fiscal year 1993. The amendment was unique because for the first time the Forest Service would be required to implement an administrative appeals process that had strict timelines for the filing and review of appeals and, perhaps most importantly, a notice and comment period for all projects, including those requiring only an EA rather than an EIS.

Idaho Republican Sen. Larry Craig offered an amendment to the Fowler amendment requiring appellants to establish standing, requiring the Forest Service to try to resolve issues through informal meetings, and shortening several timelines for processing appeals. On voice votes, both the Craig amendment and the Fowler amendment to the appropriations bill passed, and in October 1992 were enacted as part of Title III of Public Law 102-381, also known as the Appeals Reform Act.

Fowler's amendment to the Appropriations Act represented a different strategy and expanded the scope of the appeals process. Rather than trying to fight implementation of regulatory rules proposed by the Forest Service and sensing that a specific legislative proposal would be stalled or defeated, the senator attached his amendment to an appropriations measure. By expanding coverage of administrative appeals to projects covered by EAs, the measure added an entire category of Forest Service actions that would be subject to public comment. In effect, Fowler's amendment would create an actual legislative mandate for the administrative appeals process. At this point the Forest Service became the only federal agency with a legislatively mandated appeals process.

IMPLEMENTATION OF THE MANDATE: 1994

It took more than a year for the Forest Service to implement the Fowler/Craig amendments. Once again, the rulemaking process was set into motion as the Forest Service developed proposed regulations to CFR Title 36. The final rule, *Notice, Comment, and Appeal Procedures for National Forest System Projects and Activities: Requesting Review of National Forest Plans and Project Decisions,* was published in the *Federal Register* on November 4, 1993 (to become effective in January 1994). The new regulations revised Part 217 of Title 36 and added Part 215; Forest Service special permits were still covered under Part 251. (Thus, the three-part appeals system was now covered in Parts 251, 217, and 215 for permits, plans, and projects respectively, a distinction that would remain in effect until the Healthy Forests Initiative actions in 2003 and 2004). Overall, the 1994 regulations had seven major provisions:

- Establishment of a two-tier procedure for public notice and comment on national forest projects;
- Expansion by thirty days of opportunities for public involvement in Forest Service decisionmaking;

- Requirement that potential appellants provide comments or otherwise express interest in the project during the public involvement process;

- Requirement that appeals be filed and received (not just postmarked) within forty-five days of publication of a decision notice;

- Requirement that the Forest Service provide appellants with an opportunity for a face-to-face meeting within fifteen days to try to resolve issues informally;

- Establishment of a specific time limit for the Forest Service to make a decision on an appeal and, if no decision was made during that time, the original project decision would be allowed to stand; and

- Continuation of existing exemption from appeals for project decisions related to rehabilitation and recovery of forest resources and extension of the exemption to include emergency situations.[51]

Of particular importance to potential appellants were the timelines established under the rules. For Forest Service projects (covered under Part 215), the public was given thirty days in which to submit an administrative appeal; for Forest Service plan amendments, the rule provided for a forty-five-day filing period. The lengthier time frame was a response to the more complex and comprehensive structure of forest plans in comparison to projects.

One additional change to the administrative appeals process was established legislatively under the Federal Crop Insurance Reform and Department of Agriculture Reorganization Act of 1994. A small provision in the statute established a requirement that any party seeking to file litigation regarding Forest Service decisions must establish legal standing by first exhausting all administrative appeal procedures. The legislative language may have sought to reduce the number of potential litigants and "frivolous" lawsuits, but it actually had the opposite effect. Now potential litigants had no choice but to appeal first to establish standing for potential conflicts with the Forest Service.

From 1994 until 2000, a few refinements were made to the appeals process, which primarily clarified regulations, but none addressed the agency's fundamental concerns about appeals. However, numerous proposals were put forward addressing changes in national forest policy,[52] including legislation proposed in October 1997 by Sen. Craig, which would have made sweeping changes in the way the national forests were managed, including limitations on the use of appeals.[53] Perceived as a conservative attempt to return Forest Service management to a more traditional timber-oriented focus, the proposal went nowhere, although it did receive considerable attention.

At the executive level, a new Committee of Scientists was convened by the Clinton administration to revamp planning rules. This committee recommended that sustainability be a central mission of the agency despite strong criticisms that this could not be done administratively without major legislative change to the Multiple-Use and Sustained Yield Act and NFMA, and that the committee was cloaking its policy recommendations under the mantle of science.[54] The committee argued that collaborative planning and adaptive management would help alleviate criticisms of the existing appeals system, and concluded that the post-decisional appeals process was a barrier to planning with other federal agencies, as well as creating "privileged access" for those groups who participated after agreements had been reached with the larger public constituency. It recommended that the agency harmonize its administrative appeals process with other agencies. A proposed rule based on the committee's recommendations was published on October 5, 1999, and a final rule adopted on November 9, 2000, only two days after the 2000 presidential election.[55] The change from a Democratic to a Republican administration in January 2001 doomed the 2000 rules. As one of his first actions, President George W. Bush sent a memorandum to executive departments and agencies announcing a review of all new and pending regulations that had been proposed under President Clinton. The November 2000 final rule was included in the review, reopening the appeals debate.

THE WHO, WHAT, WHERE, AND HOW OF ADMINISTRATIVE APPEALS

Despite the long and controversial history of appeals within the agency, the Forest Service has not consistently maintained databases of its appeal or litigation activity. There is no tracking of appeals and the time between project inception, appeal filing, and appeal decision. No official database tracks appellants or what action the agency took on the appeals. In addition, no litigation databases are maintained to allow examination of litigation successes or failures, and no easy way exists to track the tie between appeals and litigation, that is, to determine how many appeals have been litigated and with what results.[56] No cost data exist to verify claims about the agency's financial costs of processing appeals or engaging in litigation. Moreover, because no comparable appeals process exists elsewhere in public lands management, it is impossible to compare trends in Forest Service appeal activity with other appeals processes.

To learn more about the who, what, where, and how of administrative appeals we therefore had to construct our own database.[57] We examined 4,181 appeals decided between January 1, 1997, and December 31, 2003, and available on the Forest Service's Web site, www.fs.fed.us/forum/nepa, as of January 19, 2004. The Forest Service is required to post its appeal decisions online as the result of a 1999 court settlement between the Wyoming Outdoor Council and the Forest Service.[58]

It should be noted, however, that posting does not mean that there is a searchable database; each posting is a discrete record. Moreover, there is sometimes a time lag from when a decision is made and when it is posted on the agency Web site—in some instances, newly posted decisions were more than eighteen months old. There is also inconsistency across national forests and regions; some sites did not provide information for a particular year, but it is not clear if no appeals were decided during that period or if nothing had been posted because of record-keeping difficulties.

Analysis is also limited to decisions made at the regional level and does not include decisions made by the Washington, D.C., Office of the Forest Service. Washington office decisions include appeals of forest plans as well as discretionary reviews of regional decisions. We examined administrative appeals of national forest projects only; as such, we did not include appeals of forest plans in the data set. However, forest plan amendments decided at the regional level are included in the database. A series of variables was considered and used in the development of the database: the number of appeals decided per calendar year, types of appeal (by CFR section), regional distribution, appellants, types of projects appealed, and disposition of appeal.

Despite claims that the number of appeals is increasing, the data show that number of appeals has not been increasing. The greatest number of decisions were reached in 1998 (950). Calendar year 1999 had the second-highest number of decisions, with 655; 520 were decided in 1997; 583 were decided in 2000; and 621 were decided in 2001. The fewest decisions were made in 2002 (480). As of our cutoff date in 2003, 372 appeals were posted.

Nationwide, approximately 87 percent of all appeals in recent years have challenged NEPA project decisions under 36 CFR 215 (Table 2.1). Another 16 percent related to decisions regarding special use permits and other authorizations for occupancy and use of national forests; 2 percent related to forest plan amendments reviewed at the regional level, and 1 percent were unidentifiable.

The most appeals throughout the study period were decided in the Pacific Southwest Region (Region 5), which contains all national forests in California, with a total of 742 appeals (see Table 2.2). The Northern Region (Region 1), containing Montana, northern Idaho, North Dakota, and small sections of South Dakota and Wyoming, recorded a total of 718. Together these two regions were responsible for 34.9 percent of appeals decisions posted between January

TABLE 2.1. Decisions nationwide, by CFR section, January 1, 1997, through December 31, 2003.

CFR Section	Number	% of Total
215	3,245	77.61
217	160	3.83
251	679	16.24
Undetermined	97	2.32
Total	4,181	100.00

TABLE 2.2. Total appeals decided by Forest Service Region, January 1, 1997, through December 31, 2003.

Region	Reviewed	Dismissed	Undetermined	Total
1 Northern	631	87	0	718
2 Rocky Mountain	262	112	0	374
3 Southwest	498	103	0	601
4 Intermountain	288	191	1	480
5 Pacific Southwest	453	288	1	742
6 Pacific Northwest	326	96	0	422
8 Southern	279	88	10	377
9 Eastern	243	89	1	333
10 Alaska	113	21	0	134
Total	3,093	1,075	13	4,181

1997 and December 2003. However, the Northern Region actually reviewed the most appeals, dismissing only eighty-seven appeals without review, while the Pacific Southwest Region dismissed the most appeals without review (288).

Much of the focus of the current debate over appeals has centered on the perception that environmental groups are the primary appellants using project appeals to delay Forest Service projects. The database reveals that 738 different appellants filed appeals. Private citizens filed or joined in the most appeals (Table 2.3). Of the 1,478 appeals with a private citizen listed as appellant, 1,273 were filed independently—that is, not filed in conjunction with an organization or business—and 766 of those were appeals of NEPA project decisions. Appeals filed by individuals concerned such issues as the siting of new buildings or telecommunications equipment, access to recreational areas for skiing or equestrian use, and changes in grazing allotments.

With the exception of private citizens, the most active appellants were indeed environmental organizations. The Forest Guardians and The Ecology Center filed the most appeals. The eighteen most active appellants nationally (counting individuals as one group of the eighteen) account for nearly one-half of all appeals filed. All of the most active organizations filed more than 90 percent of their appeals against NEPA project decisions.

Table 2.4 provides an overview of appeals by project type. Nearly one-third of all appealed projects related to a timber project, such as a salvage, thinning, or commercial sale—either solely or in conjunction with another type of project. Roughly 14.5 percent of appeal decisions were related to another controversial aspect of national forest management: grazing. Fuels reduction was cited as at least part of the project objectives in only 4.3 percent and restoration in only 3.7

TABLE 2.3. The eighteen most active appellant groups nationwide, by number of appeals filed[1] and total number of appeals compared to number of NEPA (215) appeals (215), January 1, 1997, through December 31, 2003.

Appellant	Total Appeals Filed	NEPA (215) Appeals	% of Total Appeals
Private Citizen	1,478	959	64.9
Forest Guardians	405	399	98.5
Ecology Center	268	265	98.9
Forest Conservation Council	210	206	98.1
Alliance for the Wild Rockies	197	195	99.0
Sierra Club[2]	182	171	94.0
The Lands Council	162	162	100.0
National Forest Protection Alliance	115	113	98.3
Native Ecosystems Council	106	105	99.1
Heartwood Forestwatch	102	96	94.1
American Wildlands	102	98	96.1
Center for Biological Diversity	89	87	97.8
Oregon Natural Resources Council	76	76	100.0
Southern Appalachian Biodiversity Project	71	64	90.1
Friends of the Clearwater	70	70	100.0
Wildlaw	57	53	93.0
Biodiversity Associates	55	55	100.0
Idaho Sporting Congress	55	55	100.0

[1] The total does not equal 4,181 (the number of appeals nationwide). This is the result of multiple appellants filing some appeals jointly. Also, Table 3.3 does not include a comprehensive list of appellants nationwide (only the top eighteen).

[2] Includes local chapters affiliated with the Sierra Club.

percent of all appeals. However, caution must be taken with these numbers. The Forest Service has no standard methodology for reporting types of projects appealed. Project type designations are not consistent between forests or regions. The coding of projects in our database was constructed based on our interpretation of appeal decision letters posted on Web sites. Whenever possible we deferred to the Forest Service label of the project to assign a project type designation. However, inconsistencies in definition limit our ability to draw conclusions about the relationship between certain categories of projects and delay in getting fuel reduction projects implemented. Moreover, because significant variations in perceptions between the agency and appellants about the actual intent and scope of a project may exist, how a project is (or should be) labeled is often highly contentious.

Typically, most appeals are denied. Of all appeals processed nationwide, the appellant's requested relief was denied in full in 56.1 percent of cases, and only granted in full 7.9 percent of the time (see Table 2.5). A significant number of appeals (25.7 percent) are also dismissed without any kind of review. There are

TABLE 2.4. Overview of appeals by project type, nationwide, January 1, 1997, through December 31, 2003.

Project Type	Number of Appeals
Timber	1,335
Grazing Allotments	606
Permits	398
Plan	248
Development	231
Travel Management	219
Fuels Reduction	179
Restoration	156
Species	145
Mining	140
Vegetation Management	136
Recreation	135
Prescribed Burn	112
Forest	100
Ecosystem	93
Trail Management	76
Undetermined	51
Land Exchange	42
Wilderness	10
Access	9
Dredging	3
Easements	3
Dam Repair	2
Demonstration Forest	2

[1] The total equals more than 4,181 (the number of appeals nationwide). This is the result of multiple project types listed on single appeals.

many reasons why an appeal is dismissed without review, including the Forest Service withdrawing the decision under appeal. Approximately one-third of appeals dismissed without review fall into this category. The database, however, cannot answer the question of why decisions were withdrawn. Was it the result of issues raised in the appeal, or was it a procedural or strategic decision by the agency? Other reasons for dismissing an appeal without review include procedural errors by the appellant (e.g., timeliness, content requirements, lack of standing) or issue resolution. Another factor affecting appeal decisions about which little is known is the informal resolution process. The Forest Service and appellants resolved issues informally in 159 cases, which accounts for 15 percent of all appeals dismissed without formal review.

Project delays are attributed to a lengthy appeals process, but because only about 36 percent of records posted by the agency include information about the date on which an appeal was filed, it was not possible to collect data that would allow generalizations to be made concerning the length of time taken to process appeals. On-line records contain no information about when a project was conceived or initiated. Moreover, no agreed-upon benchmark exists for determining what constitutes a project delay.

THE LEGACY OF A STORMY HISTORY

Mechanisms have been in place for appeal of agency decisions almost since the agency's inception a hundred years ago, and this appeals program has had a stormy history. The administrative appeals process gradually evolved from what had primarily been voluntary, cooperative arrangements early on in the agency's history, to a highly formalized, adversarial system requiring both appellants and the Forest Service to make a greater investment of resources. Informal or casual dispute

TABLE 2.5. Number of decisions nationwide by type of decision, January 1, 1997, through December 31, 2003.

Type of Decision	Number	% of Total
REVIEWED	3,093	74.0
Denied	2,344	56.1
Denied with Conditions	286	6.8
Future Appeal Potential	37	0.9
Granted	331	7.9
Partially Denied/Granted	95	2.3
DISMISSED	1,075	25.7
Appeal Withdrawn	57	1.4
Content	49	1.2
Decision Withdrawn	344	8.2
Discretionary Review	22	0.5
Issue Resolved	159	3.8
Not Decided	5	0.1
Not Subject to Appeal	75	1.8
Scope	3	0.1
Standing	223	5.3
Timeliness	138	3.3
UNDETERMINED	13	0.3

resolution was replaced by a structured, lengthy, and sometimes hostile process. There are unintended consequences of such changes. As Kerwin notes, "Certainly, each reform can be justified by a noble purpose, be it better-informed rulemaking or empowerment of those who will be affected by its results or a greater degree of management control by the president over a sprawling bureaucratic state.... Our legislators enact programs of regulation or social welfare but then encumber them with procedural requirements that will almost certainly stall their implementation."[59]

With the growth of the environmental movement and its emphasis on the importance of public input into agency decision making, the appeals process came to be regarded as an integral part of public involvement and protest strategies. However, with the growth of public access to, and influence in, decision making comes constraints on agency discretion. Agency frustration with appeals did not begin with the fire problem at the turn of the twenty-first century; for almost a quarter of a century the agency has sought to change the appeals process, concerned about delays in getting its land management plans finished and its timber sale projects approved.

Viewed as an extension of the agency's public involvement processes, it is not surprising that many difficulties with appeals have mirrored experiences with public participation more generally. The agency has long regarded its public participation processes as a way to build support for its plans and projects, while many participants have wanted to share in decision making and/or basically change those decisions. The differing expectations between public and agency have been widely reported and studies spanning a period of twenty-five years underscore the persistence of this problem.[60] Historically public participants have questioned the agency's commitment to using the input it receives in such processes. The Forest Service's own 1989 internal evaluation of its public participation efforts in forest planning concluded that the public felt the agency "did not acknowledge it [public input] ...

did not deal with it . . . did not track it . . . lost it . . . did not change anything as a result of it."[61]

During the many revisions and attempts at revision of its participation processes over the years, the agency has announced its preference for pre-decisional rather than post-decisional procedures. More recently it has embraced the benefits of up-front collaborative processes; but, it argues, the ability to hold open discussions with stakeholders is constrained by procedural barriers. This is compounded, admits the agency, by its own uneven expertise in collaboration, its lack of institutional capacity for collaboration, and its inability to keep commitments.[62] Despite many collaborative successes, the Forest Service is still perceived by many participants as treating its public participation process as consultation rather than collaboration and ignoring pre-decisional input.[63] Participants dissatisfied with the equity of public participation procedures often choose to appeal, believing appeals offer a more efficient way to object to agency proposals.[64]

The appeals process has produced both supporters and critics in the scholarly community. On the one hand, the appeal system has been called antiquated, cumbersome, working against rather than for broad public involvement, and ripe for change.[65] Indeed, there have been unintended consequences wrought by the increasingly legalistic approach to conflict resolution. By its very design NEPA is a formalistic, top-down approach to involvement. It specifically created legal mechanisms to force agencies to provide full disclosure about the environmental impact of proposed projects. Challenges to agencies often then focus on those procedures rather than project merits. Although full disclosure implies having scientific data for impact assessments, the scientific orientation often moves discussion away from values, which are at the core of most disputes over forest policy. Environmental analysis and appeals consume staff resources, but there is no way of tracking the financial costs under the current budget structure. On the other hand, appeals along with litigation have been labeled significant factors in forcing agency accountability and in catalyzing change within the agency.[66] Formal, legalistic modes of participation also compensate for power differentials, providing avenues of access for those without the political power to influence agency decisions in other contexts. Disadvantaged groups have traditionally used litigation, for example, when they felt rebuffed in legislative or bureaucratic arenas. Thus, as the appeals process became increasingly identified with the legal requirements of, and political necessities of, public participation, it is not surprising that appeals increasingly began being used to not only protest the nature and timing of particular projects but also pursue broader policy objectives.

Although appeals have been the focus of considerable political debate, there has been little comprehensive and systematic analysis of the claims and counterclaims put forward about the cost and impact of appeals. Construction of our database could not yield definitive, quantitative conclusions about those impacts. The database, however, does tell us that appeals are now used by a variety of individuals as well as organized groups to challenge a wide range of projects. The next chapter delves more deeply into the characteristics of appellants and their expectations of, and experiences with, the administrative appeals process.

NOTES

1. Martin Shapiro, "APA: Past, Present, and Future," *Virginia Law Review* 72 (1986): 452.

2. Cornelius M. Kerwin, *Rulemaking: How Government Agencies Write Law and Make Policy* (Washington, DC: Congressional Quarterly Press, 2003), 52.

3. 5 U.S.C. 551 (4).

4. Kerwin, *Rulemaking*, 3.

5. Ibid., 50.

6. Kenneth Culp Davis, *Discretionary Justice: A Preliminary Inquiry* (Urbana: University of Illinois Press, 1976), 65. See also Kenneth Culp Davis and Walter Gelhorn, "Present at the Creation: Regulatory Reform before 1946," *Administrative Law Review* 38 (1986): 511–533.

7. Much of the historical discussion in this chapter is based on research conducted by Gretchen Teich, which is reported in chapter 2 of her thesis. Gretchen M.R. Teich, "Analysis Paralysis? Examining Administrative Appeals of Forest Service Decisions," Master's thesis (Flagstaff, AZ: Northern Arizona University School of Forestry, 2003).

8. USDA Forest Service, *Manual of Procedure for the Forest Service in Washington and in District Offices* (Washington, DC: Government Printing Office, 1908).

9. Mary J. Coulombe, "Exercising the Right to Object: A Brief History of the Forest Service Appeals Process," *Journal of Forestry* 102:2 (2004): 10–13.

10. 1 FR 1092, *Regulations of the Secretary of Agriculture Relating to the Protection, Occupancy, Use, and Administration of the National Forests,* Final Rule (August 15, 1936).

11. Bradley C. Bobertz and Robert L. Fischman, "Administrative Appeal Reform: The Case of the Forest Service," *University of Colorado Law Review* 64 (1983): 372–456, at 376.

12. Allan F. Wichelman, "Administrative Agency Implementation of the National Environmental Policy Act of 1969: A Conceptual Framework for Explaining Differential Response," *Natural Resources Journal* 16:2 (1976): 261–300, at 269–270.

13. See Christopher Stone, *Should Trees Have Standing? Toward Legal Rights for Natural Objects* (Los Altos, CA: William Kaufmann, 1972).

14. Kerwin, *Rulemaking*, 119.

15. Michael J. Gippert and Vincent L. DeWitt, "The Nature of Land and Resource Management Planning Under the National Forest Management Act," *The Environmental Lawyer* 3:1 (1996): 149–208.

16. 44 FR 53966, *National Forest System Land and Resource Management Planning,* Final Rule (September 17, 1979).

17. Office of Management and Budget, *Improving Government Regulations: A Program Report* (Washington, DC: Office of Management and Budget, 1979), 6.

18. Ibid., 8.

19. Kerwin, *Rulemaking*, 120.

20. Ibid., 122.

21. 48 FR 13420, *Appeal of Decisions Concerning the National Forest System*, Final Rule (March 31, 1983).

22. 36 CFR 211.18, *Appeal of Decisions Concerning the National Forest System*; Bobertz and Fischman, "Administrative Appeal Reform," 379–385.

23. Pamela Baldwin, CRS Report for Congress, *Appeals of Federal Land Management Plans and Activities: A Report on a CRS Research Workshop* (Washington, DC: Congressional Research Service, February 20, 1990), 5.

24. Ibid.

25. Coulombe, "Exercising the Right to Object," 12. See also Ann A. Loose, David C. Williams, and Dennis L. Schweitzer, "The Public's Last Chance—Protests and Appeals to Federal Land Management Plans," *Society and Natural Resources* 14 (1988): 377–386.

26. Bobertz and Fischman, "Administrative Appeal Reform," 428.

27. 36 CFR 217, *Appeal of Regional Guides and National Forest Land and Resource Management Plans*; 36 CFR 219, *National Forest System Land and Resource Management Planning*; and 36 CFR 251, *Appeal of Decisions Relating to Occupancy and Use of National Forest System Lands*.

28. In July 2004, the name of the General Accounting Office was changed to Government Accountability Office as part of the Human Capital Reform Act of 2004. Because most reports we cite were done under the old name, for consistency we use General Accounting Office throughout.

29. U.S. General Accounting Office, *Forest Service: Information on the Forest Service Appeal System*, GAO/RCED-89-16BR. (Washington, DC: U.S. General Accounting Office, February 16, 1989).

30. Testimony of George M. Leonard, U.S. Senate, Committee on Agriculture, Nutrition, and Forestry, Subcommittee on Conservation and Forestry, May 18, 1989.

31. Testimony of Wyche Fowler, U.S. Senate, Committee on Agriculture, Nutrition, and Forestry, Subcommittee on Conservation and Forestry, May 18, 1989.

32. Pamela Baldwin and Ross W. Gorte, CRS Report for Congress, *Administrative Appeals of Forest Service Timber Sales* (Washington, DC: Congressional Research Service, April 8, 1992), 2.

33. Bobertz and Fischman, "Administrative Appeal Reform," 401.

34. 56 FR 4914, *Requesting Review of National Forest Plans and Project Decisions; Legal Notice of Decisions,* Final Rule (February 6, 1991).

35. Slade Gorton, Relief for the Northwest, 137 Cong. Rec. S. 15544 (October 29, 1991).

36. 57 FR 10444, *Review of and Comment on National Forest Plans and Project Decisions,* Proposed Rule (March 26, 1992).

37. Baldwin and Gorte, *Administrative Appeals of Forest Service Timber Sales*.

38. Ibid., 3. Also in spring 1992 yet another congressional agency, the Office of Technology Assessment, released its assessment of national forest planning. The OTA's report characterized the appeals process as an extension of public participation under NEPA and NFMA and concluded that generally appeals had been a valuable tool for the agency. U.S. Congress, Office of Technology Assessment, *Forest Service Planning: Accommodating Uses, Producing Outputs, and Sustaining Ecosystems* (Washington, DC: Government Printing Office, 1992), 95–99.

39. Baldwin and Gorte, *Administrative Appeals of Forest Service Timber Sales,* 4–5.

40. Ibid., 5.

41. Keith Schneider, "Forest Service May Alter Rule Blocking Logging," *New York Times,* late edition (April 28, 1992), A12. See also 57 FR 10444, 10445–46.

42. Schneider, "Forest Service May Alter Rule Blocking Logging."

43. Keith Schneider, "Environmental Laws are Eased by Bush as Election Nears," *New York Times,* late edition (May 20, 1992), A1.

44. Michael Goodman, "Forest Service Appeals Reform: Searching for Meaningful Review," *New York University Environmental Law Journal* (1994) at www.nyu.edu/pages/elj accessed June 19, 2002.

45. Ibid.

46. Ibid., and Ann A. Loose, "Forest Plan Appeal Decisions: Guides to the Future of the U.S. Forest Service," *Western Wildlands* 15:4 (1990): 2–6.

47. Cited in Bobertz and Fischman, "Administrative Appeal Reform," n. 114.

48. Testimony of Wyche Fowler, U.S. Senate, Committee on Energy and Natural Resources, Subcommittee on Conservation and Forestry, *Oversight Hearings to Examine the Forest Service's Proposed Changes to the Federal Administrative Appeals Process* (Washington, DC: Government Printing Office, May 21, 1992).

49. Testimony of Conrad Burns, U.S. Senate, Committee on Energy and Natural Resources, Subcommittee on Conservation and Forestry, *Oversight Hearings to Examine the Forest Service's Proposed Changes to the Federal Administrative Appeals Process* (Washington, DC: Government Printing Office, May 21, 1992).

50. Testimony of Dale Robertson, U.S. Senate, Committee on Energy and Natural Resources, Subcommittee on Conservation and Forestry, *Oversight Hearings to Examine the Forest Service's Proposed Changes to the Federal Administrative Appeals Process* (Washington, DC: Government Printing Office, May 21, 1992).

51. 58 FR 58904, *Notice, Comment, and Appeal Procedures for National Forest System Projects and Activities; Requesting Review of National Forest Plans and Project Decisions* (November 4, 1993).

52. For a summary of the many proposed changes, see Elizabeth Beaver et al., *Seeing the Forest Service for the Trees: A Survey of Proposals for Changing National Forest Policy* (Boulder: University of Colorado School of Law Natural Resources Law Center, 2000). See also Roger A. Sedjo, ed., *A Vision for the U.S. Forest Service: Goals for Its Next Century* (Washington, DC: Resources for the Future, 2000); and Donald W. Floyd, ed., *Forests of Discord: Options for Governing our National Forests and Federal Public Lands* (Bethesda, MD: Society of American Foresters, 1999).

53. J. E. deSteiguer, "Senator Craig's Public Lands Management Improvement Act of 1997," *Journal of Forestry* 96:9 (1998): 7–10.

54. For the Committee of Scientists report, see Committee of Scientists, *Sustaining the People's Lands: Recommendations for Stewardship of the National Forests and Grasslands into the Next Century* (Washington, DC: U.S. Department of Agriculture, 1999), at www.fs.fed.us/forum/nepa/rule/cosreport. Roger Sedjo, a member of the committee, offered a criticism of the report in Roger A. Sedjo, "Mission Impossible," *Journal of Forestry* 97:5 (1999): 13–14. See also other articles in the same issue of the *Journal of Forestry* as well as George Hoberg, "Science, Politics, and US Forest Law: The Battle over the Forest Service Planning Rule," unpublished paper (Vancouver, BC: University of British Columbia, 2003).

55. 65 FR 67514, *National Forest System Land and Resource Management Planning*, Final Rule (November 9, 2000).

56. Scholars, however, have systematically examined litigation. For example, Jones and Taylor analyzed U.S. Courts of Appeals cases to determine how the Forest Service fared in such cases between 1971 and 1992. See Elise S. Jones and Cameron P. Taylor, "Litigating Agency Change: The Impact of the Courts and Administrative Appeals Process on the Forest Service," *Policy Studies Journal* 23:2 (1995): 310–336. More recently Malmsheimer and his colleagues have updated and expanded this study. See Robert W. Malmsheimer, Denise Keele, and Donald W. Floyd, "National Forest Litigation in the U.S. Courts of Appeals," *Journal of Forestry* 102:2 (2004): 20–25; and Robert Malmsheimer and Donald Floyd, "U.S. Courts of Appeals Judges' Review of Federal Natural Resource Agencies' Decisions," *Society and Natural Resources* 17:6 (2004): 533–546.

57. Results from this study using data collected January 1, 1997, through September 30, 2002, are reported in Gretchen M.R. Teich, Jacqueline Vaughn, and Hanna J. Cortner, "National Trends in the Use of Forest Service Administrative Appeals," *Journal of Forestry* 102:2 (2004): 20–25. The data is further broken down for Forest Service Regions 3 (Arizona and New Mexico) and 6 (Washington and Oregon) and for four northern Arizona forests in Teich, "Analysis Paralysis?," and in Hanna J. Cortner, Gretchen M.R. Teich, and Jacqueline Vaughn, *Analyzing USDA Forest Service Appeals: Phase I, the Database* (Flagstaff, AZ: Northern Arizona University Ecological Restoration Institute, 2003).

58. Caroline Bird, "Forest Service Settles Case: Agrees to Publish Decisions on the Internet by June, but Interior Balks," *Frontline Report* (Spring 1999) at www.wyomingoutdoorcouncil.org accessed December 28, 2002.

59. Kerwin, *Rulemaking,* 107.

60. Daniel Mazmanian and Jeanne Nienaber, *Can Organizations Change? Environmental Protection, Citizen Participation and the Corps of Engineers* (Washington, DC: Brookings Institution, 1979); Ann Moote and Dennis Becker, eds., *Exploring Barriers to Collaborative Forestry: Report from a Workshop Held at Hart Prairie, Flagstaff, Arizona, September 17–19, 2003* (Flagstaff, AZ: Northern Arizona University Ecological Restoration Institute, 2003). For a summary assessment of lessons learned from the agency's public involvement, see Dale J. Blahna and Susan Yonts-Shepard, "Public Involvement in Resource Planning: Toward Bridging the Gap Between Policy and Implementation," *Society and Natural Resources* 2:3 (1989): 209–227. The evaluation of NFMA planning conducted both by the Office of

Technology Assessment and by the Forest Service itself showed similar findings regarding the agency's public involvement efforts. See U.S. Congress, Office of Technology Assessment, 20; and John W. Russell et al., *Critique of Land Management Planning, Vol. 5, Public Participation* (Washington, DC: USDA Forest Service Policy Analysis Staff, 1990).

61. Gary Larsen, *Messages from our Stakeholders. Land Management Critique: News Notes for Field Folks*, Issue 2 (Washington, DC: USDA Forest Service Policy Analysis Staff, 1989).

62. USDA Forest Service, *The Process Predicament: How Statutory, Regulatory, and Administrative Factors Affect National Forest Management* (Washington, DC: USDA Forest Service, 2002), 28–31.

63. Moote and Becker, *Exploring Barriers to Collaborative Forestry*, 4.

64. Rene H. Germain, Donald W. Floyd, and Stephen V. Stehman, "Public Perceptions of the USDA Forest Service Public Participation Process," *Forest Policy and Economics* 3 (2001): 113–124.

65. Michael J. Mortimer, Anthony V. Scardina, and Dylan H. Jenkins, "Policy Analysis and National Forest Appeal Reform," *Journal of Forestry* 102:2 (2004): 26–31.

66. Jones and Taylor, "Litigating Agency Change." See also Nancy Manring, "From Postdecisional Appeals to Predecisional Objections: Democratic Accountability in National Forest Planning," *Journal of Forestry* 102:2 (2004): 43–47; and Nancy Manring, "Locking the Back Door: The Implications of Eliminating Postdecisional Appeals in National Forests Planning," *Society and Natural Resources* 17 (2004): 235–245.

APPELLANTS, STRATEGIES, TACTICS, AND OUTCOMES

Debate over reform of the administrative appeals process was framed, in part, by undocumented examples retrieved from the institutional memories of Forest Service staff and anecdotal stories about appeals, appellants, and their motivations. They were used to prove appeals were mainly frivolous and caused untenable delays in implementing projects to reduce hazardous fuels. Just as there has been little research about trends in appeal filings by variables such as appellant, region, type, and time period, little is known about why some groups or individuals file appeals, relationships among appellants, successful and unsuccessful strategies, use of the appeals process for non-hazardous fuel-related projects, and appellants' perceptions of outcomes. Even when the data we collected are broken down by the three sections of the Code of Federal Regulations that existed through 2003, it is clear that appeals vary considerably. Data alone, however, cannot provide background and context. It is only by analyzing the project record files maintained by the Forest Service that further conclusions can be drawn regarding administrative appeals and appellants. This chapter provides a more comprehensive and complex snapshot of appellants, and then chronicles the background of individual cases and their outcomes.

Analysis is broken down initially into the types of groups that have used the administrative appeals process: environmental organizations, wise use groups, commercial and business interests, multiple appellants, Native American tribes, government agencies, and individuals. Within each of these groups, case studies provide background information on the appellant, the forest and state in which the appeal was filed, the type of appeal based on project type, the dates of both the filing and final disposition of the appeal, what further action was taken, and the date the project was implemented by the Forest Service. Of more than three thousand appeals in our database, this is only a sample of representative cases, chosen at random from appeals posted on-line by each Forest Service region from 1997–2003. They were selected to obtain an array of appellants and types of projects being appealed and for geographical diversity. Much of the argument against appeals is like a single picture showing only one point of view, but we took many pictures from several different vantage points to show the many facets of the appeals process.

The discussion of appeals is followed by a brief section on what is known about litigating administrative appeals, using the same types of variables used previously in this study. Unfortunately, little research has been done in this area for a number of reasons. Because the Forest Service had not compiled a database of court cases similar to what we developed for administrative appeals, researchers have relied upon only published court cases and may have underestimated how frequently this type of conflict resolution might be used. Some studies have combined all cases—those involving administrative appeals of projects as well as forest management plans—making comparison with our database impossible. In addition, the process of litigating cases in federal courts is sometimes glacially slow. As a result, cases may be in the pipeline for years, so it becomes difficult to trace their impact on project implementation. Nonetheless, we felt it was important to include mention of litigation and what little researchers have learned from the data they have collected. If nothing else, this points to the need for comprehensive monitoring of projects from start to finish.

Based on this examination of appellant groups and their experiences with selected appeals, we conclude that appellants vary widely in their sophistication and motives for filing an appeal, from groups that have committed significant portions of their budgets and other resources to filing administrative appeals to individuals who are not familiar with procedural rules at all.

There are also differences among groups or individuals who file multiple appeals—"frequent filers"—and those who use the appeals process infrequently—"one-shotters." Appellants vary in their expectations, from those who use the appeals process as a first order of being heard, hoping to affect the outcome of a project or establish legal standing for subsequent litigation, to those who want to advance a national goal. They also vary in their satisfaction with the results.

Finally, although these case studies provide considerable insight into the overall view of administrative appeals and how and why they are used by a wide variety of interests, we acknowledge that selected case studies do not quantitatively address the many contentious issues surrounding appeals, including how many frivolous appeals are filed , the costs of appeals, or how many appeals have led to detrimental delays in project implementation. However, we conclude that answering such questions is not merely a matter of developing an empirical test, because the questions themselves are deeply entwined in subjective assessments of "goodness" and "badness."

ENVIRONMENTAL ORGANIZATION APPEALS AND LITIGATION

It is clear from our database that environmental organizations, as an appellant category, have filed more appeals than any other type. The difficulty in attempting to make generalizations about this category of appellants is that, despite the existence of a "core" group of organizations responsible for filing appeals on a regular basis, the groups themselves differ considerably from one another. We can, however, conclude that there have been significant changes in who is filing appeals in the last three years. To corroborate our research findings, we have relied in part on a 2003 GAO study of administrative appeals of hazardous fuels reduction projects from FY 2001–2002. The methodologies of the two projects are similar, as are most of the findings.[1]

FOREST GUARDIANS/FOREST CONSERVATION COUNCIL/ NATIONAL FOREST PROTECTION ALLIANCE

The activists who represent Forest Guardians, the Forest Conservation Council, and the National Forest Protection Alliance (NFPA) are considered as a group for this discussion because of considerable overlap in their membership, leadership, and activities. They frequently appeal Forest Service projects together, and their leaders help coordinate decisions on what groups file on which projects and when.

The Forest Guardians are usually the most vilified of the three organizations because of their insistence upon a zero-cut timber policy and what is considered a confrontational form of activism. The group was founded in 1989 by activist Sam Hitt, who left Forest Guardians in April 2001 but is still active in forest issues with another group, Wild Watershed. In its 2001 report to the Internal Revenue Service, Forest Guardians listed its revenues as $350,000 (77 percent public support), which included $13,000 in non-cash contributions and $15,000 in program service revenue generated by a contract to preserve and restore the Rio Puerco. Although not identified by name, two major contributors gave donations of $50,000 and $30,000 to the organization. Its expenses for the year totaled $395,000, for a $45,000 loss (covered from net assets from previous years). The only salaried employee listed is Executive Director Susan Tixier, although the IRS report was signed by John Horning, who also is identified as executive director. The majority of Forest Guardians' expenses were directed to the Southwest Rivers Project ($172,000), the Grazing Project ($104,000), the Endangered Species Project ($30,000), and the Forest Protection Project ($19,000). The last project "monitored hundreds of activities from timber sales and roads to off-highway vehicles and herbicide application to ensure no actions would threaten ancient forests or harm sensitive species and habitats."[2]

The allocation of funds is reflected in the appeals and litigation in which the Forest Guardians has participated. Contrary to popular belief about the group's role in forest issues, there was a significant decrease in the number of Forest Guardians' appeals between 1997 and 2003, from a high of 215 appeals in 1998 to 11 in 2002 and 9 in 2003. The GAO study identified only 4 hazardous fuels reduction appeals filed by the group in 2001 and 2002, and no projects that were litigated.[3] This may reflect the fact that many projects were appealed by the Forest Conservation Council and the National Forest Protection Alliance, who filed 78 appeals of hazardous fuels reduction projects during the two fiscal years reported by the GAO. Despite the drop in the number of appeals filed and the change in where its revenues are being directed, Forest Guardians is still considered by many policymakers to be a major source of administrative appeals, and this has become part of the rhetoric surrounding the debate over the process.

The Forest Conservation Council was founded in 1986 by John Talberth in Oregon with a focus on old-growth monitoring and conservation issues, such as preservation of the spotted owl. In 1992 the group moved its operations to Santa Fe, New Mexico, and at its peak had from two to five staff who worked out of their homes, between two and ten volunteers, and about two thousand members. Forest Conservation Council also established a Southeastern Regional Office in Boca Raton, Florida, when one of its leaders, Bryan Bird, moved there for a year. The group operates three major conservation programs: the Green Spaces Initiative (to monitor and challenge new cell tower proposals harmful to migratory birds), the National Forests Program (to end logging, grazing, mining, oil and gas leasing, recreational development, and other forms of commercial activities on national forests), and the Wildlands Protection and Restoration Program. Forest Conservation Council also operates the Ecology and Law Institute to provide technical and legal expertise to other nonprofit organizations.

The organization's revenues are relatively small, ranging from $61,000 in 1998 to $93,000 in 2001. Expenses for 2002 were reported as $74,000, resulting in a $5,000 deficit and well below the $93,000 in revenues reported for 2001. Executive Director John Talberth received $14,000 as his half-time salary, while Bryan Bird, serving as secretary twenty-five hours per week, received $19,200.[4]

Even though the Forest Conservation Council is ranked third in the number of administrative appeals filed in the database, it has seen a sharp decline in appeal activity since 2001, when the group was a party in eighty-four appeals. Of the total 210 appeals filed between 1997 and 2003, only 20 were filed in 2002, and 4 in 2003. The GAO recorded fifty-one appeals of hazardous fuels reduction projects filed by the Forest Conservation Council in fiscal years 2001–2002, more than any other interest group, and two cases in which the organization appeared as plaintiffs in litigation.[5] But it seems clear that after the peak filing period (2001) the group's involvement in the appeals process has shown a significant decrease.

The National Forest Protection Alliance was launched in 1999 by Bryan Bird, whose activities have crisscrossed the three organizations and multiple appeals, including his service as secretary of the Forest Conservation Council.[6] Although the NFPA is listed in IRS records as being based in Missoula, Montana, members are active in other cities and closely monitor Forest Service projects throughout the West. In one case involving multiple appellants, the NFPA was listed at the same mailing address in Republic, Washington, as The Lands Council, another environmental organization.[7]

Under its Forest Watch program, the NFPA has called for an immediate end to corporate and commercial exploitation of public lands. The organization notes that it represents over 130 groups, including Forest Guardians and the Forest Conservation Council, and maintains twenty-seven state chapters. In 2002, NFPA organized a forest restoration conference and a second annual wildfire summit and launched the "Ten Most Endangered National Forests" campaign to educate the general public and members of Congress.

The NFPA reported its 2002 revenues as $195,000, some of which came from small individual donors, including Bird, who at the time served as vice-president of the thirteen-member board of directors. Foundation support came from Ben and Jerry's, the Fund for Wild Nature, Patagonia, the Turner Foundation, the Goldman Fund, and others. The group's overall income has fluctuated significantly since its inception, raising $109,000 in 1999 (its first year of operations), $304,000 in 2000, and $116,000 in 2001. Total expenses for 2002 were $169,000, primarily for compensation to the executive director in Colorado and field and network coordinators in North Carolina, Montana, and Virginia.[8]

Our database shows that between 1997 and 2003, the National Forest Protection Alliance filed 115 appeals total; the GAO report found 27 appeals on hazardous fuel reduction projects in fiscal years 2001 and 2002 but noted that the NFPA was not involved in any litigation during that time frame.[9]

The relationship among the three groups bears further analysis, because there is considerable overlap in staffing, board members, and affiliations. There was a period between 1997 and 1999, for instance, when Forest Guardians developed a reputation for appealing every timber sale in the United States. Bryan Bird, who has filed appeals on behalf of several organizations, reported he had been instructed by John Talberth to file in every Forest Service region as a way of gaining standing for Forest Guardians in future litigation. But the majority of those appeals, Bird says, involved a list of about ten organizations, businesses, and individuals.[10] Figures in our database confirm the high level of activity by the Forest Guardians during that period, before the Forest Conservation Council and the NFPA became active.

Typical of the Forest Guardians' appeals were seven filed on the Gifford Pinchot National Forest in Washington State from July 20, 1998, to September 21, 1998, and four others filed on the same forest on November 13, 1998.[11] In the decision letters sent to Talberth, the Forest Service official included all of the appeals together "because your Statements of Reason for each of these projects are virtually identical, and consequently, my response for each is similar." The responses to the appellant were also virtually identical in denying all eleven appeals.[12] In such an instance, it appears that neither party was interested in reasoned discourse, but rather Forest Guardians used the provisions of the administrative appeals process to make a public statement, to which the agency responded in turn with limited deliberation, perhaps illustrative of the local-level frustration that occurred more broadly within the agency.

The decline in the number of appeals filed in recent years by all three groups does not, however, indicate inactivity. The organizations may simply have shifted the lead role to other groups, as in the 2001 appeal of the Scott Able Fire Forest Health Project on the Lincoln National Forest in New Mexico. One joint appeal was filed by Bryan Bird on behalf of the NFPA and John Talberth of the Forest Conservation Council, with a separate appeal by the Center for Biological Diversity, whose activities are described below. Forest Guardians provided comments on the Scott Able project in December 2000 but did not join in the appeal with the other two organizations. However, in an October 2000 news release, Forest Guardians said there was no credible evidence to support salvage logging in the area and threatened to sue in federal court to stop the proposed sale.[13]

The Forest Service initiated its salvage logging proposal as a result of a May 2000 fire that burned an estimated 13,775 acres of national forest land near the village of Cloudcroft, New Mexico. About eight thousand acres of forest were severely burned, some of which was ponderosa pine. The draft EA for the project, developed by a private consulting firm, the Mangi Environmental Group of McLean, Virginia, was released in October 2000, revised and re-released in March 2001. In April 2001 the forest supervisor issued a Decision Notice and FONSI on a proposal to remove dead wood on thirty-four parcels, estimated to contain about ten million board feet with diameters from nine to twenty-four inches, prompting the two appeals.

The contentions raised by the Forest Conservation Council and the NFPA in their twenty-two-page appeal related primarily to alleged violations of the NEPA, an expired forest plan, violations of the NFMA and the Endangered Species Act, and "arbitrary and capricious" violations of the Administrative Procedure Act.[14] The twenty-five-page appeal of the project filed by the Center for Biological Diversity one day after the Forest Conservation Council/NFPA appeal was similar but not a duplicate of the other. The Forest Service dismissed both appeals in July 2001. Salvage logging began in fall 2001 and was completed in spring 2002.

According to Talberth, the Forest Conservation Council and the NFPA appealed jointly because he and Bird worked closely on numerous appeals, and it was both a matter of convenience and a way to bring additional weight to the contentions. Although Talberth considered the denial of the appeal a loss, saying any time "salvage logging occurs, it adds insult to injury," the appellants could argue that the project had been temporarily delayed and that the target volume was not removed by the contractor—in one sense, a victory.

THE ECOLOGY CENTER, INC.

Founded in 1988, The Ecology Center, Inc., is a nonprofit, public interest conservation center "working to protect biological diversity and ecosystem integrity, primarily in the Wild Rockies Bioregion. We also pressure agencies to conform to environmental legislation, and work to increase citizen participation in public lands management."[15] The group also participates in several other ventures, including documentary film production under the business name High Plains Films and provides maps and office space for other nonprofit organizations in Missoula, such as the Alliance for the Wild Rockies. It is governed by a seven-member volunteer board of directors and a paid executive director.

From a purely financial perspective, The Ecology Center has not been doing well in recent years. The organization's IRS return listed $239,000 in revenue for 2002 (which includes $135,000 in direct public support and $79,000 in program service revenue), with 95 percent public support. The organization's program service revenue included $29,000 from its GIS Mapping Office and $53,000 from sales of its documentary films. In comparison, the group reported income of $457,000 in 2001, and in 2000, $417,000. Expenses for 2002 were $367,000, for a loss of about $128,000. The report lists only one part-time paid employee, Executive Director Tom Platt, who received $18,000. The bulk of its expenses ($158,000) went toward other individuals' salaries and wages, although the IRS does not require that those recipients be identified. The Ecology Center's financial fortunes and activities are also reflected in its lobbying expenditures. In 2001 it spent $86,000 in lobbying, but none in 1999, 2000, or 2002.[16]

One of the nation's "frequent filers," The Ecology Center, Inc., is credited with filing 269 appeals between 1997 and 2003. According to the GAO report, the organization filed fifty-one appeals of hazardous fuels reduction projects in 2001 and 2002. All but ten of the appeals during that period were filed in Region 1 of the Forest Service, where the group is based.[17] There has been a slight decline in the number of appeals filed each year but not as dramatic a change as with other groups. Between 1997 and 2003, our database shows that the most appeals— forty-six—were filed in 1998. But forty-four appeals were filed in 2001, thirty-two in 2002, and twenty-five in 2003. It is important to note that not all appeals were related to hazardous fuel reduction projects.

Although the organization does not have an official zero-cut harvest policy on public lands, "it does have a zero-tolerance policy for degrading an ecosystem. This basically translates into a zero-cut policy in sensitive post-fire ecosystems," according to its Web site. Forest Service officials have a less benign view of the organization's goals, citing the fact that the group has targeted Montana's Helena National Forest. In twelve years, one staffer said, all but one of the agency's timber salvage/sale projects have been appealed. The majority of the appeals follow the same format, although Ecology Center staff say that each appeal is written for a specific project.

The way in which the group's strategy conflicts with Forest Service goals can be seen in a July 2, 2001, appeal filed on the Helena National Forest for the Maudlow-Toston Post-Fire Project.[18] The agency had proposed a sale of 1,449 acres of burned timber (roughly eight million board feet) resulting from a 2000 fire that burned eighty-one thousand acres of private, state, and federal lands between August 15 and September 30, 2000. The purpose of the project was to "recover the value of the burned commercial timber product before it decays and is no longer commercially viable. There is also a need to implement actions that accelerate long-term fire recovery and protect soils, watersheds, and wildlife habitat while this recovery occurs."[19]

Initially, the Forest Service had developed four alternative methods of harvesting the timber but eventually chose a fifth alternative developed from public comments on the draft EIS. The chosen alternative reduced the timber harvest to 1,351 acres and included substantial burned area rehabilitation. The Ecology Center submitted comments (co-signed by the Alliance for the Wild Rockies) on January 15 and March 20, 2001, as part of the scoping process, contending that "recent fires are a component of the forest's natural cycle of regeneration . . . [therefore] we feel that salvage logging may disrupt this natural process."[20]

The Ecology Center served as the lead appellant to the sale, joined by the groups American Wildlands (which had also submitted scoping comments); the Alliance for the Wild Rockies; and an individual, Michael Garrity (who had submitted comments on the draft EIS). The thirty-two-page letter opposing the Decision Notice also incorporated the appeal of Sara Jane Johnson, who filed on behalf of the Native Ecosystems Council.[21] The primary contentions in the appeal were that the final EIS for the salvage project failed to include a thorough economic analysis, the range of alternatives was inadequate to comply with NEPA, and the lack of scientific integrity in considering the impacts of salvage logging also violated NEPA. As relief the appellant sought complete remand of the project.

Despite comments that appeals are largely frivolous, the documents filed in this case are detailed and comprehensive, identifying fourteen points of contention. Works cited include Forest Service reports and scholarly publications pertaining to post-fire rehabilitation and the effects of salvage logging on post-fire ecosystems, along with precedent court cases and references to state and federal legislation and regulations. Analysis of the appeal contentions presumably took considerable time and resources on the part of the Forest Service. But the Forest Service denied the appeal less than a month after it had been filed. The appellants subsequently filed litigation in the District Court of Montana, where the court ruled in favor of the Forest Service,[22] and after that, in the U.S. Ninth Circuit Court of Appeals, which also ruled in favor of the agency.[23]

Despite an attempt at informal resolution of the issues in dispute, it seems apparent that the contentions raised by the groups were philosophically opposed to those of the Forest Service. One newspaper reporter described those differences as "whether to let nature take its course or to allow people to actively manage the public lands."[24] Because of The Ecology Center's history of appealing virtually all Region 1 timber projects, some Forest Service officials assert that the appeals are not really an attempt to engage the agency in a positive discussion of the management of public lands. From the perspective of one Helena National Forest official, the appeals and subsequent litigation of projects are nothing more than delaying tactics designed to make the lumber less valuable and therefore less likely to be harvested. The delays involved in this particular case, for example, resulted in an estimated 10 to 15 percent loss in the amount of timber that could be harvested and at least that much in market value. From this perspective, this figure represents a significant loss. From the perspective of those who see such logging as an ecological loss, the appeal resulted in at least a partial victory.

ALLIANCE FOR THE WILD ROCKIES (AWR)

With more than 100 organizational members and 4,400 individual members, the Alliance has become one of the most powerful, but not always visible, environmental groups in the West. Founded in 1988, its mission is "to secure the ecological integrity of the Wild Rockies Bioregion through citizen empowerment, and the application of conservation biology, sustainable economic models, and environmental law."[25] The Alliance is illustrative of the overlap of resources common to many groups in the Missoula area, where the organization is based, sharing office space with The Ecology Center. More than a dozen other Missoula environmental organizations are part of the Alliance, ranging from the Great Burn Study Group and the Wildlands Center for Preventing Roads to Women's Voices for the Earth, the Institute of the Rockies, and Friends of the Rattlesnake. The Alliance sponsors an annual Wild Rockies Rendezvous, which brings together groups from throughout the region, and has been active in promoting the Northern Rockies Ecosystem Protection Act. It also coordinates an ecosystem defense plan to reduce timber sales on roadless national forests in the northern Rockies and produces scientific reports on ecosystem protection, grizzly bear range, and bull trout habitat. Its focus is on providing public awareness materials and events, including an educational video.

A five-member board of directors oversees the Alliance's activities. Among them is Michael Garrity, a professor of economics who also has been active in the administrative appeals process filing as an individual. Garrity became executive director of the Alliance in December 2002, replacing David A. Merrill and Karen Thea, who each served for six months that year.

The group's 2002 reported revenues were $231,000, $215,000 of which came from direct public support. The primary contributors since 1998 have been the Turner Foundation, the Banbury Fund, and the Charles Englehard Foundation. Smaller foundation grants have come from the Conservation Alliance, the Glaser Family Foundation, the Wilburforce Foundation, and the Gap Foundation. AWR also reported $9,000 in income from attorney's fees awarded in a litigation settlement. Expenses for the year were $334,000—a loss of $103,000—with $272,000 allocated for programs (primarily salaries, wages, and contracted services).[26]

Although the Alliance Web site makes little mention of its involvement in the administrative appeals process, the organization has been a frequent filer, typically with other organizations. Our database shows that the group filed 197 appeals between 1997 and 2003, including some cases where the group filed independently. But as is the case with the other groups profiled, the number of appeals filed each year has been decreasing. At its peak in 2001, the organization filed thirty-nine appeals, but between 1997 and 2000 the range was from thirty to thirty-five appeals per year. In 2002, AWR appeals dropped to fifteen and in 2003, to fourteen. The GAO report indicates that thirty-six appeals of hazardous fuel reduction projects were filed in fiscal years 2001 and 2002; one project was litigated during that same period.[27]

Although many of its appeals are filed with other organizations, in 2002 AWR filed as sole appellant on the Little Blacktail Ecosystem Restoration Project on the Idaho Panhandle National Forests.[28] The project involved regeneration and selective harvesting; road work; helicopter, skyline, and tractor yarding; decommissioning unclassified existing roads; and underburning. The Forest Service contacted the Alliance to attempt an informal disposition of the matter, but a representative declined to meet. Two other appeals had also been filed on the project: one filed by an individual and another by a multiparty coalition of The Ecology Center, Lands Council, Kootenai Environmental Alliance, and Friends of the Pond.

The AWR appeal contended that the chosen alternative for the project violated NFMA, NEPA, the Clean Water Act, and the Idaho Code. In its response, the Forest Service noted that the agency had responded to expressed objections during the scoping period, the alternatives were reasonable and within management discretion, and the decision complied with all laws, regulations, and policy. The appeal was subsequently denied upon review.[29] Appeals filed by the AWR in conjunction with other groups appear to have been more successful than when the group appeals on its own.

The Lands Council

One of the oldest forest monitoring groups, the Spokane-based Lands Council is a nonprofit organization that relies totally on direct public support. According to documents filed with the IRS, The Lands Council operates four major programs in nine national forests in four states: Forest Watch (training citizens to monitor and intervene in Forest Service activities), Public Outreach (combining grassroots activism with mass media opportunities for public education), Wildfire Protection Program (educating rural communities and homeowners on how to protect their home from the dangers of wildfire), and Water Watch (educating citizens of the toxic legacy of a century of mining in the Spokane/Coeur d'Alene watershed). A part of its grassroots movement is the End Commercial Logging Campaign (ECL). The Lands Council's twelve-member board of directors includes former Washington governor Mike Lowry; ten of the board members are from Spokane. On its Web site, the group says that it uses the appeals process as a strategy for developing standing "to pressure the agency to develop logging proposals less harmful to the forest."[30]

The Lands Council's financial report to the IRS showed it received $353,000 in revenues in 2002 (about $90,000 more than in 2001), with about 9 percent of its income from membership dues. Total expenses for the year were $333,000; its full-time executive director received a salary of $33,000, with other employees as contract labor. Nearly half of the group's program expenses were for Forest Watch, with about 2 percent of expenditures directed toward its lobbying activities.[31]

The Lands Council Web site notes that the group submits formal comments on Forest Service proposals for logging, mining, grazing, land exchanges, motorized trail developments, and weed management projects. "Our comments are often used as a basis for altering timber sale proposals *before* they are so far into the process the agency cannot make substantive or effective changes." The group also claims it has "transformed the vibrant energy of a grassroots movement to end commercial logging into a targeted advocacy campaign."[32]

The database shows that between 1997–2003 The Lands Council filed a total of 162 appeals, with the numbers steadily decreasing from a high of 39 in 1998 to 12 in 2003. In the GAO study of hazardous fuel reduction projects, the group filed 29 appeals, 23 of which were in Forest Service Region 1, with the remainder in Region 6. In fiscal years 2001 and 2002, the GAO reported that The Lands Council appeared as litigants in three cases, two in Region 1 and one in Region 5.[33] The group has frequently filed appeals jointly with other environmental organizations based in Region 1 but also files appeals on its own using a staff attorney.

A typical example of an independent appeal is the 2003 Hither and Yon Beetle Project on the Idaho Panhandle National Forests in Region 1.[34] The Forest Service proposed to conduct timber harvest and prescribed burning on 253 acres of land where there had been extensive beetle kill, 59 acres of tree planting, and one-tenth of a mile of road reconstruction. The district ranger met with representatives of The Lands Council, but no resolution was reached. The appeal contended the Forest Service had violated NEPA, NFMA, and the Idaho Panhandle National Forests Plan and sought the completion of an EIS. Among the issues cited by the appellants were the lack of a proper scientific analysis of cumulative detrimental soil disturbance, inadequate analysis of the cumulative effects of activities such as increased off-highway vehicle use and increased risk of fire, and an inadequate demonstration of the continued viability of goshawk and pileated woodpecker habitat. Lastly, the appeal alleged that the proposed project was not needed because Douglas-fir beetle kill is a naturally occurring phenomenon and timber harvest could prolong outbreaks, and salvage and regeneration treatments had a potential to further degrade the environment.

The Forest Service countered that the agency had not violated NEPA because the project was not a major federal action with significant effects on the quality of the human environment, and therefore a FONSI was appropriate rather than an EIS. The agency responded to the remaining appeal contentions by explaining that appropriate studies had been conducted to determine potential impacts and that the project was needed to recover the economic value of dead timber and to promote the long-term goal of vegetative restoration.

The Appeal Reviewing Officer recommended the appellant's relief be denied, and the Appeal Deciding Officer concurred.[35] The outcome was typical of many other Lands Council appeals that have been routinely, and somewhat expeditiously, denied.

CENTER FOR BIOLOGICAL DIVERSITY

Previously known as the Southwest Center for Biological Diversity, the Center for Biological Diversity (CBD), based in Tucson, Arizona, has as its slogan "Protecting endangered species and wild places through science, policy, education, and environmental law." Three environmental activists, physician Robin Silver, biologist Peter Galvin, and philosopher Kieran Suckling, formed the group in the late 1980s. Protection of ponderosa pine forests, forest restoration and logging practices, and protection of species such as the northern goshawk all fall within the larger program areas of the organization. The group's mission statement asserts, "Combining conservation biology with litigation, policy advocacy, and an innovative strategic vision, the Center for Biological Diversity is working to secure a future for animals and plants hovering on the brink of extinction, for the wilderness they need to survive, and by extension for the spiritual welfare of generations to come."[36]

The CBD is one of the largest organizations in terms of funding but, like many of its counterparts, the center's expenses exceeded its revenues in 2002. The group reported total revenue of $1,868,000, of which $1,604,000 came in the form of direct public support—about 68 percent of total revenues. An additional $244,000 came from program service revenue, of which $204,000 was contributed by conservation organization Trout Unlimited. Expenses for the year were $2,007,000, for a deficit of about $139,000. The 2002 revenues were about $618,000 less than were received in 2001, but $725,000 more than it received in 2000. In 1997, the center generated only $625,000 and in 1998, $835,000, indicating its tremendous financial growth over the past five years. Part of the difference is the result of grants received from other organizations, which in 2002 included $40,000 from the California Native Plant Society and $43,000 from Biodiversity Associates.[37] It appears that the organization's program priorities have shifted in response to its revenue sources; its priority now is protecting trout in the western United States.

One of the factors that distinguishes the CBD from other appellants is its resources, which allow the organization to compensate its top employees relatively more than most environmental organizations. In 2002 the group's primary expense was compensation for consultants and its own employees ($841,000), followed by $157,000 for travel. Executive Director Kieran Suckling receives $47,000 per year as does board member Peter Galvin; treasurer Todd Schulke is paid $34,000.[38]

Although the organization's activities tend to focus on endangered species and their habitats, CBD has historically been one of the top twenty filers of Forest Service appeals nationwide. Our data show that between 1997 and 2003, the center filed eighty-nine administrative appeals. The group is one of the few whose overall appeal activities have increased recently, from a low of four in 2000, to fourteen in 2001, sixteen in 2002, and twenty-three in 2003. However, the 2003 GAO report shows that the center filed only five hazardous fuels reduction project appeals in fiscal years 2001 and 2002; two cases were litigated.[39] Thus, despite the increasing total number of appeals filed by CBD, the number specifically related to hazardous fuels is a small percentage of its overall activities.

The center wrote the appeal documents for three groups in a 1999 case concerning the Dry Park Vegetative Management Project, which took seven years from initial planning in spring 1995 to implementation in 2002. The project involved nearly ten thousand acres in Arizona's Kaibab National Forest, heavily forested and adjacent to Grand Canyon National Park, with both areas sharing a history of fire suppression and overgrazing. The Forest Service chose an alternative that involved thinning 6,200 trees with a diameter over sixteen inches, mistletoe control, and sixty-seven miles of road closures—proposals that would pit environmental groups against small towns that had been dependent upon local mills and the timber industry. In order to move vegetation toward the desired condition, the project was also slated to treat 7,100 acres of logging slash and existing down woody material through a combination of prescribed burning and mechanical treatment.

The EA for the project was released in July 1998, with a thirty-day public comment period. The first of two Decision Notice/Finding of No Significant Impact letters was signed in June 1999, with attempts made to discuss an informal resolution. Five contentions were identified in the first of two appeals filed in August by the CBD, the Grand Canyon Chapter of the Sierra Club, and the Southwest Forest Alliance. These contentions focused on violation of the Endangered Species Act and failure to deal with standards related to the northern goshawk, along with violations of the Administrative Procedure Act.[40] Although the Appeals Deciding Officer appeared to respond negatively to most of the appellants' claims, he did agree that the project's EA was incomplete, concluding that effects on management indicator species had not been fully evaluated and documented, and remanded the case back to the Forest Service.[41] But the second EA included only a single new paragraph that stated any deficiencies in the original document had been corrected.

In November 1999, the forest supervisor signed a second Decision Notice and Finding of No Significant Impact. The Forest Guardians filed one appeal in December 1999; the other three groups that had filed on the first EA filed a second set of appeals at the same time. The second appeal was almost identical to the first one filed by the three organizations, with comments referring to the inadequacy of the Forest Service response to the first appeal and requesting a full remand.[42] In February 2000, the Forest Service affirmed its decision, and the project was reinstated. A notice of the Dry Park timber sale appeared in March 2002, and several timber companies bid on the cut, which began in summer 2002.

The original intent of the agency project remained intact throughout the extensive public scoping process, and it appears that the appeal contentions actually had little effect on the final outcome. Delays were primarily the result of internal factors within the Forest Service rather than the appeal process. The longest delay—from March 1996 until November 1997—occurred when the project was placed on hold while the Kaibab Ranger District addressed salvage and restoration work resulting from drought conditions and two wildfires in summer 1996. Also during this time an injunction was placed on logging in the Southwest until studies could be completed on the Mexican spotted owl. In the end, the time period from the first FONSI to the final affirmation of the decision was only eight months. The outcome could be considered a loss for the CBD, but Public Lands Director Brian Segee commented that, ultimately, it comes down to "fundamental differences of what national forests are." He vowed to continue to force the agency to conduct "scientifically-based studies" to address their issues and concerns.

WISE USE APPEALS

Although the majority of criticism of the appeals process has focused on environmental groups, who have been accused of obstructing Forest Service planning, it is important to emphasize that the administrative appeals process has also been used extensively by wise use groups and their supporters.[43] However, these appeals usually fall under Section 251 and concern grazing allotments and recreational trail use rather than decisions involving the cutting of trees, whether for timber sales or fuels reduction.

Typical is the case of Sheldon Buchanan and Buchanan Ranches, represented by well-known Wyoming law firm Budd-Falen Law Offices.[44] According to the firm's Web site, it represents industry clients in Bureau of Land Management and Forest Service appeals, as well as in litigation arising under the Endangered Species Act, the Federal Lands Policy and Management Act, NEPA, the Clean Water Act, and other environmental statutes. Clients have included the Coalition of Counties for Stable Economic Growth, the New Mexico Cattle Growers Association, and private property owners represented "to protect rural traditions and ways of life, while still preserving natural resources in a manner consistent with multiple and wise use of the land."[45]

In their thirty-one-page appeal filed in 2003, the law firm argued against the district ranger's finding of noncompliance with the Buchanan's ten-year grazing permits on the Cottonwood C&H Allotment in Utah's Fishlake National Forest, which had been issued in 1996. The ranger's decision resulted in the suspension of 25 percent of permitted livestock use for the next three grazing seasons. The appellants sought to have the decision reversed or dismissed, contending that it was "arbitrary, capricious, an abuse of discretion and in violation of Federal law and Department of Agriculture regulations." The appeal also noted that the Deciding Officer did not attempt to meet with the appellants to discuss the case and violated the Forest Service Handbook's requirement not to take final action until the permittee has had an opportunity to explain actions or inactions.[46]

The appeal letter filed by the firm was more comprehensive and detailed than most other grazing appeals, making specific references to agency documents, the Administrative Procedure Act, and correspondence sent and received between the parties. The contentions, in boldface type, were well-documented, with references to prior court decisions, the U.S. Codes, and concluding with a formal request for an oral presentation and a request for mediation of the dispute.

According to Brandon Jensen, one of the attorneys who filed the appeal, the Buchanan family hired the Budd-Falen law firm because of the reputation of the company's attorneys. Although the Buchanans had made attempts to resolve the dispute, they had been unsuccessful and thus turned to legal counsel. Jensen admitted that the appeal was actually a way of getting at the larger issue of grazing on public lands because the Forest Service decision was "blatantly wrong." Jensen characterized the appeals process as unfair and ineffective because it was too informal and because it did not include a real fact-finding or hearing.[47] His view represented the firm's overall philosophy as much as it did the interests of the Buchanans.

The Forest Service Appeal Reviewing Officer reversed the decision of the district ranger on procedural grounds, although he noted that "it is clear that there was a violation of the terms and conditions of the Appellants' grazing permit. I personally have visited and reviewed the Central and Southern Utah areas and am very concerned about rangeland resource conditions resulting from the extended drought" and excess use by livestock. The ranger was instructed to closely monitor all authorized grazing on the allotment, and the Forest Service warned that any violations of use levels would be dealt with immediately.[48]

The Budd-Falen Law Offices also have filed appeals on behalf of other ranchers, such as Danny Fryar and his wife, Jacqueline, who filed eight appeals on the Gila National Forest in New Mexico between 1997 and 2003, making them the thirteenth most active individual filers. Their initial August 1998 appeal was based on a district ranger's proposal that *might* allow fences to be built around riparian areas within their grazing allotment; the law firm contended that the district ranger's action improperly reduced the season of use for the allotment and implemented mitigation measures dramatically reducing the number of cattle that could be grazed.[49] Additionally, the firm noted that the Fryars' allotment had been listed in a December 1997 lawsuit filed by the Forest Guardians that sought protection for critical habitat for the Loach Minnow and the Southwest Willow Flycatcher. Under a subsequent settlement agreement to this lawsuit, the Forest Service agreed to aggressively pursue the removal of livestock in riparian areas, including cattle on the Fryars' allotment. The appeal contended that this would cause the Fryars irreparable harm and result in serious financial injury to both them and the members of their families who depend upon them.[50] A second level appeal of the decision was filed by the firm on February 1, 1999, and was denied by the deputy regional forester on March 13, 2001.

In a summer 2003 interview, Danny Fryar said that grazing cattle is a secondary income for his family and almost a hobby. He stated his reason for filing the appeals was that he disliked the government taking action against his cattle allotment. He had attempted to reconcile his issues with the Forest Service informally in various meetings and, in his words, "both sides gave a little." But even though there was an attempt at compromise, Fryar filed his appeals because he believed he was helping fight a larger, national issue regarding ranchers' rights.

He stated that the Forest Service was "completely out of touch with the resource" and commented that the agency does what is "politically correct" rather than what is "right" for the resource.[51] Their appeals, however, were subsequently denied because the Fryars failed to show actual harm to their cattle allotment because the fencing had only been proposed.[52]

Groups associated with forest trails and off-highway vehicle use, usually considered part of the wise use movement, have filed appeals not only related to special permit uses under 36 CFR 251, but also under Section 215 relating to NEPA projects. In September 2002, Montanans for Property Rights, a group "working toward protecting property rights including public access to public lands, and sensible forest management practices which will enhance multiple-use of those lands," filed an appeal on the Lolo Post Burn Final Environmental Impact Statement. The group argued that the forest supervisor's decision, which authorized salvage logging and commercial thinning on twenty-four hundred acres out of a total thirty-five thousand burned acres and the decommissioning of 225 miles of road, did not promote "best practices" in forest management. The group accused the agency of "catering to the narrow agenda of groups promoting protection of selected plant and animal species, the selection of which is considered error-prone at best, and fraudulent at worst."

In addition to law firms like Budd-Falen, other property rights and wise use groups also play an important role in assisting those appealing Forest Service project decisions. The Web site of the Paragon Foundation, based in Almagordo, New Mexico, notes that the group is striving to offset "those forces prevailing in our society that are attempting to destroy the fundamental principles established by our Founding Fathers in the Constitution of the United States of America that guarantee individual freedom, private property rights, and protection from tyrannical government edicts; stop all productive uses of public lands; force land management decisions that are detrimental to the environment; destroy the customs, culture, and lifestyle of our rural communities."[53]

As part of its activities, the Paragon Foundation administers a litigation fund, supported through private donations, that provides financial assistance upon request for those involved in legal action in support of its mission, including groups like the Arizona Cattle Growers, the American Land Foundation, and the Apache-Sitgreaves Allottees Association.

One of the nation's most politically active wise use groups is the Blue Ribbon Coalition (BRC), which has a broad constituency of hundreds of off-road vehicle groups (including snowmobilers, equestrian groups, and jeep owners). The organization publishes information about pending legislation and projects in its newsletter and is also known for its ability to quickly mobilize individual members from the groups it represents. The BRC has not only filed appeals on its own but also encouraged members of its constituent organizations to file separately. In July 2001, the BRC filed an appeal of the North Fork Smith River Special Interest Areas Road Access EA.[54] The Forest Service also received thirteen form letter appeals filed by individuals, and their contentions were taken verbatim from the BRC. As it had with the environmental groups' appeals in the Gifford Pinchot example, the agency issued one appeal decision. Similarly, form letters of dismissal without review were sent to twenty-seven other groups and individuals who failed to file an appeal within the public comment filing period deadlines, and another form letter of dismissal was sent to seventy appellants who did file a timely appeal on the project but who had failed to participate during the scoping and notice and comment periods.[55]

As is the case with environmental organizations, wise use advocates have relied upon their own legal and financial resources in using the administrative appeals process as part of a broader strategy to advance their political agenda vis-à-vis the Forest Service and public lands management. These organizations are far less visible and given less media attention than the frequent filers profiled previously, but they are part of a social movement that has had considerable political support under the Reagan and Bush administrations.[56]

COMMODITY AND BUSINESS INTEREST APPEALS

A quick survey of both our database and GAO's listings of appellants indicates the wide spectrum of interests that have used the administrative appeals process, both for forest projects and other decisions made by the Forest Service. Although the identity and motivations of some interests can be somewhat easily identified by their name, especially regional groups such as the Friends of Mississippi Public Lands and the Hells Canyon Preservation Council, others are less transparent. Motivation for appeals filed by groups with indeterminate names like the Ambiance Project, Christians Caring for Creation, Citizens for Better Forestry, the Forest Issues Group, High Country Citizens' Alliance, and Shadow Estates Homeowners Association are not obvious based on the appellant's name alone. This is one reason why it is difficult to determine the number of commodity and business interest appeals that have been filed, but the CFR section designation identifying appeals of grazing allotments makes it somewhat easier to separate out those cases.

In the GAO report, the list of appellants in fiscal years 2001 and 2002 includes the Breckenridge Ski Resort, Potlatch Corporation, Western Radio Services Company, LSK2 Incorporated, and Minnesota Forest Industries, all of whom filed appeals related to hazardous fuels reduction projects. Commercial interests, including the Johnson Cattle Company, the Sanborn Land and Cattle Company, Rajala Industries, and smaller business entities like Earth Wisdom Tours, Sedona Photo Tours, Northern Lights Balloon Expeditions, Vallecitos Stables, and Earnhardt Ranches, are also on the list of Forest Service project appellants in our study.

Commercial and business trade groups, such as the Sacramento Grazing Association and the Sedona Airport Supporters Association, represent smaller interests that may not have the resources to file appeals on their own. One example of a trade group appeal was filed by the Intermountain Forest Association (IFA), an organization representing fifteen wood product manufacturers, timberland owners, and related businesses in South Dakota, Wyoming, and Colorado.[57] The IFA has only one staff member, a former Forest Service employee who filed five appeals for the group's members in fourteen years. In March 2001, IFA sent a comment letter to the Forest Service on behalf of Wyoming Sawmills, Inc., a locally owned and managed lumber facility in Sheridan, Wyoming. The letter requested that the agency consider a pre-burn commercial timber harvest as an alternative to the Little Bighorn Prescribed Burn on the Bighorn National Forest in Wyoming. The alternative was not included in the project, and the timber company sought help from the IFA, which appealed the decision in November 2001on the basis of five issues.[58] The appeal was dismissed in January 2002 because there was no evidence that the decision violated law, regulation or policy, although all five issues were addressed comment by comment. Although the IFA was unsuccessful, it provided a voice for the lumber mill owner, who was not familiar with the appeals process and probably would not have filed without the IFA's help.

Beside appeals of timber-related projects, business interests participate in the administrative appeals process in two other ways. First, some file appeals under 36 CFR Part 251, Subpart C, which deals with occupancy and use of national forest lands, such as rulings on special-use permits. Since 1997, Part 251 decisions have made up about 16 percent of the appeals filed. Many of the 251 appeals are related to Forest Service regulations governing the fees businesses pay to operate within a national forest. In 2003, for example, a law firm representing Doc and Al's Resort lost an appeal over $24,202 in fees owed to the agency for rent on land where their property is located in the Humboldt-Toiyabe National Forest in Nevada.[59] The Forest Service uses an external accounting team to review permits and make audit recommendations on fees and attempts to resolve cases informally whenever possible. The fee cases often involve complicated accounting and tax issues, so many appellants rely upon legal counsel to help them when they believe the fee amounts or structure should be challenged.

Because many national forest campgrounds and facilities involve concessionaires, some special-use appeals involve requests for proposals and bids for special-use permits. The president of Arizona-based Recreation Resource Management, for example, filed an appeal in 1998 over the selection of another firm to manage the Chugach National Forest campgrounds in Alaska. The appellant contended that his firm should have been rated higher and that the evaluation panel was biased toward the competing firm in their scoring. The appeal was denied by the acting regional forester, who ruled that although the point spread between the two firms was close, the appellant had not been as effective during a teleconference interview, and four of the five panelists had no prior knowledge about his company.[60] In this case, the appeals process provided the company owner with a formal opportunity to air his grievances about the selection process that might not otherwise have been available to him without resorting to litigation.

Other special-permit appeals deal specifically with complaints and non-compliance related to business operations. An example of this appeal type is one filed by a law firm on behalf of Nunatek Kennels, Inc., which operated commercial, guided dogsled tours on the Juneau Icefield under a special-use permit granted by the Tongass National Forest in Alaska. The company received its first permit in 1997, and evaluations of its performance showed problems serious enough for the district ranger to consider denying a 1998 permit altogether. In order to ensure that Nunatek Kennels' operations would be conducted safely and in accordance with Forest Service goals and policies, several stipulations were added to the 1998 permit. The agency's evaluation of the company's 1998 operations found performance to be unacceptable on several key criteria, and the company subsequently filed its appeal of the designation, which was denied.[61]

A second way commodity interests, such as timber companies, have participated in the appeals process is when they serve as "interested parties" to an appeal. (As will be discussed in Chapter 6, the designation of interested party was eliminated in 2003.) In these cases, a letter is sent to the Forest Service noting the individual's or group's desire to be informed of all actions taking place during the appeals process. For example, in appeals filed on the Hume Vegetation Project on the Sequoia National Forest in California in 1998, Sierra Forest Products was listed as the sole interested party. The company, based in Terra Bella, California, has an extensive history of logging in the area and was forced to shut down one of its mills and lay off 100 employees when the Clinton administration declared much of the area a national monument. It also operates a biomass electrical generating station near the project.[62] The company was one of ten respondents during the public scoping period and, after the appeals were denied, was the successful bidder to begin mechanical thinning in spring 2000. By becoming an interested party to the appeals, Sierra Forest Products was kept informed of each stage of the process and was able to monitor project decisions from start to finish. It is not possible to determine whether their role gave them an advantage in the bidding process once the appeal was denied, but the information they gleaned certainly provided them with the most up-to-date status reports on when bidding might proceed and an overall understanding of Forest Service plans.

CASES WITH MULTIPLE APPELLANTS

A Forest Service decision can be appealed multiple times and multiple appellants can be parties to an appeal, which accounts for the fact that there are more appeals in both our database and the GAO study than there are decisions. The GAO study found that of the 197 appealed decisions reported, there were 285 appeals with 559 appellants, including 482 appeals by 85 different interest groups and 77 appeals by 53 private individuals. Of the interest groups, seven appeared as appellants twenty or more times. Similarly, multiple plaintiffs can be parties to a lawsuit.

Case studies indicate that including multiple appellants to an appeal usually results from one of two strategies: a desire to create the perception that multiple appellants equal more support for the appeal, or the provisions of different types of resources and expertise by the various appellants in development of the appeal. However, it is difficult to determine the level of public interest in a Forest Service project solely on the basis of the number of appeals filed. For example, two appeals were filed on the Trough Springs Fuel Break Project in the Mendocino National Forest in California in 2001. One appeal was filed jointly by the Forest Conservation Council and the Environmental Protection Information Center,[63] with a second appeal filed by Clark Frantzen. Frantzen claimed in his appeal letter that he represented more than a hundred families and individuals in the region "that share a common interest in public lands issues and the preservation of public access and multi-purpose recreation opportunities on public lands."[64] But the Forest Service notes in its denial of the requested relief that Frantzen did not identify an organizational name or those he claimed to represent. This leaves open the question of if the agency would have responded differently if separate appeals had been filed by each interested person Frantzen mentioned. However, the Forest Service letter also notes that a notice of the proposal had been mailed to thirty individuals and groups that had previously expressed an interest in management of the project area; six comments were received prior to the EA review, but only the appellants responded during the review and comment period.[65]

This is in sharp contrast to the approximately 1,200 appeals filed on the Open Road and Open Motorized Trail Travel Plan for Targhee National Forest in 1998. In this project, the appellants included a wide range of concerned citizens and competing interests, state and local government representatives, the Greater Yellowstone Coalition, and the Blue Ribbon Coalition. In general, the appellants argued that the forest supervisor's decision was flawed because site-specific decisions were made without public participation or review in violation of NEPA, agency policy, and regulations. But individual appeals raised issues ranging from the agency's failure to consider a reasonable range of alternatives, violations of the Americans with Disabilities Act, age discrimination, denial of access to public property, and an unclear definition of the term "snow machines."[66] In this instance, the Appeal Review Officer reversed the forest supervisor's opinion to allow for additional public review and comment.

Aside from the "frequent filers" among environmental groups, smaller regional groups often join together in multiparty appeals, combining their mutual interests and resources and sometimes relying upon a larger organization as the lead appellant. In October 2001, four local groups filed an appeal over the Manter Restoration Project in the Sequoia National Forest in California.[67] The project was a result of the July 2000 Manter Fire that burned nearly seventy-five thousand acres, including fifty-five hundred acres within the Sequoia National Forest. The area is one of the most active fire forests in the United States, averaging two hundred fires per year, usually as a result of lightning.

The Forest Service project called for removing hazard trees, selling salvage timber on 1,337 acres, restoring and burning of fuels. The multi-appellant appeal was filed by Ara Marderosian (executive director of Sequoia ForestKeepers), the Sequoia Forest Alliance, the Tule River Conservancy, and the Kerncrest Audubon Society—grassroots organizations whose members frequent the Sequoia area. Included in the same appeal as individuals were Carla Cloer, chair of the Sierra Club Sequoia Task Force and recipient of the organization's John Muir Award for her efforts in protecting the Sequoia National Forest, and Ronald and Carol Wermuth, area residents who frequently file as individuals with the Sequoia Forest Alliance.[68]

The 125-page appeal had more than a dozen separate contentions, including the Forest Service's alleged failure to specify a cumulative watershed effects model for ensuring the viability of the Pacific fisher. The appeals document was comprehensive and covered such a wide range of issues that the Forest Service had to prepare a sizeable decision comment letter in response. Marderosian also participated in a conference call with several Forest Service staff members in an attempt to try to reach a resolution, but the parties were unsuccessful. Although the appeal was denied, the groups and individuals continue to work together on projects in the area and frequently interchange appellants and appeal language. The Tule River Conservancy has used introductory statements in subsequent appeals that are almost identical to those used by Marderosian and Carla Cloer.[69]

One of the stereotypes surrounding the administrative appeals controversy relates to "template" or "boilerplate" appeals (where multiple appellants file identical or nearly identical documents). Our case study analysis found evidence that this strategy has been used by various environmental groups. An example occurred in the Crimson Tide Forest Health Project (CTFHP), initiated in 1998 to thin dense forest stands and reduce the fire hazard on a small parcel (less than two hundred acres) in California's Eldorado National Forest. The Forest Service categorically excluded the project from the NEPA process as a small-scale salvage of timber at high risk of loss from wildfire, and a timber sale contract was issued. However, a 2000 Circuit Court case, *Heartwood v. U.S. Forest Service*,[70] placed an injunction on all sales of this type, forcing the agency to prepare an EA for the project.[71]

The EA was released in June 2000 and a decision was made in August to implement an alternative that called for commercial understory thinning, whole tree yarding, and other treatments such as prescribed burning. The decision was appealed in a multiparty action by the Forest Conservation Council, National Forest Protection Alliance, and an individual, Scott Schroder, on October 9, 2000.[72] The appeal presented seven contentions, six of which were carried forward, often verbatim, from comments filed on the EA. The contentions did not acknowledge the Forest Service response as documented in the supplement to the EA even though regulations about the appeal content state that it must show "how the Responsible Official's decision fails to consider comments previously provided."[73]

Nonetheless, the Appeal Review Officer reversed the forest supervisor's decision based on inadequate analysis of effects on wildfire and wildlife. The reversal came as a surprise to staff who prepared the EA because it had been based on standard actions used in other projects by the forest for which EAs had been prepared and projects that had been categorically excluded. They concluded that the appeal process for the project "rewards Appellants who fail to properly engage in scoping or commenting to projects and it allows Regional Office reviews to unilaterally reverse decisions without the benefit of dialog or discussion with the Responsible Official or the project interdisciplinary team."[74] A second EA was prepared and expanded to address issues highlighted during the appeals process and agency review and was released on July 2, 2001. Three months later, a second appeal was filed, this time by the Forest Conservation Council, the National Forest

Protection Alliance, and Chad Hanson of the John Muir Project, who joined the appeal when Scott Schroder dropped out. Four of the five items listed in the appellant's request for relief from the 2000 appeal were repeated in this appeal; three of the six contentions were again carried forward virtually verbatim. The written recommendation of the Appeal Reviewing Officer was issued on October 31, 2001, and affirmed November 9, 2001. The Crimson Tide Timber Sale contract, representing about $112,000 in stumpage revenue, was subsequently delayed because the logging firm had accepted other contract obligations in the interim that needed to be met.

It is difficult to determine the impact when multiple appeals are filed. For example, twenty appellants filed regarding the decision notice for the Phelps Snowmobile Trail Project on the Eagle River-Florence Ranger District in Wisconsin's Chequamegon-Nicolet Forest in 2002. Just days later, the district ranger withdrew his decision on the project, so the appeal record was closed without review of the merits of the appeals. It is unknown whether the appeals influenced withdrawal of the decision.[75]

In another case involving multiple appellants, the appeals process definitely changed the Forest Service's decision. Forest Guardians, Prescott National Forest Friends, and three individuals (two of whom were husband and wife) appealed the EA of the Baker's Pass Ecosystem Management Project on the Prescott National Forest in Arizona in August 1997. The appeals varied in their complexity and contentions and apparently were filed without consultation among the parties. One of the individual appellants, Robert Grossman, contended that the EA did not meet NEPA requirements because it failed to adequately consider the project's economic costs.[76] A month later, Forest Service officials met with Mr. Grossman and agreed to resolve his appeal by conducting an environmental analysis that would be prepared jointly by the appellant and a Forest Service staff member. A representative of the Prescott National Forest Friends also met informally with the Forest Service three weeks after the group's appeal was filed.[77] The group had expressed concern over wildlife monitoring and, during the discussion, a mutual agreement was reached to develop a cooperative effort, resolving the appeal. Forest Guardians declined to meet regarding informal disposition, and the other two appellants apparently were not involved in further discussions after their appeal was filed.[78]

On October 8, 1997, the Forest Service withdrew its decision in order to consider information that the appellants had brought to light during the appeals process. The agency said it would amend its analysis and reconsider the decision after the appellants' contentions and data were analyzed. In this instance, the processing time was very short; the decision notice was issued July 8 and the letter announcing withdrawal of the project was issued October 8. In just ninety days, the Forest Service had met with two of the four appellants, resolved two appeals informally, and agreed to take the comments and concerns of all parties under further consideration.

Some appeals involve organizations that are well-versed in the administrative appeals process, but they also rely upon external legal assistance, sometimes adding that organization to the appeal. In January 2003, the Hell's Canyon Preservation Council filed a joint appeal with The Ecology Center for the Orion Mine Project on Oregon's Wallowa-Whitman National Forest. The third appellant in this case was the Northwest Environmental Defense Center, a nonprofit public interest organization in Portland, Oregon. The center provides legal support to individuals and grassroots organizations and has frequently assisted the two other appellants in filing appeals and litigation. Generally, law firms are hired on a contract basis, serving several clients at a time. They may or may not be added as parties to the appeal, so it is difficult to determine whether or not external legal assistance has been sought by an individual or organization. Some organizations, such as the Sierra Club and the Oregon Natural Resources Defense Council, have extensive legal staff resources and provide assistance to others on an informal basis. Although it is not necessary to have a law degree to file an appeal and it is not possible to determine whether legal assistance increases an appellant's chance of success, the expertise of attorneys and other professionals, such as wildlife biologists, economists, and foresters, can definitely create the perception that an appeal is stronger than one without the inclusion of these resources.

NATIVE AMERICAN TRIBAL APPELLANTS

Our database found that several Native American groups and tribal organizations have participated in the scoping process or as appellants, although none were identified as having appealed or litigated projects in the 2003 GAO study. Because tribal land boundaries often overlap those of national forests, we would expect Native American groups to be part of the planning process. But issues of tribal sovereignty and the Forest Service's sensitivity to cultural traditions and beliefs of Native American peoples show that appeals in this category are handled differently than those filed by other environmental or commercial interests.

Illustrative of those differences is the Copwood Timber Sale in the Winema National Forest of Oregon.[79] In 1995, the Forest Service issued a schedule of proposed actions and conducted scoping on its proposal to conduct commercial thinning of green trees and salvage of dead, dying, and diseased timber on approximately 7,800 acres, along with conifer planting and road obliterations to improve hydrological function. The draft EA was released in May 1996 and reissued in August 1996 after a determination was made that the project did not meet the criteria established in the Rescissions Act, which would have allowed for a shortened comment period and disallowed administrative appeals.[80] A Decision Notice, the EA, and a FONSI were issued in November 1996, and in January 1997 an appeal was filed by the Sierra Club Legal Defense Fund and Oregon Legal Services Native American Program on behalf of the Klamath Tribes.[81]

The Klamath Tribes are a confederation consisting of the Klamath, the Modoc, and the Yahooskin Band of Snake Indians in south-central Oregon. The appellants contended that the tribes had entered into a treaty with the United States in 1864 in which they ceded their aboriginal title to lands, reserving for themselves a homeland that became the Klamath Indian Reservation. In addition, the tribes reserved hunting, fishing, and gathering rights for their members on the reservation, which now included lands managed by the Forest Service. The tribes were terminated from federal recognition in 1954, thus ending their right to government-to-government relations with the United States. But in 1974 the tribes won a U.S. Supreme Court case that ruled tribal members retained their rights from the original 1864 treaty in perpetuity. In 1986 federal recognition was restored. By 1995 when the Copwood Timber Sale was proposed, considerable tension had been created between the tribes and the federal government, and tribal leaders attempted to stop any project they believed infringed upon their rights. The appeal contended that the timber sale involved a massive harvest within the treaty rights area, with significant adverse impact on the watershed and the fish and wildlife resources on which the tribes depend. In addition to the issue of treaty rights, the appellants alleged that the Forest Service had failed to consult with the tribes, failed to share relevant information regarding the sale, failed to ensure that tribal resources would be protected and enhanced, and failed to adequately disclose and analyze the impact of the sale on the human environment. They sought a stay of all activities until the appeal was resolved.[82] The district ranger said in an interview, "They appealed everything. . . . [T]hey felt cheated."[83]

This appeal represents more than just a difference of opinion on the economic or scientific viability of a timber sale. The Klamath Tribes have their own Department of Natural Resources and employ specialists in forestry, conservation biology, hydrology, habitat evaluation, and other disciplines to monitor projects slated for reservation land. As the length and comprehensiveness of the appeal attests, the tribes were supported by not only their own scientific expertise but also the substantial legal resources of two non-tribal organizations. One major issue was whether or not the Forest Service had, in fact, been in active consultation with the tribes in disclosing environmental consequences, as required by NEPA.

The EA for the Copwood Timber Sale extensively chronicled the agency's attempts to involve tribal leaders throughout the process, although subsequent communications indicated there was confusion over an "official" response from the tribes to the Forest Service. The appeal contended that the tribes had not been kept informed, lacked sufficient maps and other details of the sale, and did not have sufficient time to coordinate a recommendation. The tribes also communicated their "government-to-government concerns" to the Chief of the Forest Service, Jack Ward Thomas, noting that the district ranger's letters had been "patronizing" and spoke "to our people as if we were children who don't quite understand what is going on rather than as the staff of a sovereign governmental body with its own scientists, experts, and painstakingly developed technical information. Suffice it to say that the manifestation of such an attitude by your staff is unprofessional and counterproductive."[84]

One and a half months after the appeal was filed, both the Appeal Deciding Officer and the Appeal Review Officer for the Forest Service made a determination in letters in February 1997 that the decision to implement the timber sale be reversed. The reason given in both letters was that the EA violated NEPA by not providing an adequate disclosure of the proposed action's cumulative effects, with no mention of the other contentions. More importantly, the appeal triggered a series of events that had less to do with NEPA and more to do with the tribes' treaty rights. The administrative appeal in this case was used in an unorthodox manner compared to many other Forest Service appeals. But the way in which the tribes used this tool speaks volumes about the importance of appeals to the public. In this case, if an appeal process had not been available, the project would likely have gone to litigation resulting in increased costs and resources for both parties.

Since the Klamath appeal, no other Forest Service project has gone through in the area. The Forest Service and the Klamath Tribes signed a Memorandum of Agreement (MOA) in February 1999 that illustrates the impact of the Copwood decision. The tribal chairman now works directly with the regional forester rather than negotiating with the local districts.

The MOA states clearly that the tribes's role is more than that of another interested public; that the Forest Service and the Klamath Tribes work as cooperative governments in policy and management decisions affecting tribal sovereignty, making them equal entities in the formation of forest policies in the area.

GOVERNMENT AGENCY APPEALS

Among the thousands of appeals in our database, less than forty have involved government agencies as appellants. The majority of appeals in this category were filed by county-level government bodies, such as county boards of commissioners. Most were filed in Forest Service Region 3 (Arizona and New Mexico). Government appellants from this region include Catron County, Los Alamos County, and Otero County—all in New Mexico. None of the 818 appeal decisions on projects involving fuels reduction activities in the GAO study involved government entities, and none were involved in litigation in fiscal years 2001 and 2002.

The primary role of government in the administrative appeals process is during the scoping period, when agencies like county governments or state agencies are routinely sent announcements of proposed projectes, field trips, public meetings, or other elements of the public comment phase. Some federal regulations, such as NEPA and the Clean Air Act, require federal agencies to review proposed projects.

The Forest Service usually works from a predetermined list of agencies, organizations, and persons to whom copies of the project's documents (especially EAs and EISs) are sent. For example, in the proposed Agua/Caballos Projects in the Carson National Forest in New Mexico, the draft EIS and the final EIS were sent to eighteen tribes, twelve federal agencies and elected officials, five state agencies, five local governments, one college, forty-five organizations and businesses, and nearly two hundred individuals. Between April 19 and October 16, 1995, sixteen comment letters were received on the Agua/Caballos draft EIS, including one from the U.S. Environmental Protection Agency, one from the New Mexico Department of Game and Fish, and one from the U.S. Department of the Interior. Between February 1999 and November 2000, the Forest Service received thirty-four comment letters, five of which came from government bodies (U.S. Department of the Interior, U.S. Environmental Protection Agency, State of New Mexico Environment Department, New Mexico Department of Game and Fish, and the Navajo Nation). The government agency letters provided technical information, sought additional data, or recommended that the agency consider other options and alternatives.[85]

A government body's resources clearly have an impact on its ability to file administrative appeals where the technicalities of forest health are concerned. Smaller communities are unlikely to have the staff or expertise to track pending projects or provide expert commentary. In June 1998, for instance, the Town of Bartlett, New Hampshire, filed a short appeal on the Sugar Hill and C. L. Graham Overlooks Improvement Project in the White Mountain National Forest. Within six weeks, the Forest Service denied the town's appeal without review, noting that the Office of Selectmen in the town of 2,512 people had not indicated any interest in the project despite two attempts at contacts to solicit involvement and numerous mailings of scoping materials, the draft EIS, and the final EIS.[86]

This does not necessarily mean, however, that smaller government entities are unlikely to influence Forest Service projects. In another New Hampshire case, the Conway Board of Selectmen appealed the Diana's Bath Trailhead Project, also in the White Mountain National Forest. The Forest Service had reached a decision on the project on October 23, 1998, which was appealed on November 24 by the Town of Conway, New Hampshire. Three weeks later, the Forest Service and the Board of Selectmen reached an agreement for an informal disposition of the appeal, which was then subsequently withdrawn the following day.[87] Conway has a population of about 1,700 people and is in the same ranger district as the Town of Bartlett. But many factors may influence the success of one community compared to another: relationships between the district ranger and community leaders; the staff available to monitor national forest activities; the importance of the project to the town's mission or interests; the size of the project; or even the willingness of a town to participate in scoping activities and to negotiate a solution.

Some government appeals are denied even when the local entity is deeply involved in the decision making process and has substantial resources available. In 1997 the Lawrence County Board of Commissioners filed an appeal of the Dalton Piedmont Project Area that covered nearly thirty-five thousand acres in South Dakota. The county contains several towns, including Spearfish and Deadwood on the state's western border, and has a population of about twenty-two thousand. The county commissioners and the Committee on Recreation, Wildlife and Tourism of the Lawrence County Environmental Review Plan had been involved at virtually every stage of the project's development. The county had submitted four sets of comprehensive comments on the project, and a public meeting of the commissioners with a Forest Service representative had been held. The Forest Service responded to many of the county's comments during the scoping process and made changes as a result. For this reason, the Forest Service Appeal Review Officer said that there had been sufficient local participation in the plan's development. The agency also reviewed but dismissed the county's eight other appeals contentions dealing with mountain pine beetle infestation, tree harvesting, calculation of thermal cover, preferred alternatives, snag habitat, prescribed burning, old growth, and hardwood and grassland restoration.[88]

Lawrence County's resources were substantial, with fire science and forestry expertise within its County Fire Advisory Board and a USDA Forest Service fire sciences laboratory located in the area. The county has an extremely comprehensive wildland interface ordinance, and the contentions it presented were specific and detailed. Although the appeal was eventually denied, the county's comments were considered and incorporated into the final project.

Government entities seeking to influence Forest Service projects have advantages over individuals or groups—they are routinely part of the planning and scoping process and often have developed close working relationships with district-level staff. The Forest Service needs the cooperation of local, regional, and state governments early on, and some consult and confer processes are mandated for federal agencies. But given the breadth of issues government entities must deal with on a daily basis, they are less likely to commit resources to appeals or litigation and choose to participate in pre-decisional activities instead.

INDIVIDUAL APPELLANTS

One issue frequently mentioned in discussions of the administrative rulemaking process is the impact of individuals who file appeals on their own. Concerns have been raised about the ability of individuals to influence Forest Service decisions as much as large, well-organized environmental groups or business interests can, and the potential delays their participation in the decision making process may have. There is also a perception that individuals file "nuisance" or "frivolous" appeals simply to take up the agency's time and resources without raising substantive contentions or participating in the scoping process during the pre-decisional phase. Many appellants are what one law professor refers to as "one shotters"—people who do not routinely use the rule making or legal process and who seldom win against established organizations or agencies (or "repeat players").[89]

In our database, appellants were designated as "private citizens" if there was no indication that they were filing on behalf of or representing a group. In these appeals, no group affiliation was noted in the appellant's return address, although it was impossible to determine whether or not the person might have held membership in an organization. Some individuals filed on their own, and some were represented by legal counsel. In our database, we identified 1,478 appeals filed by individual appellants between January 1, 1997, and December 31, 2003. The majority (958, or 64.8 percent) were filed on NEPA projects under Section 215, 56 (3.8 percent) related to Section 217 (forest plan revisions and amendments), and 422 (28.6 percent) related to Section 251 permits and authorizations. The CFR section used as the basis for the appeal could not be determined in forty-two appeals.

In our analysis, one individual, John Swanson of Minneapolis, filed the most appeals in cases that were decided and posted on-line during the study period. The second most frequent filer was Erik Ryberg of Moscow, Idaho, who filed twenty-six appeals in Forest Service Regions 4 and 6. Although Ryberg filed appeals as an individual, he has served as director of the Payette Forest Watch and works with another environmental group, the Idaho Sporting Congress. Third in line as frequent filers are Thomas Manning, who as a private citizen filed eighteen appeals on grazing projects in Arizona's Gila National Forest, and Scott Schroeder, who filed eighteen appeals in Region 5. Manning, who lives in Silver City, New Mexico, files as an individual but in multiparty appeals frequently is joined by the environmental groups Gila Watch and Wilderness Watch. Schroeder, of Nevada City, California, files as an individual and on behalf of the Forest Conservation Council and the National Forest Protection Alliance. Two additional individuals, Jeff Burgess and Jim Bensman, each filed sixteen appeals; all of Burgess's appeals were related to grazing. Nine of Bensman's appeals were filed on the same projects as nine appeals filed by Carla Cloer on the Sequoia National Forest; Cloer filed by herself on only one project.

Case studies of individuals filing Section 251 appeals, primarily based on disagreements over the terms of grazing permits, show that these appellants appear to have little interest in issues beyond their own. Although some have become familiar with the process by filing numerous appeals, there is little evidence they use their expertise to assist others in similar circumstances. Thomas Manning, the third most active individual filing appeals, and Jeff Burgess, the fifth most active filer, use the appeals process to oppose the Forest Service's grazing policies but file as individuals even though they may be working directly or indirectly with an established environmental organization.

There has long been a perception that individuals have used appeals to obstruct a Forest Service project, but this is not always the case, based on interviews and case studies we examined.[90] In all but one instance, the appellants either took part in or attempted to informally resolve their grievances with the Forest Service. The evidence shows that the appellants truly sought a resolution in their favor rather than simply trying to stall Forest Service actions. If the appellant had wanted to slow down the project, there would have been no need to meet in an attempt to work things out. By refusing to meet with agency officials, the Forest Service would have been forced to commit more resources to addressing the appeal— actions that potentially could have delayed project decisions and implementation. But if an informal resolution could be reached, the project or actions would then be able to proceed without further delay. The willingness of individual appellants to participate in this informal process indicates their desire to solve the issue at hand rather than to cause it to drag on indefinitely.

Several persons who were interviewed after they had individually filed appeals seem to have done so for philosophical reasons based on their perceptions of how western resources should be managed. Although they do not represent specific groups, some believe that they are representing a larger interest, such as ranchers who object to what they perceive as unreasonable Forest Service restrictions on their grazing privileges. Others appeal because they disagree with the actions of the Forest Service on a regional or national level and choose to express their views using the administrative remedies available to them. Some, but not all, of those appeals involve issues unrelated to hazardous fuel reduction projects.

For example, in June 2000, William Conway filed a Section 251 administrative appeal against the Tonto National Forest in Arizona because the Forest Service had notified him of the agency's intention to reduce the number of cattle allowed to graze on his Greenback Valley Ranch allotment. Conway argued the reduction would prevent him from running an economical operation and would jeopardize the ability of the operation to support the two families that relied upon the cattle ranch.[91] Conway's family had been ranching in the area since the late 1800s and had a history of poor relations with the Forest Service. In August 2003 one of his relatives had been charged with shooting at, and hitting, a Forest Service fire-fighting helicopter that was dipping water from a stock tank on his property.[92] Over the years, Conway had unsuccessfully filed several grazing-related appeals.

Conway was straightforward in his appeal letter and used materials from the local county extension office to back up his claim. He appeared to be legitimately concerned that the actions proposed by the Forest Service would destroy his traditional way of life and that of his family. Like many in the rural West, Conway shares a perceived belief in "local ownership of public lands" based upon the length of time involved in local residents' relationship with that land. He felt that because his family had been ranching in the Greenback Valley area for more than a century, they should be allowed to determine the best uses of the land regardless of any evidence presented by the government. He noted that he had not been adequately noticed of his appeal rights on the decision and asked for a stay of the decision until the appeal was decided. He attempted an informal resolution by meeting with district-level officials several times and also requested, and was able to obtain, a meeting at the forest supervisor's office.

During an interview, Conway said that he felt totally ignored and did not expect much when he filed his appeal because of past experiences. According to Conway, all his previous appeals had been handled "pretty much the same," and district-level meetings were pointless because he felt that projects were merely rubber-stamped after the decision on what to do had already been made. He says he did not intend for his appeal to be part of a national movement; rather, he only wanted to solve the issues related to his own allotment.[93]

The overall impression he provided was that he just wanted to be left alone to do his ranching without interference from the Forest Service. It should be noted, however, that Conway copied his appeal letter to the Arizona congressional delegation, the Arizona Cattlemen's Association, and the University of Arizona Extension Office, apparently seeking the assistance or support of other groups and officials. His appeal was denied by the acting forest supervisor, who concluded that the district ranger's decision to limit the number of cattle was warranted.[94]

Some individuals file appeals as a form of protest against the Forest Service's overall forest management policies. Charles Chapman of Brookhaven, Mississippi, who has filed six appeals of timber projects on the Homochitto National Forest in Mississippi, first became involved in filing appeals from "looking at the destruction and lack of concern by the Forest Service."[95] He is the fourteenth most frequent filer in our private citizen database. Chapman believes that the agency does not care about the clearcuts taking place, so he files appeals in order to tell the government that "we can do better." In that sense, he sees himself as a leader because, he says, "Nobody ever said anything until I started asking questions." But he also notes that although he feels he is helping the Forest Service to improve, he does not feel that he is playing a part in a larger picture. In one appeal letter, Chapman noted that he had provided specific comments on a project, some of which were addressed in the EA, "but several of them wasn't address [sic] at all."[96] His outlook is that he just wants to improve the health of the forest in the county were he lives and that appeals are his method of doing so.

Chapman attempted an informal resolution in each case before he filed an appeal and said, despite "lots of talks every time," the issues he raises are never resolved, and he has no other option but to file appeals. He believes that the national forest staff has a "cut and slash mentality" and that "every one of them considers this a game." His major complaint is that the Forest Service is "still too tied to money" and that it would plan projects differently if it was not so concerned about making money from timber projects. Chapman's view is that "everyone knows you need to cut timber—just don't massacre the land."[97]

Chapman has personally written each of his own appeal letters, crediting the knowledge he gleaned from his father, a retired Forest Service employee. But analysis of the letters shows that they are not persuasively written and are riddled with spelling and grammar errors that might make it difficult for the appeals to be taken seriously. Another major flaw that has caused the appeals to be dismissed is never seeking a remedy but merely stating his opposition to a project. Simply disagreeing with the Forest Service, without a request for relief, is grounds for dismissal.

Evidence indicates that although a person may file an appeal independently as an individual, appellants also rely upon others for assistance. In March 2002, Ralph Brewington and Ken Kantorowicz each filed Section 215 appeals against the Lewis and Clark National Forest in Montana over the Big Snowy Mountains

Access and Travel Management Plan.[98] The Forest Service had proposed limiting off highway vehicle (OHV) travel within the project area in order to help reduce resource impacts. The agency had issued a FONSI for the project.

The appeals filed by Brewington and Kantorowicz were exactly the same, even though the two men did not know each other. A mutual friend had separately asked each man to appeal. They were given a form letter with a blank line for the appellant's name and address. Kantorowicz filled in the blank in his own handwriting; Brewington typed his. The form letter included specific references to trails that had been open to motorized access since the 1960s and included a portion of a regional map. The letter describes the Forest Service project as "an abuse of discretion, arbitrary and capricious" and claims that public comments were not taken into account, therefore violating the Americans with Disabilities Act, the Constitution, and the decision reached in *Montana Wilderness Association v. United States Forest Service.* Although various contentions are cited, the appeal letters do not seek a specific remedy but note that the findings "should be deleted, changed, or modified" without identifying what the agency should do. Both men included with their form letters reproductions of photographs of themselves and their families or friends using OHVs. Less than a week after the appeal letters were received, the Forest Service dismissed both appeals without review because neither Brewington nor Kantorowicz had participated in the public comment period on the project.[99]

Neither man had ever filed an administrative appeal before and indicated they did so because their mutual friend had warned them that the Forest Service had a project related to one of their favorite OHV riding spots. The friend, they said, was "all worked up" about the trails' proposal and separately gave each man a form appeal, which they signed. Both appellants were relying upon second-hand information and had no idea what stage the project was at, or what the appeal process involved. Brewington actually admitted that he signed the letter because he felt intimidated and wanted to avoid a confrontation with his friend, not thinking that it would actually amount to anything. After he received a reply from the Forest Service, he said that he felt it was "a big mistake to get involved." In this situation, he said, the opposition was the result of "two or three people getting disgruntled and thinking they are going to change the whole thing." He himself was in favor of banning OHVs from some trails.[100]

Another individual appellant, Renick Atkins, filed a Section 215 appeal in July 2000 against the Monongahela National Forest in West Virginia, objecting to the use of herbicides in an area known as Panther Run.[101] The herbicide spraying was part of a project that included some logging and the removal of underbrush. In an interview, Atkins said he had never filed an appeal before but appealed because he has a second home near the project that has an "open" springwater source. He was concerned the herbicides would pollute his spring and worried about the impact on wildlife, especially brook trout in a creek in the area. He said he filed the appeal in an attempt to try and force someone to hear what he had to say and that he just wanted his local area to be taken care of.[102]

Atkins said that it was his perception that he had not filed a formal appeal. But his letter to the Forest Service, which was just three paragraphs long, clearly states that it was in fact an appeal, and he referred to himself as the appellant. He said he felt he was exercising his right to be heard and that he has a good relationship with the Forest Service; he was not attempting to obstruct the agency's actions. Even though his appeal was denied because the agency contended that the effects of the herbicide spraying had been addressed, he was satisfied because "somebody listened to me."[103]

There are a few appellants who have been labeled "nuisance" or "mystery" filers by critics of the administrative appeals process because they do not participate in the public scoping process, are not known to be part of established interest groups, and have refused to be contacted by representatives of other groups or the Forest Service.[104] As noted previously, one of these individuals is John Swanson, the most frequent filer in our database, who truly acts independently. His appeals are almost always handwritten and casually written, seeking no relief but providing his commentary and views on water and wildlife. In one appeal, he argued that the issue of solitude was not considered in a project's Record of Decision.[105] Appeals filed by individuals such as Swanson are routinely dismissed on procedural grounds according to Forest Service response letters, but even casual review of their appeals does consume staff time and resources. In one case, Swanson's appeal was denied a month later.

In contrast, Sara Jane Johnson, who incorporated the Native Ecosystems Council with five members of her family, makes part of her living filing appeals and litigation. But unlike Swanson, Johnson uses her expertise to raise what she feels are legitimate arguments and issues pertaining to Forest Service policy. A reporter described her as looking "more like a rancher than an eco-warrior," a portrait perhaps not in keeping with her job as the owner of a campground near Willow Creek, Montana.[106]

Johnson has a Ph.D. in biology and worked as a Forest Service biologist for six years in the Targhee National Forest and for eight in the Gallatin National Forest. Her job was eliminated in 1988, which she suspects was the result of her disagreements with the forest supervisor. Initially, she worked for the group American Wildlands but, when the group decided it would no longer focus on the Black Hills of South Dakota, where she lived, she founded her own organization.

Her work for the agency has given her an insider's perspective on Forest Service operations. She admits to having been naive about the political process and acknowledges she is for zero cut on public lands. She has filed numerous Section 215 appeals with American Wildlands on the Helena National Forest, the majority of which have been decided against her. She has also litigated a handful of cases and says, "I'm not doing this because I don't have anything better to do. I love to recreate, I love to ride. But I want to make a difference. So this is my new strategy: going to court. I'm only here because nothing else worked. The Forest Service has no one but themselves to blame."[107]

Forest Service officials say that Johnson is someone who appeals under the guise of science but really is using that as a cover for her zero-cut philosophy. One forest supervisor said he was exasperated that Johnson professes to file appeals for the "members" of her group, even though the group is composed only of Johnson and her family in South Dakota. "Sara Jane—she never participates in the discussions. She just says 'We disagree and you will end up in court,' so all us idiots sit around and invest our time and effort."[108]

Johnson spends her summers managing the campground and, in her spare time and winters, reads reports and files appeals and litigation. Under the Equal Access to Justice Act, the prevailing party can request that court costs and legal fees be paid for by their opponent, in this case, the Forest Service. In one case Johnson won against the Helena National Forest, she was awarded $24,000 in costs and attorneys fees. After paying the lawyer she had hired and American Wildlands, she ended up with about $11,500. She also relies upon grants from groups like the Turner Foundation, the Cinnabar Foundation, and the Kongsgaard-Goldman Foundation.

But it does not appear that many individual appellants actually make their living filing administrative appeals. Our data and case studies provide a sense of the number and concerns of appellants, showing that individual filers are quite diverse in their widely varying motivations, skills and resources, and different roles they play in the decision making process. However, the majority of those studied do appear to have a genuine personal interest in forest issues, whether they use national forests for recreation, as a source of income, or as a site for meditation and ritual.

LITIGATION

Our study provides a considerable amount of data related to administrative appeals, but much less is known about what happens to appeals that are subsequently litigated. Much rhetoric surrounding appeals has focused on "frivolous" lawsuits that allegedly tied up the courts and delayed project implementation. Although a few researchers have looked at judicial opinions on Forest Service projects and management plans (primarily at the frequency of cases, litigant characteristics, and success rates), most studies have dealt with the period prior to 1992, when the appeals process was substantially changed by Congress and the Forest Service.[109]

In the most comprehensive study to date, researchers at the State University of New York, Syracuse, analyzed all published courts of appeals cases decided between January 1, 1970, and December 31, 2001, in which the Forest Service was a defendant in a case involving management of one or more national forests. During the thirty-one years that were examined, the study found 119 cases meeting the criterion, or about four per year. Overall, the Forest Service won sixty-eight (57.1 percent).[110]

Other findings from the study indicated that the number of cases have steadily increased since 1970 (in line with increases of other natural resource agencies' projects), with cases evenly distributed among the agency's regions. The number of litigated cases increased since 1992, with a spike in cases during the first Clinton administration. When litigants were classified as representing an environmental or commodity interest, 86.6 percent of the plaintiffs in national forest management cases and 71.4 percent of project appeals cases were filed by environmental interest groups. Commodity interests were plaintiffs in 13.4 percent of cases, and the Forest Service was the appellant in 21.8 percent.

Environmental interests won 48.2 percent of district court cases they appealed, but commodity interests won only two of the sixteen cases they appealed. The Forest Service won 42.3 percent of the twenty-six cases it appealed from the district courts. There was a distinct difference in the types of cases that the Forest Service won or lost, with the agency most successful in cases involving the Wilderness Act and least successful in cases involving logging.[111]

As part of its larger study of administrative appeals of hazardous fuel projects, the GAO study found that twenty-six interest groups and one individual were involved in litigation over projects involving hazardous fuels reduction in fiscal year 2001–2002. The groups that litigated the most cases in this category were The Ecology Center (ten cases), followed by the Sierra Club (five), Hell's Canyon Preservation Council (four), Native Ecosystems Council (four), and the Oregon Natural Resources Council (four). As the GAO points out, all Forest Service decisions can be brought to court and, during the study period, about three percent (twenty-five) of the decisions were litigated. More than one decision can be litigated in one court case; in 2001 and 2002, the twenty-seven parties were involved in a total of twenty-one court cases. The litigated decisions affected about 111,000 acres, or about 2 percent of the lands managed by the Forest Service.[112]

What remains to be studied in depth, however, is the kind of case study–level analysis that has been discussed in this chapter. So far, we know very little about the litigation of appeal decisions except on the macro level. Further research needs to be done on the specifics of who litigates and why, and how litigation fits into the larger picture of forest management. This is also essential as the debate continues on the impact of legislative reforms such as the Healthy Forests Restoration Act and its implementing regulations that include provisions changing the judicial review process associated with appeals (discussed in Chapters 5 and 6).

THE COMPLEXITY OF ADMINISTRATIVE APPEALS

All kinds of interests have used the appeals process. Many are sophisticated frequent filers; others are not. Although environmental groups have put significant resources into appeals, the resources of several high-profile filers have declined over recent years along with the stock market. The decline in total number of appeals and shifts to other strategic goals and projects has probably as much to do with finances as it does with any other factor.

The GAO study found scant evidence of inordinate delays in the processing of appeals, but the question of delay is more complicated than simply measuring the time between project decision and settlement of an appeal. First, there are difficulties with automatically assuming that a delay in implementing an agency's project is ipso facto a negative event. Delays are used as strategic tools in all sorts of venues, from filibusters in Congress to time-outs in football. A project delay might enable participants to simultaneously pursue other entry points in the political process to achieve their goals before a final decision forecloses options that are undesirable to the group. For example, a delay might allow time to pursue legislative solutions that protect an area to be logged or time for studies to be completed that cast doubts on the agency's assertions. Delays are not always an undesired outcome or perceived the same way by different interests. Instances have been cited of lost jobs or a fire occurring before a fuel reduction project can be implemented, but for the most part determining whether delays are a gain or a loss is primarily a matter of political perspective.

Moreover, there is a multiplicity of reasons why projects get delayed, which might not totally be related to a filing of an appeal. Simply calculating in isolation the length of time it took for an appealed project to be implemented sheds no light on the role of these other factors—for example, funding, drought, or the effect of a lawsuit decided elsewhere (as in the Dry Creek project)—in moving a project through the planning, environmental review, and implementation processes.

Cases involving "frivolous" appeals can indeed be cited, but a significant portion of appeals are not frivolous. Sometimes appeals are filed simply as a procedural vehicle to get standing to litigate. Other times it is apparent that individuals do not have the savvy to meet the minimal requirements for filing an appeal—asking for specific relief, prior participation in the planning process, or filing in a timely manner. Such appeals take time to process and therefore impose economic and administrative costs on the agency, but lack of sophistication does not equal frivolity. Moreover, some groups repeatedly use appeals as a way of making a strategic point and raising public awareness about the values at stake. Frivolous perhaps from one perspective, but part of a group's public education strategy from another. Use of the term "frivolous" may make for good political rhetoric, but it is more difficult to operationalize a definition of a frivolous appeal.

Agency personnel have expressed frustration because appeals do not just focus on improving a site specific project but press forward a sweeping national goal, such as zero cut. However, commodity and wise use groups have used appeals for similar strategic purposes, despite goals often aligned more with retention of an existing set of institutional arrangements (for example, grazing privileges or recreational vehicle access). Whether it is a legitimate use of the appeals process to press forward a broader public policy goal rather than working with an agency to improve a particular project is again a matter of political perspective.

Individual appellants often file independently of organized groups and are not assisted by outside groups or litigating entities. Their assessment of the efficacy of appeals also varies. Regardless of outcomes, some individuals filing appeals view the process as a way to allow a point of view or concern to be raised and heard by the government, while others say the process is useless because they believe the Forest Service already knew what it wanted and nothing would change its course. For every Sara Jane Johnson making appeals and litigation a crusade or reaping some financial gain, there are more individuals who infrequently file or are one-shotters and almost always "lose."

A simple accounting of decision results often does not tell "the rest of the story." The impact of the Klamath Tribe's appeal of the Copwood Timber Sale extended beyond the particular contested project to affect tribal-agency relationships. Was the ultimate result—withdrawal of the timber sale—a loss for the agency, or were both parties ultimate winners? Outcomes can be tangible and intangible in both time and space. When the Buchanan family's appeal was granted, it did not necessarily mean that they had won the larger war with the agency, as their allotment would continue to be closely monitored.

Finally, what neither the GAO studies nor our database and case studies of actual appeals show is the intangible impact appeals might have on projects before they are even announced. Scholars call this the "Rule of Anticipated Reaction."[113] For instance, does the mere existence of an appeals process force the agency to pay greater attention to environmental concerns, knowing the decision will be carefully scrutinized to ensure compliance? Are certain kinds of options not pursued because of fear of appeals? Do appeals prompt the agency to broaden or narrow the range of alternatives it addresses, or to modify a project even before it is proposed? Or are up-front delays inevitable as agencies try to "bullet proof" documents so they will meet legal and regulatory tests of adequacy? Are "good" decisions not made because of fear of appeals, or are "bad" projects not proposed at all because of the potential of appeals? Also harder to document and evaluate include the effects of an appeal process on dialogue, on accountability, and on the processes of organizational learning and professional development.[114]

Any analysis of the appeals process needs to be placed within the context of all other decision processes and factors that contribute to what the Forest Service does or does not do, including NEPA analyses, litigation, funding, organizational culture, and interest group pressure. The complex reality of administrative appeals is like forest management itself. Appeals represent a mutually interdependent set of problems that are fuzzy, ambiguous, and equivocal.

NOTES

1. In the General Accounting Office's October 2003 report on appeals and litigation, which only covered fiscal years 2001 and 2002 (contrasted with our data that sorted by calendar year), the five groups filing the most appeals on fuels reduction activities were The Ecology Center, the Forest Conservation Council, The Lands Council, the National Forest Protection Alliance, and the Oregon Natural Resources Council. United States General Accounting Office, *Forest Service: Information on Appeals and Litigation Involving Fuels Reduction Activities* (Washington, DC: General Accounting Office, October 2003), 53–55. The document is referred to hereafter as the U.S. GAO Study.

2. Forest Guardians, Internal Revenue Service Form 990 (2002), at www.guidestar.org accessed February 1, 2004.

3. U.S. GAO Study, 53.

4. Forest Conservation Council, Internal Revenue Service Form 990 (2002), at www.guidestar.org accessed February 1, 2004.

5. U.S. GAO Study, 53.

6. Some of the materials and analysis of the three groups were prepared by Andrew J. Meador, *Case Study of Appeals Filed Against the Scott Able Fire Forest Health Project* (Flagstaff, AZ: Northern Arizona University Department of Political Science, 2003).

7. Appeal No. 01-06-0005 (November 6, 2000). The other parties in the appeal of the Buck Vegetation Management Project in the Wallowa-Whitman National Forest included

the Hells Canyon Preservation Council, the Idaho Sporting Congress, and an individual who originally submitted the appeal, Erik Ryberg.

8. National Forest Protection Alliance, Internal Revenue Service Form 990 (2002), at www.guidestar.org accessed February 1, 2004.

9. U.S. GAO Study, 54.

10. E-mail correspondence from Bryan Bird, January 9, 2003, and telephone interview on February 20, 2003. Bird subsequently took a position as Appeals and Litigation Coordinator for the Sierra Club National Forest Campaign and then with Forest Guardians, although he remained in close contact with the other organizations' leaders and activities.

11. Some of the materials and analysis of Forest Guardians and the Forest Conservation Council were prepared by Rod Parish, *A Case Study of the Spring Valley Wildland/Urban Interface Fuels Reduction Project* (Flagstaff, AZ: Northern Arizona University Department of Political Science, 2003).

12. Decision letters to John Talberth, December 15, 1998, and December 31, 1998.

13. Forest Guardians, "Forest Guardians Fights Salvage Timber Scalp in Lincoln NF," News Release, (October 19, 2000).

14. Appeal No. 01-03-00-0033 (May 29, 2001).

15. Some of the materials and analysis of The Ecology Center were prepared by Franklin Pemberton, *Maudlow-Toston Post-Fire Salvage Sale* (Flagstaff, AZ: Northern Arizona University Department of Political Science, 2003).

16. The Ecology Center, Inc., Internal Revenue Service Form 990 (2002), at www.guidestar.org accessed February 1, 2004.

17. U.S. GAO Study, 53.

18. Appeal No. 01-01-00-0050 (July 2, 2001).

19. USDA Forest Service, *Final Environmental Impact Statement and Record of Decision: Maudlow-Toston Post-Fire Salvage Sale,* May 7, 2001.

20. Letter from Lauren Buckley, The Ecology Center, to District Ranger Joni Packard, Townsend Ranger District, March 20, 2001.

21. Appeal No. 01-01-00-0051.

22. *Native Ecosystems Council, The Ecology Center, Inc., and The Sierra Club v. United States Forest Service,* CV 01-177-M-DWM (2002).

23. *Native Ecosystems Council, the Ecology Center, Sierra Club v. United States Forest Service,* U.S. Ct. Appeals, 9th Cir., No. 02-35687 (2003).

24. Eve Byron, "Maudlow-Toston Salvage Sale Questioned," *Helena Independent Record* (October 24, 2001), at www.helenair.com accessed February 2, 2002.

25. "AWR Mission Statement" at www.wildrockiesalliance.org/about accessed February 1, 2004.

26. Alliance for the Wild Rockies, Internal Revenue Service Form 990 (2002), at www.guidestar.org accessed February 1, 2004.

27. U.S. GAO Study, 53, 56.

28. Appeal No. 02-01-00-0049 (appeal date unknown).

29. Decision letters to Liz Sedler, Alliance for the Wild Rockies, April 11, 2002, and April 23, 2002.

30. The Lands Council, "Forest Watch Program," at www.landscouncil.org/fwatch accessed December 21, 2003.

31. The Lands Council, Internal Revenue Service Form 990 (2002), at www.guidestar.org accessed January 31, 2004.

32. Ibid.

33. U.S. GAO Study, 54, 56.

34. Appeal No.03-01-00-0042 (April 30, 2003).

35. Decision letters to Karen Lindholdt, The Lands Council, April 30, 2003, and May 12, 2003.

36. Center for Biological Diversity, "About the Center for Biological Diversity," at www.sw-center.org/swcbd/aboutus accessed February 2, 2004.

37. Center for Biological Diversity, Internal Revenue Service Form 990 (2002), at www.guidestar.org accessed February 2, 2004.

38. Ibid.

39. U.S. GAO Study, 53, 56.

40. Appeal No.99-03-00-0107 (August 11, 1999).

41. Decision letter to Brian Segee, Center for Biological Diversity, September 27, 1999.

42. Appeal No.00-03-00-0015 (December 21, 1999).

43. For the purpose of this book, the term "wise use" refers to groups and individuals whose formal or informal mission adheres to the Wise Use Agenda developed in 1989. See Alan Gottlieb, ed., *The Wise Use Agenda: The Citizen's Policy Guide to Environmental Resource Issues* (Bellevue, WA: Free Enterprise Press, 1989).

44. Karen Budd-Falen, an aide to former Secretary of the Interior James Watt under the Reagan administration, is best known for developing a series of ordinances for Catron County, New Mexico, that affected grazing rights and public rangelands. Before establishing her current legal offices, she worked for the Mountain States Legal Foundation.

45. Budd-Falen Law Offices, "About Us," at www.buddfalen.com/about accessed February 3, 2004.

46. Notice of Appeal for Sheldon Buchanan and Buchanan Ranches (September 8, 2002).

47. Telephone interview with Brandon Jensen, July 14, 2003.

48. Letter to Brandon L. Jensen, Budd-Falen Law Offices, regarding Appeal 1570-1 (March 17, 2003).

49. The proposal is outlined in a series of letters from District Ranger Michael Gardner to the Fryars in summer 1998, describing the Annual Operating Plan for cattle on their allotment.

50. Appeal No. 98-03-06-0010 (August 10, 1998).

51. Telephone interview with Danny Fryar, August 1, 2003.

52. Letter to Brandon Jensen, Budd-Falen Law Offices, regarding Appeal No. 10-03-0001/0002 (March 13, 2001).

53. Paragon Foundation, "Mission," at www.paragonfoundation.org/mission accessed February 3, 2004.

54. Appeal No. 01-05-00-0079 (July 9, 2001).

55. Generic letter to appellants regarding North Fork Smith River SIA Road Access Project (August 20, 2001).

56. For an overview of the role of wise use and property rights groups, see Jacqueline Vaughn Switzer, *Green Backlash: The History and Politics of Environmental Opposition in the U.S.* (Boulder, CO: Lynne Rienner, 1997); David Helvarg, *The War Against the Greens: The "Wise Use" Movement, the New Right, and Anti-Environmental Violence* (San Francisco, CA: Sierra Club Books, 1994); and Paul R. Ehrlich and Anne H. Ehrlich, *Betrayal of Science and Reason: How Anti-Environmental Rhetoric Threatens Our Future* (Washington, DC: Island Press, 1996).

57. Some of the materials and analysis of this case were prepared by Kristina Fernandez, *Little Bighorn Prescribed Burn* (Flagstaff, AZ: Northern Arizona University Department of Political Science, 2003).

58. Appeal No. 02-02-02-003 (November 21, 2001).

59. Appeal No. 02-04-00-0041 (March 12, 2002).

60. Appeal No. 98-10-00-13 (May 18, 1998).

61. Appeal No. 99-10-00-0011 (December 23, 1998).

62. Some of the materials and analysis of this case were prepared by T. C. Eberly, *Hume Timber Sale/Hume Vegetation Project* (Flagstaff, AZ: Northern Arizona University Department of Political Science, 2003).

63. Appeal No. 01-05-00-0229 (appeal date unknown).

64. Appeal No. 01-05-00-0228 (September 21, 2001).

65. Letter to Clark D. Frantzen regarding Appeal No. 01-05-00-0028 (November 8, 2001).

66. Generic letter to appellants regarding Open Road and Open Motorized Trail Travel Plan (January 14, 1998).

67. Some of the materials and analysis of this case study were prepared by Chris Seck, *The Manter Restoration Project* (Flagstaff, AZ: Northern Arizona University Department of Political Science, 2003).

68. Appeal No. 02-05-00-0006 (October 9, 2001).

69. Appeal. Nos. 90-05-00-0067 and 98-05-00-0068 (appeal dates unknown).

70. *Heartwood v. U.S. Forest Service,* 230 F 3d.947 (7th Cir., October 18, 2000).

71. Some of the materials and analysis of this case study were prepared by Jonathan D. Bakker, *The Crimson Tide Forest Health Project: A Case Study of the Role of NEPA Documentation and the Forest Service Appeal Process in Forest Health Projects* (Flagstaff, AZ: Northern Arizona University Department of Political Science, 2003).

72. Appeal No. 01-05-00-0002 (October 9, 2000).

73. 36 CFR 215.14(b(5)).

74. Don Yasuda, "Rebuttal to Joel Pagel, Ecosystem Conservation," Unpublished report to Regional Office, USDA Forest Service, Eldorado National Forest, Placerville, CA (2001): 5.

75. Generic letter to appellants regarding Appeal of the Decision Notice and Finding of No Significant Impact for the Phelps Snowmobile Project (July 31, 2002).

76. Appeal No. 97-03-00-0053 (September 18, 1997).

77. Appeal No. 97-03-00-0054 (August 23, 1997).

78. Appeal No. 97-03-00-0055 (August 25, 1997).

79. Some of the materials and analysis of this case study were prepared by Jason Kirchner, *The Copwood Timber Sale Project* (Flagstaff, AZ: Northern Arizona University Department of Political Science, 2003).

80. Public Law 104-19.

81. Appeal No. 97-06-0069 (January 7, 1997).

82. Ibid.

83. Telephone interview with Kent Russell, April 10, 2003.

84. Letter to Jack Ward Thomas, December 9, 1996.

85. USDA Forest Service, *Record of Decision and Final Environmental Impact Statement for the Agua/Caballos Proposed Projects, Carson National Forest* (2003), 267–269, 282–283. See also *Sixteen Comment Letters and Responses on the Agua/Caballos DEIS* (copied documents provided by the Forest Service).

86. Appeal No. 98-09-0032 (June 12, 1998).

87. Appeal No. 99-09-0021 (November 24, 1998).

88. Appeal No. 98-02-03-0026 (January 22, 1998).

89. Marc Galanter, "Why the 'Haves' Come Out Ahead: Speculations on the Limits of Legal Change," *Law and Society Review* 9:1 (1994): 95–160.

90. Some of the materials and analysis of the individual appellant case studies were prepared by Jason Kirchner (Flagstaff, AZ: Northern Arizona University Department of Political Science, 2003).

91. Appeal No. 00-03-12-009 (June 26, 2000).

92. Telephone interview with William Conway, July 17, 2003.

93. Ibid.

94. Letter to William Conway regarding Appeal No. 00-03-12-0009 (September 26, 2000).

95. Telephone interview with Charles Chapman, July 20, 2003.

96. Letter from Charles Chapman to the USDA Forest Service Appeals Deciding Officer, August 15, 2000.

97. Telephone interview with Charles Chapman, July 20, 2003.

98. Appeal No. 02-01-00-0037 (March 8, 2002).

99. Letters to Ralph Brewington regarding Appeal No. 02-01-00-0037 and Ken Kantorowicz regarding Appeal No. 02-01-00-0032 (March 12, 2002).

100. Telephone interviews with Ralph Brewington and Ken Kantorowicz, July 24, 2003.

101. Appeal No. 00-09-0024 (July 10, 2000).

102. Telephone interview with Renick Atkins, July 15, 2003.

103. Ibid.

104. Some of the materials and analysis of these filers was prepared by Tara Tribuna, *Case Study: Jasper Fire Value Recovery Project* (Flagstaff, AZ: Northern Arizona University Department of Political Science, 2003).

105. Appeal No. 01-02-03-0015 (May 29, 2001).

106. Eve Byron, "Working Through a Log Jam," *Helena Independent Record* (March 3, 2002), at www.helenair.com/articles/2002 accessed March 29, 2003.

107. Ibid.

108. Ibid.

109. See, for example, Lettie Wenner, *The Environmental Decade in Court* (Bloomington, IN: Indiana University Press, 1982); and Elise S. Jones and Cameron P. Taylor, "Litigating Agency Change: The Impact of the Courts and Administrative Appeals Process on the Forest Service," *Policy Studies Journal* 23 (Summer 1995): 310–336.

110. Robert W. Malmsheimer, Denise Keele, and Donald W. Floyd, "National Forest Litigation in the US Courts of Appeals," *Journal of Forestry* 102:2 (2004): 20–25. See also Robert Malmsheimer and Donald Floyd, "U.S. Courts of Appeals Judges' Review of Federal Natural Resource Agencies' Decisions," *Society and Natural Resources* 17:6 (2004): 533–546.

111. Ibid.

112. U.S. GAO Study, 15.

113. Paul J. Culhane, *Public Lands Politics: Interest Group Influence on the Forest Service and Bureau of Land Management* (Baltimore, MD: Johns Hopkins University Press, 1981).

114. Nancy J. Manring, "From Postdecisional Appeals to Predecisional Objections: Democratic Accountability in National Forest Planning," *Journal of Forestry* 102:2 (2004): 43–47; and Nancy J. Manring, "Locking the Back Door: The Implications of Eliminating Postdecisional Appeals in National Forest Planning," *Society and Natural Resources* 17 (2004): 235–245.

THE WILDLAND-URBAN INTERFACE
AND THE FIRE-APPEALS INTERFACE

FIRE HAS BEEN A PART OF HUMAN EXISTENCE LONG BEFORE RECORDED TIME. ACCORDING TO one eminent fire historian, the earth has burned for more than four hundred million years. "For almost all the span of terrestrial life, fire has continued, to varying degrees, as an environmental presence, an ecological process, and an evolutionary force."[1] But when humans started to control fire—to begin fires under varying circumstances, or halt unwanted fires—entire landscapes could be shaped and changed. From an estimated one billion acres of forests in the United States in 1600, only 730 million acres were left just four hundred years later. Colonization meant a demand for wood for homes, railroads, and shipbuilding, which aided the development of a powerful timber industry. Sheep and cattle destroyed some of the flammable landscape, and overcutting made its own contribution.[2]

Government officials began to extinguish non-anthropogenic (i.e., lightning-caused) fire during the mid-1800s, well before the Forest Service was established in 1905. At that time, fire became a focal point for the Forest Service's management of its own lands as well as its cooperative activities in state and private forestry. The agency soon convinced policymakers that it could combine the conservation ethic of the utilitarian value of trees with its technological ability to manage fire.

Fire policy essentially emphasized rapid suppression of all fires.[3] For many years the agency struggled with the role of prescribed fire to reduce fuel loads and fire hazards, but essentially fire exclusion and rapid attack of ignitions ruled the day.[4]

By the late 1960s, however, fire suppression was considered "intrusive," and the theory that fire was natural and therefore belonged in the forests became more broadly accepted. Researchers began to examine more closely the Native American practice of using fires to maintain the landscape and actively explored whether or not there was a way to "restore" natural fire regimes. Forest and fire experts debated whether lightning-caused fires should be allowed to burn and, if so, for how long and to what extent. Should natural resource agencies use "prescribed" fire to imitate natural fires, or stop all burning to preserve the aesthetic quality of the land and protect valuable timber resources?

In 1968 the National Park Service made a dramatic change in its fire policy by agreeing to allow "prescribed natural fires"—that is, lightning-caused fires would not be suppressed under certain conditions when officials could control the burning. By the mid-1970s "fire management" had begun to supplant "fire control" in the lexicon of the professional forester. Concern over escalating fire budgets, coupled with increasing knowledge about the detrimental ecosystem effects of strict fire suppression policies, led to reassessing policy and establishing a revised fire policy in the Forest Service in 1978.[5] The risk stance in forest fire management changed from aggressive fire suppression to a stance where managers would be expected to be more sensitive to efficiency tradeoffs. However, when a prescribed fire to improve habitat for the endangered Kirland's warbler escaped in north-central Michigan's Mack Lake Fire in 1980, burning forty-four homes and summer cottages and killing one Forest Service fire fighter, risk adversity increased.[6] "Fire management" in areas where prescribed fires could potentially escape or where less than all-out suppression would endanger lives and property was still problematic.

The explosive mixture of people, wildlands, and fire hazards is not a new problem. Although fire managers grew increasingly concerned about the wildland-urban interface fire hazard, the public still had only limited awareness of the problem or the serious threat it posed until the mid-1980s. For many years the interface problem had been perceived as mainly affecting Southern California, an area that sits at the intersection of millions of people, fierce Santa Ana winds, and fire-prone chaparral vegetation.[7] Fires in the mid-1980s, however, opened a window of opportunity to increase awareness of the problem's national scope. In 1985 the United States experienced the most severe wildland fire losses of the century up to that point. More than eighty-three thousand fires burned approximately three million acres, destroyed or damaged in excess of fourteen hundred structures, and killed 44 people.[8] Florida's Palm Coast Fire destroyed ninety-nine expensive homes in only a few hours. The public began to recognize that in varying degrees and forms the interface problem could be found in virtually every state.

In response to heightened awareness, the Forest Service, the National Fire Protection Association, and the U.S. Fire Administration formed a partnership in early 1986 to focus discussion and resources on wildland-urban interface problems.[9] These three groups were soon joined by the Bureau of Land Management and the National Association of State Foresters. The interface initiative's theme, "Wildfire Strikes Home," encompassed a number of activities, including conferences, videotape preparation, satellite broadcasts, news conferences, and development of a new series of public service ads focusing on the potential danger of loss or damage to personal property and life. Other related activities on the interface theme followed.[10]

Concerns about the interface fire situation were heightened again during the 1987 and 1988 fire seasons. The agencies' new flexible fire policies were fiercely tested in 1988, when thirty-one fires burned about 45 percent of Yellowstone National Park—including vast swaths of old-growth forest—and threatened nearby communities and historic visitor facilities within the park. The controversy over the decision to allow fires to burn throughout the park pitted fire ecologists against loggers, nature lovers, property owners, and average citizens who thought the government had lost its environmental mind. In addition to the Yellowstone fires, the sixth largest fire in California's history burned 145,000 acres, destroyed 28 structures, and caused one death in Stanislaus County, and two destructive wildfires destroyed seventeen homes near Rapid City, South Dakota, in July 1988. As of October 13, a total of 72,750 wildfires had burned over five million acres. Compared to the previous five years (1983–1987), the 1988 fire season represented a 30.6 percent increase in the number of fires and a 137.75 percent increase in acres burned.[11] Suppression efforts cost over a half billion dollars.[12]

The 1988 wildfires in Yellowstone National Park resulted in a substantial volume of studies and policy reviews but no fundamental change to the overarching policy related to wildfires until the mid-1990s. After thirty-four fire fighters were killed in 1994, the government completely altered its philosophical and on-the-ground approach to wildfires with the 1995 Federal Wildland Fire Management Policy, the first comprehensive statement of fire policy coordinated between the Departments of Interior and Agriculture. In this policy, support for fire suppression was replaced by policies that recognized fire's role as a management tool for achieving the goals of ecosystem management and ecosystem health.[13] This policy was revisited in 2000 following the Cerro Grande fire in New Mexico, which started as a 900-acre prescribed fire set by the Park Service in Bandolier National

Monument near Los Alamos; almost 250 structures were destroyed, forty-eight thousand acres burned, and eighteen thousand people evacuated.[14] Although the federal interagency working group reviewing the 1995 fire policy found it to be essentially sound, several policy changes and additions were made in 2001 to address issues of ecosystem sustainability, science, communication, and ongoing evaluation.[15] In addition, President Bill Clinton proposed (and Congress subsequently funded) the National Fire Plan (NFP), which provided additional funding for fire control, community assistance, fuels treatments, and burned area rehabilitation. In 2002 the Ten-Year Comprehensive Strategy Implementation Plan endorsed by the Secretaries of Agriculture and Interior, the Western Governors' Association, the National Association of State Foresters, the National Association of Counties, and the Intertribal Timber Council broadened the collaborative aspects of the National Fire Plan. The Secretaries of Agriculture and Interior also created a new Interagency Wildland Fire Leadership Council to further implement the National Fire Plan.[16] Thus, by the time of President Bush's Healthy Forests Initiative, fire policy was already in a state of transition.

TRENDS AFFECTING WILDLAND FIRE POLICY

In this time of significant policy change, two trends have collided. First, development continues to infringe upon wildland areas. People move to wildland settings but often are unprepared to live in fire hazard zones and often add to the hazard problem by building location and design (siting on steep slopes in heavy fuels, using wood shake roofs, and having inadequate water). Managers have also become increasingly concerned over fire fighter safety, because the presence of structures alters basic fire fighting strategies. Both wildland fire crews, who are not equipped or trained to fight structural fires, and structural fire fighters, who are not equipped or trained to fight wildland fires, are endangered. There are concerns that dollars and workforce resources are being diverted from ecological to structural objectives.[17] Moreover, the values at risk have increased considerably. Expensive homes and resorts now sprout in areas where once only rustic cabins in the woods existed. Even so, the agency has estimated that the cost of protecting private structures often exceeds their value.[18]

A second trend has been the continuing deterioration of forest ecosystems. At the same time development continues to infringe upon wildland areas, those areas have become more prone to fire. Fires have been increasing in size, occurrence, and intensity. In the fire-adapted forests of the southwestern United States and in areas such as the Blue Mountains of eastern Oregon, for example, low intensity fires historically removed excess fuels and provided needed nutrients for future growth.[19] Tree ring data and fire scars show repeated low-intensity fire occurrences until around the time of European settlement. Almost a hundred years of fire exclusion, high-grade logging, and overgrazing, however, have fundamentally altered these historic fire regimes. Without fire, numerous small-diameter trees have proliferated. They compete with one another and larger old-growth trees for water, light, and growing space. Stressed trees invite insects and disease. Conditions are ripe for catastrophic crown fires that burn hotter and damage the basic soil infrastructure. During the early 1990s, the forest health emergency began to receive considerable attention and study, with scientists warning of forests unraveling and the prospect of larger and more frequent catastrophic fires.[20]

Extended drought throughout the West has only exacerbated the problem. By August 2002—the year of Arizona's Rodeo-Chedeski Fire—the state was in the seventh year of what University of Arizona scientists predicted might be a thirty-year drought cycle.[21] Less winter snowpack and fewer spring rains have left forests tinder dry and with fire seasons that start earlier than normal. Less moisture also makes it more difficult for already-stressed trees to resist insects such as the bark beetle. The dead vegetation adds even more fuel. Climate—a critical variable in fire occurrence—is further complicating the forest health picture.

Concerns about solving the forest health crisis have coincided with the growing professional movement of ecological restoration, which focuses on ecosystems (e.g., wetlands and riverine systems as well as forests) that have been degraded, damaged, or destroyed directly or indirectly by human activity. In the case of forests, restorationists strive to bring the structure, function, and composition of forest ecosystems back to conditions resembling their historic ranges of variability.[22] A central goal is to create forest conditions where fire can again play a constructive rather than destructive role.

The ideal of forest restoration offers opportunities for building coalitions among community-based groups who see advantages in demonstrating forest stewardship while restoring their communities, environmentalists who see a need to bring forests and fire back into ecological balance, and businesses and workers who see economic opportunities in ridding overstocked forests of excess small-diameter trees. Yet, the ideal of restoring forests is not without controversy. The greatest fear is that what really is driving the push for ecological restoration is a hidden agenda—the desire to bring back the ecologically damaging large, industrial, and unsustainable timber management levels of prior decades. Foresters, for example, speak of the need for active management, arguing that it can not be assumed that the forest will take care of itself.[23] This is, in part, a response to those who argue that the forest can heal itself. It is also in response to those who argue that passive restoration, such as eliminating the activities that degrade ecosystems (road and dam building, livestock grazing, fire suppression, fish stocking, commercial logging, and the introduction of non-native species) is a more effective and efficient use of resources than active restorations requiring further ecosystem manipulations. Critics view the term active management as a code word for the kinds of forest management practices and human manipulation of nature that created the forest health crisis in the first place. For many, fire exclusion has been about saving trees so they could be cut, but the new mantra seems to be about cutting trees to save them from fire. In either case, the solution is still a timber program. Everyone argues about the size of the trees that should be thinned, where thinning should take place, and what to do with wood removed from the forest. Consequently restoration has moved slowly. Forest restoration is intuitively attractive but "the devil is in the details."

The 2000 and 2002 fire seasons raised public concerns about the magnitude of the fire problem, deteriorating forests, and the need for fuels reduction to restore forests and protect communities. The 122,827 fires of the 2000 fire season burned 8.43 million acres—the worst fires in the last fifty years, eclipsing earlier records. Federal agencies alone spent $1.36 billion in fire suppression costs, almost three times what had been spent in 1999. With flames racing toward the town of Los Alamos, New Mexico, where the Los Alamos nuclear laboratory is located, the Cerro Grande Fire became symbolic of the potential damage that might face other communities surrounded by forests if something was not done, and soon.

In 2002—the second worst season—7.1 million acres burned, and 21 fire fighters lost their lives. Three states, Arizona, Colorado, and Oregon, had their largest wildfires in this century. Yet again images of more than a thousand homes burning and the devastation of valuable forest resources—such as the White Mountain Apaches' loss of over 60 percent of their standing timber in the Rodeo-Chediski Fire—were deeply imprinted on the public's memory.

Some suggested reasons for why the recent fire seasons had been so damaging and costly include the following:

- Natural causes (like the long-term drought in the West) and human-induced global warming that created climatic conditions conducive to fire;
- Policies that led to over-grazing;
- Decades of fire exclusion policies that allowed undergrowth to build up and fuel mega-fires;
- The Forest Service's failure to implement basic recommendations of the 2000 National Fire Plan focusing on fuel reduction in the wildland-urban interface;

- Homeowners' refusals to take basic steps to fire-proof and protect their homes and property, especially in areas surrounded by or near forests;

- Logging practices that focused primarily on large tree removal; and

- Budget maximizing propensities of the Forest Service.[24]

But the explanation that garnered much of the attention from elected officials and the media is that environmental groups were using the administrative appeals process and litigation to delay or block implementation of proposed hazardous fuels reduction projects, thus leading to massive wildfires.

DATA, RHETORIC, AND FOCUSING EVENTS

Like the long history of frustration with administrative appeals, wildland-urban fire issues were not new on the political agenda. However, beginning with the fires of 2000, appeals and fires became visibly entwined, an appeals-fire interface if you will. The appeals-fire interface allowed the problem to be framed so that it affected the political construction of policy reform. Members of Congress and the Bush administration were successful in achieving three goals:

- Demonizing environmental groups through the use of rhetoric, synecdoches, and repetition of unconfirmed data to reduce their influence and credibility in the forest and fire policy debate;

- Placing blame for damage on environmental organizations that misused the administrative and legal processes to promote a radical agenda leading to the loss of lives, property, and valuable natural resources; and

- Attaching a desired solution to a predetermined problem by capitalizing upon a series of focusing events.

In this instance, the desired solution was reform of the administrative appeals process to reduce regulatory red tape that was perceived as delaying reduction of hazardous fuels in the national forests, resulting in catastrophic wildfires.

Several factors frame an issue as it becomes part of the legislative policy agenda. Three critical factors are the use of empirical data, the role of rhetoric, and the occurrence of focusing events. These three factors were instrumental in helping Congress and the administration achieve their goals.

First, let's take a look at empirical data. In the most recent controversies over wildfires and forests, members of Congress have relied heavily upon empirical data, with both those seeking change and those attached to the status quo using studies to appeal to public values that support their positions. As one scholar who studies how issues reach the political agenda notes, "In general, the role that empirical knowledge plays in the policy process is going to be based on the public's perception of that information, not the raw data itself. The raw data means little; it is the public's interpretation which will play the role. Of course, agents with a stake in the outcome will struggle to move public interpretations of new data in directions more conducive to the outcome that they think desirable."[25]

Empirical data (or the lack of it), especially when it is conflicting or cannot be corroborated, is filtered through the media,[26] organizational press releases, and public debate. Data become fodder for political posturing and rhetoric in an attempt to control policy direction and outcomes. An important element of the policy debate in this case has been the reification of data related to administrative appeals, litigation, and the role of environmental groups. Once a statistic or finding has been published, especially if it comes from a government agency, the data are used and re-used repeatedly, with few attempts at verification or analysis. There are multiple instances where elected and appointed officials have referred to data that research later determined to be subject to sampling bias or otherwise unreliable. Substantial discrepancies exist between data compiled by the Forest Service and provided to the GAO and the way that data were used by the Forest Service in its own reports. The dynamics of data use and misuse by stakeholders illustrate how attempts were made to assess blame for failed forest and fire policies, with environmental groups eventually losing ground.

Rhetoric, the second factor, is another technique by which various actors attempt to define and redefine problems. Rhetorical strategy involves reliance on and selection of specific terms that relate to emotional appeals, allusions, metaphorical substitutions, repetitions, and techniques of argument. Of particular relevance to this study is the technique of "synecdoche" or the "substitution of part for whole, genus for species, or vice versa."[27] Commonly used in a political setting, the synecdoche includes rhetoric where a single example is used to characterize a typical instance that is then used to frame and define a larger problem.[28]

In the wildfire policy debate, the numerous appeals filed by two groups— Forest Guardians and The Ecology Center—were portrayed as exemplary of the tactics of every environmental organization to oppose all forest thinning projects. As the previous chapter shows, this broad-brush characterization is inaccurate and significant differences exist in the types of projects where appeals are filed. Many environmental groups, in fact, support thinning forest lands in the wildland-urban interface.

Another extremely important aspect of rhetoric is the emergence and diffusion of symbols.[29] Just as Smokey Bear symbolizes the nation's policy of preventing and suppressing forest fires, visual cues and symbols became an important element in the appeals debate. President Bush crumbled the dead black bark of a Douglas fir in the palm of his hand when he announced his healthy forests policy near the site of the Squire Fire in southeastern Oregon. In a vivid image covered widely by the press, the president kicked his boots at the ashen soil, challenging his critics to "come and stand where I stand."[30] Reaching out to shake the hand of a state fire fighter, Bush said he was trying to bring a little "common sense" to forest policy, noting, "We must discourage the endless delays that prevent good forest policy from going forward."[31]

The phrase "paralysis by analysis" also became a rhetorical symbol. James Watt, interior secretary under President Ronald Reagan, used the phrase to describe the "conservation consensus" that would end with the Reagan Revolution. It resurfaced in 1999, the thirty-year anniversary of NEPA, which brought about calls for change. Rep. James Hansen (R-UT), chair of the House Resources Committee, said that Congress should take another look at NEPA to ensure the law accomplishes its intended goals. Charging that "the implementation of the law has become a sham," Hansen said NEPA "crushes the process with paperwork—a paralysis of analysis that can take years and years and millions of dollars."[32] The phrase "analysis paralysis" would later be repeatedly used by elected leaders and Forest Service officials as a way to label the administrative appeals process as problematic.

A third factor framing discussion of an issue is a disaster or crisis that serves as a focusing event. A focusing event is like an early warning: attention is called to something that could be considered a problem if subsequent events really establish that there is a widespread condition that needs attention.[33] Different factors, termed *drivers*, combine with focusing events to create a sense that action must be taken immediately. Drivers of natural resource–based political conflict include issues such as scarcity, importance of place, scientific disagreement and uncertainty, electoral politics, political and interest group strategies, and media framing.[34] The occurrence of several major wildfires within a short period of time was not only a focusing event but also served to create awareness of a nationwide problem of fire danger, enhancing the prospects of new policies being formulated and adopted. The fires drove policymakers to move more quickly on legislative and regulatory solutions.

SHOW METHE DATA!

Almost as soon as the flames ignited in 2000, public officials began to politicize the wildfires and demand action. This process involved the emergence of policy entrepreneurs—individuals both in and out of government who invest their resources (such as time, reputation, political status) in exchange for what is hoped to be some form of future return.[35] Montana governor Marc Racicot blamed the fires on the Clinton administration's "lack of balanced stewardship," with a reminder that he had warned a Senate subcommittee in March 2000 about forest conditions in the West. "The Clinton administration didn't cause these fires, but their policies have left the Forest Service under-funded and under-prepared for this crisis."[36] Racicot, who was rumored to be a potential nominee for Secretary of the Interior under presidential candidate George W. Bush, later backed down, saying that some people wanted "to continue to make this a war of words and political positions. I would say that the time has come for all those swords to be laid down."[37]

Timber trade groups, such as the American Forest and Paper Association, called for a new Forest Service fire management plan for designated wilderness areas that included tree thinning. The Northwest Forest Association said that "[c]urrent well-intentioned but misguided regulations require exhaustive environmental documentation, delaying harvests of diseased or burned timber indefinitely."[38]

Sen. Ron Wyden (D-OR) countered with a study he had requested from the Congressional Research Service (CRS) that concluded that logging in national forests does not protect against devastating forest fires, and that logging activities often increase a forest's fire risk. "My sense is that this is a problem that cries out for an examination that goes far deeper than the next election," Wyden said.[39] The CRS study, along with another from the Pacific Biodiversity Institute, were frequently cited in the media as evidence that refuted claims that logging and road-building could have prevented or reduced the severity of the 2000 wildfire season.[40]

Environmental group representatives such as Mike Bader, executive director of the Alliance for the Wild Rockies, urged congressional leaders to hold hearings on what he called "a transparent attempt to gain access to the National Forests for the express purpose of logging. This fiscally irresponsible and ecologically damaging charade must be stopped."[41] A press release distributed by four other environmental groups said that "the arguments for additional logging are self-serving attempts to exploit emotions and human tragedy for corporate profit. The facts simply don't support the political rhetoric."[42]

The summer's blame game and finger-pointing opened the policy window—an opportunity for advocates of new proposals to seek support. When this happens, it allows policy entrepreneurs to attach solutions to problems and take advantage of politically propitious focusing events. Policy windows open infrequently, and they do not stay open long. The wildfire policy window opened in late 2000 with criticisms of the government's handling of the Cerro Grande Fire and the 1995

National Fire Policy, allowing new policies, such as the 2001 Fire Policy, to be proposed.

Congress also used this opportunity to criticize the administration's response to the deadly wildfires. At meeting of a House Budget Committee task force on natural resources and the environment, Rep. George Radanovich (R-CA) waved a 1994 report from the National Commission on Wildfire Disasters at Forest Service officials. Radanovich questioned why the agency and the Clinton administration had a "minimal response" to years of warning about wildfires. He also cited a 1999 GAO report that concluded that the Forest Service had not yet developed a general strategy for selectively reducing fuels in America's national forests.[43] President Clinton, himself a policy entrepreneur, responded by directing his staff to develop a series of recommendations that were released in September 2000 as the National Fire Plan. Congress followed with a $2.9 billion appropriation for the NFP's implementation.[44] Research dollars were also made available under the National Fire Plan, which augmented the stepped-up funding for fire research under the Joint Fire Science Program initiated in fiscal year 1998. In essence the Clinton administration threw money at the problem.

Environmental groups supported the National Fire Plan at the outset because it helped diffuse criticism that blamed them for holding up projects, delays some officials believed contributed to the destructiveness of the massive fires of 2000. Environmental leaders could also support the NFP because it focused on fire fighting preparedness, ecosystem restoration, and working with communities damaged or potentially affected by wildfire. This policy sought to solve the wildfire problem by shifting the issue to protecting the wildland-urban interface rather than to large-scale back country tree-cutting projects that would reduce fuel loads but were also likely to attract appeals and litigation.

Several conservative members of Congress used the opening of the policy window to move in a totally different policy direction. In summer 2001, Sen. Larry Craig (R-ID), a member of the Senate Subcommittee on Forests and Public Lands, and Rep. Scott McInnis (R-CO), chair of the House Subcommittee on Forests and Forest Health, expressed their concern that administrative appeals and litigation were delaying implementation of the NFP and the Forest Service's hazardous fuels reduction projects. The two members of Congress asked the GAO to identify the number of hazardous fuels reduction projects the Forest Service had proposed, analyzed, and funded for implementation in fiscal year 2001; the number of those projects that had been appealed or litigated; and who had appealed or litigated project decisions. The GAO sought this information from Forest Service headquarters in Washington and each of the nine regional Forest Service offices in July and August 2001.

In its August 31, 2001, response letter, the GAO noted that the requesters asked for the information as quickly as possible and, as a result, the data were not verified. The GAO letter stated that the Forest Service had decided to implement 1,671 hazardous fuels reduction projects, of which twenty (about 1 percent) had been appealed and none litigated.[45] The GAO data indicated that appeals and litigation were not delaying implementation of hazardous fuels reduction projects, a finding that was not consistent with the congressional members' concerns. For the next ten months, the GAO letter lay virtually buried, and questions about administrative appeals and litigation did not resurface until the 2002 wildfire season began. The policy window closed, but only temporarily.

It opened again with one of the summer's early blazes, the 138,000-acre Hayman Fire in Colorado, which raged from June 8 through July 19. The wildfire was the largest in the state's history, destroying more than 130 homes and causing an estimated $13 million in damage. Although the fire was human-caused (a Forest Service employee was sentenced to six years in prison in 2003 for deliberately starting the blaze), its proximity to Denver refocused attention on the potential for catastrophic fire in the wildland-urban interface. The window opened just as policymakers received copies of a new forty-page Forest Service report that set up the policy and media skirmishes leading to the summer's "data debate."

Titled *The Process Predicament: How Statutory, Regulatory, and Administrative Factors Affect National Forest Management,* this report began by noting that "despite a century of devotion to conservationism, the Forest Service today faces a forest health crisis of tremendous proportions," outlining the risks to national forests from severe wildland fires, insects and disease, and invasive species. The executive summary stated that the agency operates within a statutory, regulatory, and administrative framework that makes it unable to effectively address rapid declines in forest health because of three factors:

- Excessive analysis—confusion, delays, costs, and risk management associated with the required consultation and studies;
- Ineffective public involvement—procedural requirements that create disincentives to collaboration in national forest management; and
- Management inefficiencies—poor planning and decision making, a deteriorating skills base, and inflexible funding rules, problems that are compounded by the sheer volume of the required paperwork and the associated proliferation of opportunities to misinterpret or misapply required procedures.[46]

Acknowledging that part of the solution would be internal, the report also singled out external forces that created an atmosphere that prevented the agency from focusing on "the new era of public land management." The most frequently cited argument was that regulations—"process delays"—keep the agency from producing on-the-ground results. Congressional action "seems to have favored a complex public process over other, more efficient management methods." All of this created "a costly procedural quagmire," and management uncertainty based on the possibility that a case may go to court. One section singled out problems caused by the administrative appeals process, noting that appeals can greatly delay a project and discourage collaboration.[47] Much of the report's language echoed the comments made by Rep. Hansen in 1999.

In the discussion of the problem's scope, the Forest Service cited several examples related to project workloads, time spent on a project, and costs—analysis that later served as the basis for comments from several elected officials. The report said that the entire process from scoping to implementation normally takes more than a year. Although noting that it was not possible to find exact figures on the time spent on planning, analysis, and documentation, *The Process Predicament* cited a 1999 report by the National Academy of Public Administration (NAPA) that estimated that planning and assessment consume 40 percent of total direct work at the national forest level. The agency noted that NAPA estimates were based on "educated guesses by Forest Service professionals."[48] *The Process Predicament* also cited a 1997 GAO report that again relied upon an internal Forest Service estimate that "inefficiencies within this process cost up to $100 million at the project level alone."[49] Guesstimates of Forest Service personnel were thus presented in reports by other entities, which were, in turn, then cited by the agency in its own reports, and then repeated by other officials.

The NAPA report was based on interviews with Forest Service personnel and focused on implementation of the agency's new financial system, budget and appropriation structure, organizational structure and design, strategic planning and performance measurement, and leadership. The 40 percent figure was an estimate of overall planning and assessment costs and was not specifically related to just appeals or subsequent litigation phases. But in an *Arizona Republic* opinion piece published just after *The Process Predicament* was released, Rep. Jeff Flake (R-AZ) asserted that "40 percent of our Forest Service's budget is swallowed up just fighting lawsuits filed by 'environmentalists.'"[50] A day later, the newspaper printed an opinion piece by Arizona senator Jon Kyl (R) in which he also repeated the 40 percent budget statistic, which he said was devoted to regulatory compliance, anticipating legal battles, and fighting pending lawsuits. Their interpretation of what the 40 percent figure meant focused on the problem as they perceived it, rather than how it was used both by the NAPA report and in *The Process Predicament*.

One of the curious correlations cited by the Forest Service was a figure showing that although the number of appeals filed from 1995 to 2001 had been going up, the number of board feet of timber harvested during that same time frame had been cut in half. From a methodological perspective, one clearly visible flaw was that the number of appeals filed was based on a year, while the number of board feet was based on a fiscal year. More importantly, the report simply asserted a cause-and-effect correlation without any evidence to support the claim.[51]

The message of *The Process Predicament* was clear, if not explicit. The Forest Service sought the assistance of its partners to "find collaborative ways out of this process predicament."[52] By framing the issue in terms of process, the agency implied that the devastation caused by wildfires could be avoided by revising statutes and regulations, setting the stage for the next phase of policymaking. Legislators used data in the document to further their contention that the appeals process and litigation were eating up the agency's budget—another reason for a change in policy.

As expected, environmental groups responded angrily to *The Process Predicament,* adding their own rhetoric. One press release accused timber groups of "cashing in their chips" after Bush raised $1.7 million in contributions from timber executives at a Portland fundraising event. The Oregon Natural Resources Council called congressional hearings on *The Process Predicament* "a set-up for the Bush administration to cook up a 'solution' to the problem that will undoubtedly be a timber industry 'wish list' to weaken our environmental safeguards." A representative of Cascadia Wildlands Project referred to the report, noting, "'Analysis paralysis' is a Forest Service term for public input. The problem isn't the process, it's the product. The public doesn't support an old-growth product. We need to focus on restoring forest health, not logging dwindling old-growth forests."[53]

The availability of accurate data continued to be an essential element of debate and became a factor in legislation that would be proposed in September 2002. On July 9, 2002, the GAO sent a follow-up letter to Rep. McInnis in response to his request that the agency clarify how the data in the August 31, 2001, report were developed. The GAO responded with a letter that sought to explain a number of methodological issues that had been encountered and reiterated that, because members had requested the information be provided as quickly as possible, the GAO did not verify the information the Forest Service had provided.[54]

A day later, on July 10, 2002, the Forest Service released its own report, *Factors Affecting Timely Mechanical Fuel Treatment Decisions.* The report concluded that almost half (48 percent) of all decisions made in fiscal years 2001 and 2002 for mechanical treatments of hazardous fuels were appealed. The Forest Service said that of 326 decisions subject to administrative appeals, 155 were appealed and, in addition, 21 decisions had also been litigated—figures that were contradictory to the GAO's findings. The Forest Service noted that all data could not be completely verified and "are subject to further verification."[55]

Based on the new data, the report concluded that "it takes substantial time to plan for, make decisions on, and begin implementing Forest Service projects (including fuels hazard reduction projects)."[56] The factors cited for the planning and decision delays included management uncertainty surrounding appeals and litigation, changing standards and guidelines, changing court interpretations, and supplementing documents to meet new requirements.

NO, SHOW *US* THE DATA!

The dueling data became the basis for questions by environmental groups, members of Congress, and the media about discrepancies between the widely circulated and quoted GAO and Forest Service reports. One of the first responses came the same day the July 10 report was released when the National Forest Protection Alliance filed a Freedom of Information Act (FOIA) request for details on the Forest Service report, including a request for a list of the mechanical treatment projects that were appealed. The Forest Service report had not listed which projects it had included in its tally, which made verification of the statistics impossible. The organization asked that the request receive expedited processing because "[t]his is a breaking news story of general public interest."

Frederick Norbury, director of Ecosystem Management Coordination for the Forest Service's Washington Office, denied the request for expedited processing and, as a result, the agency did not mail its response to the FOIA request until September 6, 2002. In his letter, Norbury said that the time frame for gathering the information in the report was "limited to hours" with much of the information provided orally in telephone interviews. The Forest Service was unable to find any electronic or hard copies of the interviews but did provide some e-mail responses to the verbal inquiry, along with a "more up-to-date list of decisions which is subject to further verification and change."[57]

A review of the Norbury letter and the FOIA documents shows the inconsistencies in Forest Service tracking systems, the somewhat casual attitude of some of the staff who responded to the internal request for data on appeals and litigation, and the reliance upon institutional memory rather than scientific methodologies. For example, one staff e-mail starts, "Here's the best I can come up with," and continues, "I would feel comfortable saying 100% of all appealable vegetative management decisions are appealed and 95% of all appealable decisions are appealed. As for nonappealable decisions . . . cat exs . . . I do not have numbers.

Based on a few responses from the forests this morning, I'm guessing that . . ."
Another regional report included the statement: "However, without checking all
the appeals I do not recall an appellant that used prescribed burning or mechanical
treatment of fuels as a reason to appeal a project." Another region's response was
based on reports from seventeen of its eighteen forests, and two regions provided
only three sets of numbers without any other documentation.[58]

The Forest Service's inability to provide documentation of its reporting
methodology and the alacrity of the study itself seem to have been somewhat
overlooked, except by a handful of environmental activists who made the effort
to seek verification of the data. At issue was not only the accuracy of the data
itself but, more importantly, the flaws in how the information was compiled and
verified by the Forest Service before the report was released to the public. Despite
those factors, the 2002 report would be cited extensively and would later become
part of the rationale for changes to administrative rules and congressional
legislation.

One organization, The Wilderness Society, released its comments on the
discrepancies on July 12, 2002, relying upon the data in the GAO's 2001 report
and saying that the Forest Service report "is a poor attempt to shift blame. . . .
The Forest Service issued a different report that utilized Enron-inspired
accounting."[59]

Congressional interest in the accuracy of the Forest Service and GAO reports
appears to have begun at a July 11, 2002, hearing convened by the House
Subcommittee on Forests and Forest Health that focused on the National Fire
Plan. Much of the meeting focused on the Forest Service study, which had been
released a day earlier, and the resulting headlines that repeated the idea that
environmental activists delayed forest thinning projects and played a role in the
season's wildfires. At the hearing, Reps. Jay Inslee (D-WA) and Tom Udall (D-
NM) asked for a full list of projects referred to in the Forest Service report and
were told by an agency official that a list would be provided to them. When the
project list was not forthcoming, members of the committee staff made repeated
requests to various agency personnel.

On July 25, Inslee and Udall sent a follow-up letter to Forest Service chief
Dale Bosworth, noting that they were "deeply troubled" by the Forest Service's
actions.

> We have now been informed that the promised list of the specific projects that
> supposedly were the basis for the report does not exist—and never existed—
> and that the Forest Service is working on a new, "more accurate" report. We
> have also been told that for purposes of preparing the report only numbers of
> projects were collected from the regions, rather than the names of projects. If

this is correct, it is of course troublesome because there is no way to assess or verify the number and types of projects that were the subject of the report.[60]

Another report was produced by The Forest Trust,[61] an environmental group that performs research on forest management and works collaboratively with the Forest Service at the local level, but does not file administrative appeals. Its September 3, 2002, study concluded, "Our analysis . . . reveals a sampling bias, unreliable data, and unsupported conclusions. The discrepancies between the data the Forest Service provided to the GAO and the data it used for its own report reveal that the agency lacks a consistent system for tracking and analyzing its projects."[62]

Keeping up the pressure for the government to document its findings, Inslee and Udall made a joint announcement, expressing their opinions about the validity and credibility of the earlier Forest Service and GAO findings. Udall commented, "Cooking the books and advancing misleading statistics, as the US Forest Service apparently did, gets in the way of sincere bipartisan efforts to find common ground to the shared problem of wildfire risk, and the need to create a sustainable forest economy that provides tools to restore fire-adapted forests. To attempt to score political points by using selected data to reach a predetermined outcome does not address the serious problem this country faces with regard to wildfires."[63] Inslee implied duplicity on the part of the Forest Service, saying "[t]his report shows that the attempts by the U.S. Forest Service to cut large trees located deep within our forests for commercial profit under the guise of fire prevention efforts often meet with appeals."[64]

Although the controversy over the data continued throughout the 2002 fire season, the Forest Service study was frequently referred to, giving the report additional visibility and credibility. Articles praising and denouncing the Forest Service report, along with the text of the report itself, appeared on the Web sites of a wide spectrum of organizations, from Taxpayers for Common Sense to groups like Truthout, Native Forests, and the Inland Empire Society of American Foresters. Distribution of the report on the Internet led to the involvement of more stakeholders but little discussion about the report's veracity. Because the National Forest Protection Alliance did not receive a response to its FOIA request until September 2002, almost all references to the Forest Service report were made before the flaws in the agency's methodology were known.

Four environmental groups produced a joint press release that referred to the "hastily produced report." A spokesperson for the group Native Forests commented, "This level of research may be OK for a middle school project, but when the U.S. Forest Service quickly pieces together a report and then uses it as Exhibit A to justify suspending our environmental laws to increase logging in national forests, it approaches fraud." The executive director of the National Forest Protection Alliance referred to the earlier GAO study and stated, "The Forest Service didn't like the findings of the GAO report, so they cooked up numbers more to their liking. This is unconscionable behavior on the part of the Forest Service but not a big surprise." The Forest Conservation Council also referred to the GAO report, and a representative from the group Heartwood concluded the press release by commenting, "This report is an example of why our laws should not be suspended. The Forest Service cannot be trusted to do adequate and accurate analysis on their own."[65]

There was virtually no coverage or references to the groups' press release, although the on-line publication *Greenwire* published a staff article on October 3, 2002, that covered not only the results of the FOIA request, but also a response from Forest Service spokeswoman Heidi Valetkevitch. She said the report was compiled as a "speedy response" to a congressional inquiry. "Regardless, we've gone back and fact-checked and it's quite a bit higher, the percentage appealed." Valetkevitch told *Greenwire* that the Forest Service had changed its numbers; 143 of 206 mechanical thinning treatment projects slated for fiscal years 2001 and 2002 were appealed (rather than the initial report of 155 of 326 projects), increasing the percentage from 48 percent to 69 percent.[66] The "new" study's results had not been corroborated by the reporters who published the revised figures—they appear to have relied upon the agency spokesperson's comments.

An Associated Press story that was published in several newspapers repeated the advocacy groups' contention that the report was assembled in haste and contained misleading information. One of the groups' spokesperson was quoted, saying "[t]his is amateur hour and they released this to a committee of Congress. This was obviously put together for political reasons to make political hay over this issue and we view this report as a sham."[67] Colorado-based Forest Watch Campaign also called the Forest Service report "a sham" and again referred to the GAO study, which had been cited frequently by environmental groups and widely reported in the media.[68]

Ironically, the 2001 GAO letter to Congress that was widely cited by environmental organizations was just as methodologically unsound as was the July 2002 Forest Service report. Both documents relied upon hastily collected, agency-reported data that would later be determined to be inaccurate. The results of the GAO research were more favorable to the argument of environmental groups that very few forest projects were appealed and litigated and, thus, GAO data were used extensively in their press releases and commentary. Similarly, both *The Process Predicament* and the Forest Service report, which indicated that projects were frequently appealed and litigated, were used by members of Congress, the administration, and agency officials as a rationale for needing process change.

RHETORIC AND FOCUSING EVENTS AS POLICY DRIVERS

Anecdotal stories, generalizations, synecdoches, and rhetoric were used to frame the issue and underscore the contention that something was wrong with an administrative appeals process that "allowed" policy to be manipulated by environmental organizations. This theme was pervasive throughout the media and in comments by many elected officials and critics of the NEPA process. Like in the childhood game Gossip the media used statements by one official that would be repeated by another official, even though the information was rarely checked for accuracy. Anecdotal information and guesstimates slowly worked their way into the policy debate as "factual" information.

The 2002 Rodeo-Chediski Fire in Arizona—the largest wildfire in the state's history—was widely covered by the media and shows the media's power to frame issues. The *East Valley Tribune* noted that its investigation found that "plans to cut fire danger by thinning trees in an Arizona forest now being destroyed by the nation's largest active wildfire were blocked for three years by a Tucson environmental group." The article connected the fire in the Apache-Sitgreaves National Forest to an appeal and subsequent litigation by the Center for Biological Diversity, quoting a regional forest coordinator as saying "[w]e're litigating while the forest burns." A CBD representative countered that it was wrong to blame his group or other environmental organizations for the inferno. "It's sheer scapegoating," the representative said. "These guys want to use this to further whatever their political agenda is."[69] The use of the Rodeo-Chedeski Fire as a synecdoche for wildfires caused by interventionist environmentalists had been firmly established; a public television state poll in Arizona found that 61 percent of Arizonans blamed the Rodeo-Chediski Fire on environmentalists' legal maneuvering.[70]

Another example of the use of a generalization, which was later repeated in a somewhat different form, was a statement made by Forest Service chief Dale Bosworth in an interview. When asked why more had not been done to thin out the forests, Bosworth said, "We go through an awful lot of process and spend an awful lot of money working through environmental impact statements and public review and then appeals and litigation."[71] Bosworth never defined what "an awful lot" meant, but the concept crept into the debate, underscoring the perceived problem of administrative appeals by environmental groups that policymakers had identified.

Several policy entrepreneurs within Congress used anecdotal information to promote their agenda for a change in the appeals process. Sen. Kyl said that environmental groups protested and stopped a forest thinning program in Arizona's Coconino National Forest in 1996 to protect a single bird's nest. He noted that a crown fire burned through the forest later that same year, engulfing the tree that housed the bird the groups were trying to protect. "Now these radicals are singing a different tune," he said.[72] Kyl's information came from *The Process Predicament*, which included a snippet of a similar story from *The Sacramento Bee*.[73] The executive director of the Center for Biological Diversity then alleged that the information Kyl used was an exaggeration of "an account given by Bush's new chief of the Forest Service. The chief's report is an exaggerated retelling of a California newspaper story. And the newspaper story was wrong to begin with."[74]

The same theme and statistics were used by Colorado senator Ben Nighthorse Campbell in his opinion piece for the *Pueblo Chieftain*. Campell wrote:

> [T]he constant threat of lawsuits from environmentalists has resulted in a near
> halt to fire management efforts. Instead of working toward the already
> enormous task of reducing unmanageable fires, the U.S. Forest Service is now
> forced to tailor its studies and assessments for proposed actions in anticipation
> of a hailstorm of lawsuits and appeals from those who purport to protect our
> forests. In fact, an estimated 40% of the U.S. Forest Service's work at the
> national forest level, about $250 million each year, is spent on extra analysis to
> insulate the forest service from future frivolous lawsuits.[75]

A handful of Congressmembers joined the debate with rebuttals. Rep. Inslee responded that the wildfires in Arizona were a result of the failure to understand the necessity of periodic fires coupled with extreme drought. "Environmentalism did not cause these forest fires," he said. "What we do not know is why the administration is blaming the environmentalists for the fires, rather than working to prevent further global warming in our own country."[76]

After the Forest Service report was published in July 2002, members of the House Resources Committee, of which Jeff Flake was a member, met to consider whether delays by environmental groups had contributed to the West's wildfires. Flake responded to the Forest Service study by saying "[t]hese numbers show that some so-called environmentalists want nothing more than to stop all forest thinning."[77]

Reactions to the summer's political rhetoric came from both environmental organizations and timber industry groups, along with newspaper editorials and op-ed pieces calling for reasoned discussion and restraint. Many environmental groups tried to distance themselves from the generalized view that they opposed all fuels reduction in national forests, while still accusing the administration of exploiting the fear of fires in order to roll back environmental protections and boost commercial logging. Colorado Wild, for example, supported legislation to direct National Fire Plan funds to projects in the wildland-urban interface, while pointing out that environmental groups play a critical role in keeping the Forest Service from "simply trying to appear to be doing something about forest fire."[78]

On July 18, 2002, more than 150 environmental groups signed a letter sent to Forest Service chief Dale Bosworth, every member of Congress, and the Western Governors' Association that explained, "In recent weeks, some politicians and some U.S. Forest Service officials have repeatedly misrepresented the conservation community's position on wildfires, home protection and fuel reduction. . . . The conservation community has always supported common sense approaches designed to effectively protect homes and communities from fire." The letter also stated that the groups played a leading role in educating homeowners about the importance of treating flammable material adjacent to homes and communities.[79] According to one of the leaders of the effort, "this got nearly zero media coverage even though it was in direct response to all the blaming that was going around. And this was following extensive outreach to the press . . . they just didn't see it as 'newsworthy.'"[80]

John Horning of Forest Guardians, one of the groups that had filed numerous administrative appeals in the 1990s, wrote an opinion piece for the *Albuquerque Tribune* that said the underlying causes of the catastrophic wildfires in the Southwest were past logging practices, a history of fire suppression and overgrazing, along with intense drought and global warming. "Blaming Forest Guardians and other environmental groups for these wildfires is grossly irresponsible, inaccurate and ignores the scientific reality." He used the GAO's 2001 report to bolster his arguments but did not mention the conflicting results of the Forest Service report.[81] A Sierra Club official also referred to the GAO report, urging Arizona governor Jane Hull, Sen. Kyl, and other elected officials "to get their facts straight before pointing fingers. . . . What we don't need is more rhetoric which serves only to fan the flames of hate and divisiveness."[82]

Debate was not limited to the West, where wildfires were raging. Jack Swanner, president of the North Carolina Forestry Association and general manager of a timber company, quoted Arizona governor Hull's widely reported comment, "The policies that are coming from the East Coast, that are coming from environmentalists, that say we don't need to log, we don't need to thin our forests are absolutely ridiculous." Adding his own sentiments, Swanner stated:

> The Forest Service's ability to implement management tools in a timely
> manner is limited by conflicting environmental laws and mandates that are

manipulated by environmental groups. They wield their power in courts with a legal strategy to tie up projects in endless appeals and lawsuits. Unclear goals and the threat of lawsuits leave professional land managers with few options. The environmental legal machine files more than 500 appeals and lawsuits annually against the Forest Service. Environmental studies and documentation required on every activity on federal lands costs U.S. taxpayers between $179 and $329 million annually. . . . The resulting delays exact an incalculable human and environmental toll.[83]

From time to time, the media advised the stakeholders in the debate to stop the war of words. A *New York Times* editorial called for a truce in what it called the "ideological wars" and said that "this is no time for partisan sniping." Citing the 2001 GAO study, the editorial called "absurd" the notion that environmental lawsuits have hindered fire-prevention projects.[84] The *Washington Post* quoted environmental leaders' use of the GAO statistics in an article published before the Forest Service study was released and noted, "All the players in western land debates have begun asking whether this year's fires are also fueled by another factor: politics."[85] An editorial in the *Arizona Republic* referred to the "blaze of competing sound bites" and called for leaders to "curtail rhetoric and thin the trees."[86] *High Country News* was one of the few publications to state that both the GAO study and the subsequent Forest Service report were "slim on details" and "a lot like dueling with flamethrowers: a lot of sizzle, but awfully short on precision. . . . The lack of details about what really happened with thinning projects the last two years means the debate could be based more on hype than facts."[87]

Policymaking moved forward quickly while the controversy lingered on. Taking advantage of an opening in the policy window, President Bush presented his Healthy Forests Initiative on August 22, 2002, calling for stepped-up efforts to prevent the damage caused by catastrophic fires by reducing unnecessary regulatory obstacles that hinder active forest management, working with Congress to pass legislation that addresses the unhealthy forest while expediting procedures for forest thinning and restoration projects, and fulfilling the promise of the 1994 Northwest Forest Plan to ensure sustainability and appropriate timber production.

The National Association of State Foresters immediately announced its support for the Healthy Forests Initiative, praising the president's commitment to the National Fire Plan and also applauding efforts to streamline "the process for completing environmental regulations and decreasing the amount of time that agencies spend dealing with litigation."[88] Groups like the Oregon Natural Resources Council said they accepted the idea of thinning but wanted to make sure it would be done where it could do the most good and did not become an excuse to cut old-growth timber.[89] In a formal statement, the Natural Resources Defense Council said, "The administration is asking Congress to torch our most basic environmental protection law under the guise of fire prevention. Rolling back rules for the timber industry and eliminating public participation represent yet another cynical attempt by perhaps the most anti-environmental administration in U.S. history to line the pockets of its corporate friends at the expense of public safety and our natural heritage."[90]

FRAMING THE WILDFIRE "PROBLEM"

The debate over Forest Service administrative appeals is exemplary of the way in which empirical data, rhetoric, and focusing events can be used to frame policy and how process reform can be brought to the political agenda. The image of fire became an important symbol of the debate over forest and wildfire policy beginning in the mid-1990s, gaining increasing salience during the 2000 and 2002 fire seasons. The psychological fear of fire, coupled with dramatic imagery of the destruction of forests and property, opened the policy window for stakeholders seeking a solution to a perceived problem: legislation enacted in 1992 that mandated the Forest Service use an administrative appeal process to resolve conflicts over forest projects. Government policymakers believed that the appeals process and subsequent avenues for litigation delayed projects designed to reduce hazardous fuels in forests. There was also a perception that environmental groups were misusing the process by filing frivolous appeals to stop thinning in national forests as part of a zero-cut policy. This misuse of process created hazardous forest conditions for residents in the wildland-urban interface who had not taken the necessary steps to reduce their fire risks, thus threatening fire fighters and the larger community.

Environmental groups saw the issue from other perspectives. Some organizations felt the appeals process was an important element of public participation that allowed them to monitor and challenge Forest Service actions they believed to be contrary to the spirit and procedures of NEPA. Others viewed appeals as a necessary step in order for them to gain legal standing for potential litigation of forest projects. There was also support for the idea that Congress and the administration were seeking reform of the appeals process as a way of sidestepping public scrutiny so that timber companies could return to logging large trees under the guise of fire prevention.

Both government officials and environmental groups used empirical data and analyses that were methodologically questionable to support their perceptions of the problem, and those data were then repeated and published without corroboration. Rhetoric was an important strategy used by both sides as they sought to frame the issue in terminology that reflected their position. Problems became identified with value-laden terminology that intensified the salience of wildfire. Fire-related terms provided an additional element framing the discussion, as references were made to the "ignition" of the debate, "fanning the flames," "blowing smoke," "incendiary accusations," "heated discussions," "adding fuel," and "inflammatory rhetoric." Synecdoches were used to generalize from one incident to a pattern of problems, regardless of accuracy.

Additionally, policymakers successfully shifted the debate from the "problem" of wildfire policy—eclipsing from public discussion the decades of ineffective human attempts to simplify and control nature by such policies such as fire exclusion and all-out fire suppression as well as the consequences of continued human development in the interface—to the "solution" of process reform. A series of focusing events in 2000 and 2002—massive wildfires that caused substantial property and resource loss—encouraged the president and Congress to capitalize on a sense of urgency and the certainty of catastrophic wildfire. With the opening of the policy window, policymakers demonized environmental groups as the parties responsible for delay and irrational responses, while the president and Congress argued for "common sense" reform that would protect the nation from devastation and lengthy court battles.

As a result, both Congress and the Bush administration were able to propose new legislation and regulatory changes that would repeal or severely restrict the use of administrative appeals of Forest Service projects. By framing the problem as the result of actions by overzealous or misguided environmental groups who misused the process, policymakers were able to recast the agenda in terms more to their liking and, potentially, to negatively affect the perception of environmental organizations in the larger natural resources debate. We will now turn to the development of the Healthy Forests Restoration Act and the significant regulatory changes initiated in response to the fire-appeals interface.

NOTES

1. Stephen J. Pyne, *Fire: A Brief History* (Seattle: University of Washington Press, 2001). This is one of the suite of books in the *Cycle of Fire* series published under the editorship of William Cronon. For another perspective, see Stephen F. Arno, *Flames in Our Forest: Disaster or Renewal* (Washington, DC: Island Press, 2002).

2. For a history of early American use of forests and the role of fire in changing the landscape, see Stephen J. Pyne, *Fire in America: A Cultural History of Wildland and Rural Fire* (Princeton, NJ: Princeton University Press, 1982); Michael Williams, *Americans and Their Forests: A Historical Geography* (New York, NY: Cambridge University Press, 1989); John Perlin, *A Forest Journey: The Role of Wood in the Development of Civilization* (Cambridge,

MA: Harvard University Press, 1991); and William Cronon, *Changes in the Land: Indians, Colonists, and the Ecology of New England* (New York, NY: Hill and Wang, 1983).

3. The objective (adopted in 1935) was to put enough suppression forces on a fire to control it by 10:00 A.M. of the following morning. The 10:00 A.M. policy was formally amended in 1971 by the 10 Acre Policy, which set ten acres as a pre-suppression goal for wildfire containment. These policies remained in effect until 1978.

4. Pyne, *Fire in America*. Ashley Schiff's classic public administration study of the Forest Service's suppression of scientific reports that discussed the benefits of prescribed fire details the controversy over prescribed fire within the agency. Ashley Schiff, *Fire and Water: Scientific Heresy in the U.S. Forest Service* (Cambridge, MA: Harvard University Press, 1962).

5. For example, there was a 57 percent real increase in pre-suppression expenditures in the Forest Service from 1970 through 1975. In the same period—characterized by a series of severe fire years—the number of fires and acres burned also increased. It was becoming increasingly apparent that deployment of pre-suppression resources did not necessarily avert fire-induced damages and suppression costs. Reducing the proportion of fires less than ten acres in size by 2 percent would have taken an estimated 90 percent increase in pre-suppression expenditures. Robert D. Gale, *Evaluation of Fire Management Activities on the National Forests,* Policy Analysis Staff Report (Washington, DC: USDA Forest Service, 1977). The 1978 change in fire policy is described in Thomas C. Nelson, "Fire Management Policy in the National Forests: A New Era," *Journal of Forestry* 77:1 (1979): 723–725.

6. Albert J. Simard, Donald A. Haines, Richard W. Blank, and John S. Frost, *The Mack Lake Fire,* General Technical Report NC-83 (St. Paul, MN: USDA Forest Service North Central Forest Experiment Station, 1983).

7. Prominent California fires included, for example, the 1961 fire in Bel Air, the 1966 Wellman Fire in Santa Barbara, the 1970 Laguna Fire in San Diego, the 1977 Sycamore Fire in Santa Barbara, and the 1980 fire in San Bernardino. Jack A. Blackwell and Andrea Tuttle, *California Fire Siege 2003: The Story* (Sacramento, CA: California Department of Forestry and Fire Protection, and Washington, DC: USDA Forest Service, 2003).

8. Gary O. Tokle, "The Wildand/Urban Interface: Design for Disaster," *Fire Command* 54:1 (1987): 17–19, 17.

9. The National Fire Protection Association (NFPA) is a private, nonprofit group of seventy-five thousand individuals and eighty national trade and professional organizations whose traditional focus has been codes and standards related to structural fire. (However, since the mid-1980s the association has published a standard related to the wildland-urban interface: NFPA 1144, *Standard for Protection of Life and Property from Wildfire, 2002 Edition* [Batterymarch Park, MA: National Fire Protection Association].) The U.S. Fire Administration of the Department of Homeland Security and the Federal Emergency Management Agency's primary goal is to improve fire safety, again largely with regard to structural fire. The decision of these three groups to jointly tackle the wildland-urban fire problem was the first formal coordination activity ever to occur between structural and wildland fire interests.

10. See USDA Forest Service, National Fire Protection Association, U.S. Fire Administration, *Wildfire Strikes Home* (Batterymarch Park, MA: National Fire Protection Association, 1987); William C. Fischer and Stephen F. Arno, eds., *Protecting People and Homes From Wildfire in the Interior West: Proceedings of the Symposium and Workshop,* General Technical Report 251 (Ogden, UT: USDA Forest Service Intermountain Research Station, 1988); and Robert D. Gale and Hanna J. Cortner, eds., *People and Fire at the Wildland Urban Interface: A Sourcebook* (Washington, DC: USDA Forest Service, 1987).

11. Boise Interagency Fire Center, *Fire Season Statistics and Summary* (Boise, ID: Boise Interagency Fire Center, 1988), 7.

12. Fire Management Policy Review Team, *Report on Fire Management Policy* (Washington, DC: Department of the Interior and Department of Agriculture, 1988).

13. U.S. Department of the Interior and U.S. Department of Agriculture, *1995 Federal Wildland Fire Management Policy and Review* (Washington, DC: U.S. Department of the Interior and USDA, 1995).

14. Historical Wildland Fire Statistics, National Interagency Fire Center, at www.nifc.gov/stats/wildlandfirestats accessed June 24, 2002.

15. U.S. Department of the Interior, U.S. Department of Agriculture, U.S. Department of Energy, U.S. Department of Defense, U.S. Department of Commerce, U.S. Environmental Protection Agency, U.S. Federal Emergency Management Agency, and National Association of State Foresters, *Review and Update of the 1995 Federal Wildland Fire Management Policy* (Boise, ID: National Interagency Fire Center, 2001).

16. U.S. Department of the Interior and U.S. Department of Agriculture, *Managing the Impacts of Wildfire on Communities and the Environment: A Report to the President in Response to the Wildfires of 2000* (Washington, DC: Department of the Interior, 2001).

17. Hanna J. Cortner, Robert M. Swinford, and Michael R. Williams, *Emergency Assistance and Mutual Aid Policy Analysis* (Washington, DC: USDA Forest Service Policy Analysis Staff, 1990); Hanna J. Cortner and Theodore Lorensen, "Resources Versus Structures: Fire Suppression Priorities in the Wildland/Urban Interface," *Wildfire* 6:5 (1997): 22–33; and Ron H. Wakimoto, "National Fire Management Policy: A Look at the Need for Change," *Western Wildlands* 15:2 (1989): 35–39.

18. USDA Forest Service, *Fire Suppression Costs on Large Fires—A Review of the 1994 Fire Season* (Washington, DC: USDA Forest Service, 1995).

19. Nancy Langston presents a compelling history of human attempts to simplify nature and how ideology trumped science and led the Forest Service down a path of management with severe unintended consequences. Nancy Langston, *Forest Dreams, Forest Nightmares: The Paradox of Old Growth in the Inland West* (Seattle, WA: University of Washington Press, 1995). See also Herbert E. McLean, "The Blue Mountains: Forest Out of Control: Bugs, Disease, and Well-Intentioned Mismanagement Have Turned an Enormous Swath of Northeastern Oregon to Tinder," *American Forests* 98:9–10 (1992): 32–35, 58, 61.

20. USDA Forest Service, *Restoring Ecosystems in the Blue Mountains: A Report to the Regional Forester and the Forest Supervisors of the Blue Mountain Forests* (Portland, OR: USDA Forest Service Pacific Northwest Region, 1992); Gerald J. Gray, ed., "Health Emergency Imperils Western Forests," *Resource Hotline* 8:9 (1992): 1–3; Jay O'Laughlin et

al., *Forest Health Conditions in Idaho* (Moscow, ID: University of Idaho, Idaho Forest, Wildlife, and Range Policy Analysis Group, 1993); R. Neil Sampson and David L. Adams, eds., *Assessing Forest Ecosystem Health in the Inland West* (1994), Papers from the American Forests Workshop, November 14–20, 1993; W. Wallace Covington, "Concepts of Forest Health: Utilitarian and Ecosystem Perspectives," *Journal of Forestry* 92:7 (1994): 10–15; Jack Ward Thomas, "Concerning the Health and Productivity of the Fire-Adapted Forests of the Western United States," Statement by the Chief of the Forest Service before the Subcommittee on Agricultural Research, Conservation, Forestry, and General Legislation, Committee on Agriculture, U.S. Senate, *Wildfire* 4:1 (1995): 18–21. It is not as if the Forest Service had done nothing previously to deal with the buildup of fuels. For example, former Congressional Research Service analyst Bob Wolf has estimated that, during the past twenty-three years, the agency has conducted fuel treatments such as light burning on 12,206,000 acres (personal communication, October 17, 2003).

21. Reported at www.ispe.arizona.edu/climas/fire/overview/connection accessed October 29, 2004.

22. Society for Ecological Restoration International Science and Policy Working Group, *The SER Primer on Ecological Restoration* (2002), at www.ser.org. accessed September 18, 2002; W. Wallace Covington et al., "Restoring Ecosystem Health in Ponderosa Pine Forests of the Southwest," *Journal of Forestry* 95:4 (1007): 23–29; Wallace W. Covington, W. A. Niering, Ed Starkey, and Joan Walker, "Ecosystem Restoration and Management: Scientific Principles and Concepts," in *Ecological Stewardship: A Common Reference for Ecosystem Management,* Vol. II, Robert C. Szaro, N. C. Johnson, William T. Sexton, and A. J. Malk, eds. (Oxford, UK: Elsevier Science, 1999), 559–617.

23. Jay O'Laughlin, "Wildfire: Is the Forest Service the Culprit or the Solution?" *Idaho Falls Post Register* (September 1, 2002).

24. For various explanations and studies see Russell T. Graham, *Hayman Fire Case Study,* Gen. Tech. Rep. RMRS-GTR-114 (Fort Collins, CO: USDA Forest Service Rocky Mountain Research Station, 2003). For perspectives by environmental groups see Peter Morrison and Kirsten Harma, *Analysis of Land Ownership and Prior Land Management Activities Within the Rodeo and Chediski Fires, Arizona* (Winthrop, WA: Pacific Biodiversity Institute, 2002); Center for Biological Diversity, Sierra Club, and Southwest Forest Alliance, *Prelude to Catastrophe: Recent and Historic Land Management within the Rodeo-Chediski Fire Area* (nd); Sierra Club, *Forest Fires: Beyond the Heat and Hype* (Washington, DC: Sierra Club, nd). For an explanation of arguments claiming that weather is the prime reason for widespread fires and that lack of institutional incentives to control budgets is the major reason for increased fire costs, see Randal O'Toole, *Reforming the Fire Service: An Analysis of Federal Fire Budgets and Incentives* (Bandon, OR: The Thoreau Institute, 2002).

25. Michael A. Smith "The Interpretative Process of Agenda-Building: A Research Design for Public Policy," *Politics & Policy* 30:1 (2002): 9–31.

26. For a discussion of the media's role in agenda setting, see Maxwell McCombs and Donald Shaw, "The Agenda-Setting Function of Mass Media," *Public Opinion Quarterly* 36 (1972): 176–187; Shanto Iyengar, *Is Anyone Responsible? How Television Frames Political*

Issues (Chicago: University of Chicago Press, 1991); and James W. Dearing and Everett M. Rogers, *Communications Concepts 6: Agenda-Setting* (Thousand Oaks, CA: Sage, 1996).

27. Richard A. Lanham, *A Handlist of Rhetorical Terms* (Berkeley, CA: University of California Press, 1991), 148.

28. See Deborah Stone, *Policy Paradox and Political Reason* (New York, NY: HarperCollins, 1988), 116. President Reagan, for example, was noted for his singling out an instance and making sweeping generalizations in defense of his policies based on this one example. He highlighted the perversities of welfare reform by citing cases of welfare abuse. When an example provided an exemplar he showcased the individual in his State of the Union address.

29. See Murray Edelman, *Politics As Symbolic Action* (New York, NY: Academic Press, 1971); and Edelman, *The Symbolic Uses of Politics* (Urbana, IL: University of Illinois Press, 1972); Charles D. Elder and Roger W. Cobb, *The Political Uses of Symbols* (New York: Longman, 1983); and William H. Riker, *The Art of Political Manipulation* (New Haven, CT: Yale University Press, 1986).

30. "Bush Urges a Hands-On Forest Policy," *Winston-Salem Journal* (August 23, 2002), at www.journalnow.com/wsj accessed August 24, 2002.

31. Paul Fattig, "The Tour: Pushing 'Common Sense' At Fire Site," *Medford Mail Tribune* (August 23, 2002), at www.mailtribune.com accessed February 14, 2004.

32. The phrase is attributed to Watt in C. Brant Short, *Ronald Reagan and the Public Lands* (College Station: Texas A&M Press, 1989), 55. James V. Hansen, "Does the National Environmental Policy Act Need to Be Rewritten?" *Roll Call* (April 19, 1999), at www.web.lexis-nexis.com/universe/document accessed February 6, 2003.

33. John W. Kingdon, *Agendas, Alternatives, and Public Policies,* Second edition (New York: Longman, 2003), 98. See also Thomas A. Birkland, *After Disaster: Agenda Setting, Public Policy, and Focusing Events* (Washington, DC: Georgetown University Press, 1997).

34. Martin Nie, "Drivers of Natural Resource-Based Political Conflict," *Policy Sciences* 36 (2003): 307–341.

35. See Jack L. Walker, "Performance Gaps, Policy Research, and Political Entrepreneurs," *Policy Studies Journal* 3 (Autumn 1974): 112–116.

36. Editorial, "Racicot Wrong to Blame Clinton for Fires," *The Missoulian* (August 15, 2000), at www.missoulian.com accessed January 27, 2003; Larry Fish, "Montana's Governor Denies Blaming Wildfires on Clinton," *Philadelphia Inquirer* (August 26, 2000), at www.philly.com accessed January 27, 2003.

37. Fish, "Montana's Governor Denies Blaming Wildfires on Clinton."

38. Cat Lazaroff, "Logging Does Not Reduce Fire Risk, Two Studies Conclude," *Environmental News Service* (September 5, 2000), at www.ens.com accessed January 27, 2003.

39. Ibid.

40. See, for example, Ken Picard, "Very Political Science," *Missoula Independent* (September 14, 2000), at www.missoulanews.com accessed January 27, 2003.

41. Alliance for the Wild Rockies, "Groups Request Congressional Hearings on Forest Service $12 Billion Forest Proposal," News release (August 29, 2000), at www.wildrockiesalliance.org accessed January 27, 2003.

42. Center for Biological Diversity et al., "Scientific Report Shows Logging and Road Building Will Not Protect Forests From Fire" (September 5, 2000), at www.sw-center.org/swcbd accessed January 27, 2003.

43. Brian Hansen, "Wildfires Debate Engulfs Congress, Western States," *Environmental News Service* (September 15, 2000), at www.ens.com accessed January 27, 2003.

44. For a discussion of the two policy initiatives from an administrative perspective, see Charles R. Wise and Christian M. Freitag, "Balancing Accountability and Risk in Program Implementation: The Case of National Fire Policy," *Journal of Public Administration Research and Theory* 12 (2002): 294–523.

45. U.S. General Accounting Office, *Forest Service: Appeals and Litigation of Fuel Reduction Projects*, GAO-01-1114R (Washington, DC: General Accounting Office, August 31, 2001).

46. USDA Forest Service, *The Process Predicament*, 5.

47. Ibid., 27–28.

48. Ibid., 35. The NAPA study on restoring managerial accountability to the Forest Service was presented to the House Committee on Appropriations, Subcommittee on Interior and Related Agencies, in testimony by Dall Forsythe. The recommendations of the NAPA focus primarily on implementation of a new financial system, budget and appropriation process, organizational structure and design, strategic planning and performance management, and leadership. Forsythe's testimony is available on-line at www.napawash.org/resources/testimony/testimony_02_16_00 accessed February 3, 2003.

49. U.S. General Accounting Office, *Forest Service Decision-Making: A Framework for Improving Performance*, Report to Congressional Requestors, GAO/RCED-97-71 (April 1997), 102.

50. Jeff Flake, "Costly Lawsuits Provide Kindling for Forest Blazes," *Arizona Republic* (June 25, 2002): B7.

51. USDA Forest Service, *The Process Predicament*, 37.

52. Ibid., 40.

53. Oregon Natural Resources Council et al., "Environmental Safeguards Under Attack by the Bush Administration," News release (June 11, 2002), at www.onrc.org.

54. U.S. General Accounting Office, Letter to Rep. Scott McInnis, *Forest Service: Scope and Methodology Used to Determine Number of Appeals and Legal Challenges to Fiscal Year 2001 Fuel Reduction Projects* (Washington, DC: General Accounting Office, July 9, 2002).

55. USDA Forest Service, *Factors Affecting Timely Mechanical Fuel Treatment Decisions* (Washington, DC: USDA Forest Service, July 2002).

56. Ibid.

57. Letter from Fred Norbury to Jeannette Russell, September 6, 2002.

58. The comments from the e-mail correspondence are taken from documents provided by the Forest Service in its response to the National Forest Protection Alliance FOIA request.

59. The Wilderness Society, *Forest Service Continues to Blow Smoke: Why the USFS Report on Appeals Is Wrong* (Washington, DC: Wilderness Society, July 12, 2002).

60. "America Needs A Credible Forest Service," News release (July 26, 2002), at www.house.gov/inslee/enviro_forest_service_letter accessed January 24, 2003.

61. In fall 2004, this organization changed its name to The Forest Guild.

62. Jeffery Morton and Laura McCarthy, *A Comparison of Two Government Reports on Factors Affecting Timely Fuel Treatment Decisions* (Santa Fe, NM: The Forest Trust, September 3, 2002).

63. "U.S. Reps. Tom Udall and Jay Inslee Release Report Clarifying Differences Between Fuel Reduction Statistics," News release (September 4, 2002), at www.house.gov/inslee/enviro_fuel_reduction accessed January 24, 2003.

64. Ibid.

65. Native Forest Network, "Freedom of Information Act Request Reveals Info U.S. Forest Service 'Report' Was Gathered in Hours," News release (October 1, 2002), at www.nativeforest.org/press_room/release_10_01_02 accessed December 28, 2002.

66. Brian Stempeck, "Study Was Quick, But It Also Low-Balled Appeals Estimates—USFS," *Greenwire* (October 3, 2002), at www.eenews.net/sample accessed December 28, 2002.

67. Robert Gehrke, "Environmentalists, Forest Service Agree That Fire Report Was Rushed, Figures Were Off," *Las Vegas Sun* (October 2, 2002), at www.lasvegassun.com/sunbin/stories/text/2002/oct/02 accessed December 28, 2002.

68. Forest Watch Campaign, "Another Summer of Fire—and Deception," at www.coloradowild.org/fwc/fwc accessed January 21, 2003.

69. Mark Flatten and Dan Nowicki, "Green Group Lawsuit Blocked Forest Thinning," *East Valley Tribune* (July 8, 2002), at www.eastvalleytribune.com/rodeofire accessed July 8, 2002.

70. Mary Jo Pitzl, "Wildfire Finger-Pointing Rampant," *Arizona Republic* (July 26, 2002): B7.

71. "Seven Questions You Need Answered," *Arizona Republic* (June 30, 2002): V1.

72. Jon Kyl, "Environmental Activists Place Forests At Risk," *Arizona Republic* (June 26, 2002): B9.

73. Tom Knudson, "Playing With Fire: Spin on Science Puts National Treasure at Risk," *Sacramento Bee* (April 25, 2001), quoted in USDA Forest Service, *The Process Predicament*, 9.

74. Kieran Suckling, "Dear Senator Kyl: Get the Facts About the Fires," *Arizona Republic* (July 16, 2002): B7.

75. Ben Nighthorse Campbell, "Environmental Extremists Fan Forest Fires," *Pueblo Chieftain Online* (July 7, 2002), at www.chieftain.com/sunday/editorial/index/article/4 accessed January 25, 2003.

76. "Environmentalists Not Responsible for Forest Fires: 'Fifty Years of Bi-partisan Ignorance to Blame,'" News release (June 26, 2002), at www.house.gov/inslee/enviro_wildfire accessed January 24, 2003.

77. Billy House, "Forest Service Adding Fuel to Debate on Tree Thinning," *Arizona Republic* (July 11, 2002): A7.

78. "Politicians Blowing Smoke Over Colorado Fires," at www.coloradowild.org/coloradofires accessed January 21, 2003.

79. "Conservation Groups Set Record Straight," News release (July 18, 2002).

80. Personal communication from Matthew Koehler, January 27, 2003.

81. John Horning, "Don't Flame Tree-Huggers," *Albuquerque Tribune* (July 18, 2002), at www.abqtrib.com/print/index accessed August 27, 2002.

82. Sandy Bahr, "Faulty Practices, Logging Methods Fanning Flames," *Arizona Republic* (June 25, 2002): B7.

83. Jack Swanner, "Restore the Health of Our Forests Before They Go Up in Smoke," at www.ncforestry.org/docs accessed January 25, 2003.

84. Editorial, "Scorched-Earth Politics," *New York Times* (June 30, 2002), at www.nytimes.com accessed July 19, 2002.

85. Rene Sanchez and William Booth, "Did Politics Put a Match to West's Wild Lands?" *Washington Post* (June 27, 2002): A3.

86. "Time to Put Up the Money and the Muscle," *Arizona Republic* (June 26, 2002): B8.

87. Matt Jenkins, "Blame Game Sheds Little Light on Fires," *High Country News* (August 19, 2002), 3.

88. National Association of State Foresters, "NASF Commends Presidential Forest Health Initiative," News release (August 23, 2002), at www.stateforesters.org/news accessed August 26, 2002.

89. Jeff Barnard, "Forest Plan Faces Obstacles," *The Missoulian* (August 26, 2002), at www.missoulian.com accessed August 26, 2002.

90. Natural Resources Defense Council, "Bush's Forest Proposal a 'Smokescreen' Says NRDC," News Release (August 22, 2002), at www.nrdc.org/media accessed August 24, 2002.

REFORM BY LEGISLATION
The Healthy Forests Restoration Act

BY DEFINING THE FIRE-APPEALS PROBLEM IN TERMS OF PROCESS AND POINTING BLAME AT environmental groups misusing appeals procedures, Congress and the Bush administration were able to cast environmentalists as a major threat to the health of the nation's forests. Rather than having to defend decades-old policies of fire exclusion or deal with broader questions of fire management and forest restoration,[1] the Forest Service became an active partner with the president and Congress in calling for process reform that would give it more management discretion to implement fuel reduction and forest thinning projects as well as limit public participation in decision making. The emphasis on process, rather than the content of existing forest and fire management policies, also provided a reasonable explanation for the administration to take a lead in seeking regulatory as well as legislative change. Between 2001 and 2003 the Bush administration used parallel strategies—legislative and regulatory—to substantially alter the direction of forest policy.

Legislation is but one type of policy instrument and, in this case was combined with a strategy of administrative rulemaking to achieve a desired outcome. From the perspective of the Bush administration and its supportive interests, a principal sought-after outcome was reducing regulatory constraints under NEPA. Specific to that goal was the repeal of provisions allowing for administrative appeals of Forest Service project decisions. More broadly, some stakeholders sought repeal of NEPA altogether. This chapter documents the legislative history of the Healthy Forests Restoration Act (HFRA), and Chapter 6 focuses on regulatory changes enacted at the same time the legislative approach was being formulated and adopted.

THE 107TH CONGRESS

The legislative process is perhaps the most common way in which elected representatives seek to solve demanding policy problems. It is relatively visible, highly procedural and formalized, and what constituents expect their elected officials to do in Washington. What is not known (but subject to considerable speculation) is how the legislative process is influenced by external forces. Cynics believe that much of what the public sees, whether at public hearings or on cable television channels like C-SPAN, has been carefully orchestrated by congressional staff who are themselves manipulated by powerful stakeholders that have an interest in a particular issue. Others believe the central government has been reduced to a position where it simply coordinates and bargains with other centers of power, whether state and local governments or networks of other actors in the public and private sectors. Lobbies—organized interests that use their resources to influence the political process—compete for legislators' attention and are part of the decision making process, although the extent of their influence varies considerably.[2]

During the second session of the 107th Congress and the first session of the 108th Congress, President Bush used his allies in Congress to push forward his administrative goals—including the Healthy Forests Initiative—in the legislative arena. As explained in the previous chapter, some problems rise quickly to the top of the decision-making agenda and wildfire was no exception during the second session of the 107th Congress. The 2002 fire season, along with massive insect infestation of forests, provided several members of Congress with a rationale for introducing new legislation to fight the fiery menace working its way across the West. With the nation's worst fire season as backdrop for their expedited efforts, Congress moved forward rapidly in an attempt to implement this element of the president's environmental agenda. As is typical in the legislative process, several small and often less expansive bills are introduced at the beginning of the policy debate, literally getting the discussion going prior to the introduction of more comprehensive measures.[3]

In the case of forest policy and wildfires, one of the more publicly controversial proposals came in July from Sen. Tom Daschle (D-SD), whose amendment to

H.R. 4775 addressed the Supplemental Appropriations Act. Daschle's bill was limited to seven identified timber sale analysis areas—all of them in South Dakota—and sought to expedite the projects "notwithstanding NEPA." Although the senator had worked with environmental organizations, the governor, and local stakeholders to fashion the proposal, he was quickly criticized for promoting legislation benefiting only his home state.[4] President Bush even referred to Daschle's maneuver when he announced his Healthy Forests Initiative, noting "[t]here's so many regulations, and so much red tape. My attitude is, if it's good enough for that part of South Dakota, it's good enough for Oregon."[5] Another short bill, H.R. 5358 or the Community Protection Against Wildfire Act of 2002 (introduced by Rep. Jay Inslee, D-WA), authorized grants for community and private wildfire assistance but did not address wildfire protection on federal lands.

A more defined political agenda began to form in late July as the fire season progressed. Rep. Dennis Rehberg (R-MT) sought to have the Secretary of Agriculture take prompt actions to address the risk to the national forests in H.R. 5214, the National Forest Fire Prevention Act. The measure pointed the finger at administrative and legal processes that were holding up immediate actions to create a defensible fuel zone in fire hazard or insect-infested areas and authorized additional timber treatments as needed.

His colleague, Rep. John Shadegg (R-AZ), sought to deal with the problem by authorizing regional foresters to exempt tree-thinning projects from administrative appeals and legal actions that delayed or prevented projects from moving forward in H.R. 5309, introduced July 26, 2002. The bill, the Wildfire Prevention and Forest Health Protection Act of 2002, noted that there was an extraordinary wildfire threat to national forests and cited the Forest Service's July 2002 Forest Service *Factors Affecting* report that found 48 percent of projects involving mechanical tree-thinning had been subject to challenge and appeal. The Forest Service report provided Shadegg with statistical information that had been lacking in earlier attempts at reform, even though, as discussed in the previous chapter, there were substantive questions about the study's methodology.

The Healthy Forests Initiative proposed by President Bush on August 22 provided Congress with a blueprint for the administration's preferences on forest and wildfire policy. As the 2002 fire season wound down, the president had little difficulty in securing support for his package among most members of Congress from western states, who had already felt the political heat after the 2000 fire season. The 107th Congress was filled with incumbents who were serious about satisfying their rural, resource-focused constituencies, even though there were fewer than a dozen seriously contested House seats at stake in the 2002 election.

Just two weeks after Bush's August speech, the administration delivered a four-part legislative proposal to Congress. It was designed to "streamline unnecessary red tape that prevents timely and effective implementation of wildfire prevention and forest health projects on public lands. Delays of these projects can have devastating environmental and social consequences when catastrophic fires strike." Two of the four proposals called for expediting the reduction of hazardous fuels in critical areas through collaborative processes and developing long-term stewardship contracts to thin trees and remove dead wood. The third proposal would repeal the Appeals Reform Act that had mandated an administrative appeals process for Forest Service projects, and the fourth proposal "would establish common sense rules for courts when deciding on challenges to fuels reduction projects."[6]

Forest Service chief Dale Bosworth echoed the president's sentiments by calling for the repeal of legislation that "forces the U.S. Forest Service to accept citizen appeals of all land-management decisions. . . . We've spent way too much time and way too much money doing analysis and paperwork. . . . I don't need my people sitting in windowless rooms doing paperwork. I need them out on the ground, getting the job done."[7]

The president's proposals also began to pick up support among western governors and the Western Governors' Association—a powerful stakeholder in the fire-appeals debate. Colorado governor Bill Owens said that the "changes in the way we manage our federal forest lands are long overdue, as evidenced by the devastating fires this summer."[8] Montana governor Judy Martz, who had succeeded Marc Racicot in office and served as the chair of the Western Governors' Association, told reporters, "I would like to do away with appeals, period."[9]

By September 2002 the administration had effectively framed the debate to show that administrative appeals were keeping the Forest Service from doing its job. The implication was that environmentalists cause fires. The only solution, it appeared, would be to do something about the appeals process itself.

Congress responded with several bills designed to implement the president's forest policy agenda that went far beyond the July proposals. In the House, the Healthy Forests Reform Act of 2002 (H.R. 5319), sponsored by Rep. McInnis, gained the most momentum. The bill, introduced September 4, 2002, called for collaborative dispute resolution to replace the existing appeals process, although it allowed opponents of Forest Service projects to challenge agency actions in federal court. Reps. Shadegg and Rehberg abandoned their own proposals to join in sponsorship with McInnis.

The speed at which the House sought to move forward on the president's proposal is indicated by the fact that the first hearing on the McInnis bill took place September 5, 2002—the day after it was introduced. Concern about the timing of the hearing was posed in the first set of questions raised by Rep. Peter DeFazio (D-OR), who stressed that the wildfire issue required more time for members to prepare and who requested that another hearing be offered on the same issue.

At the hearing, McInnis called his bill "a reasoned and prudent approach to getting our arms around the West's wildfire crisis." He went on, contending that it takes projects "upwards of several years to work their way through the NEPA process and any subsequent appeals and lawsuits" and calling for the existing Forest Service appeals process to be replaced with a pre-decisional procedure.[10]

The first panel of witnesses at the hearing, Agriculture Secretary Ann Veneman and Interior Secretary Gale Norton, discussed the social and environmental devastation caused by the year's wildfires. Veneman emphasized the time and cost and warned that the president's Healthy Forests Initiative was essential to implementing the Ten-Year Collaborative Strategy to reduce wildfire risk. Developed in response to congressional direction in the FY 2001 Interior appropriations bill and in collaboration with a number of citizen and governmental groups, the strategy, Veneman pointed out, had been endorsed by the two secretaries, the Western Governors' Association, the National Association of State Foresters, the National Association of Counties, and the Intertribal Timber Council. Norton took a somewhat different approach, noting that the initiative was needed to guard against catastrophic wildfires, not all wildfires, and describing the benefits of thinning forests. Thinning, she said, resulted in numerous benefits besides reducing hazardous fuels.

The second panel of witnesses began with Charles H. Burley, representing the American Forest Resource Council, a group composed of forest product manufacturers and forest landowners. He testified that the appeals process "was well intentioned when instituted. Unfortunately, over time, it has become a process too often abused by individuals and organizations that wish to delay or stop Forest Service activities from being implemented—this is particularly acute if the project involves harvesting trees." Burley went on to cite the Forest Service's *Factors Affecting* report and concluded "the appeals period is increasingly being used to simply block or delay projects."[11] Support for repeal of the appeals process also came from the Forest Counties Payments Committee, an advisory committee to Congress. In its testimony, a group representative outlined the frustration of individuals and groups who tried to work collaboratively with the Forest Service. "Many of these citizens depend on timely decisions that affect their communities, and they are concerned about solving forest health problems. The work they do together, and with the Agency, can be un-done by someone who did not make the effort to find solutions for addressing forest management issues."[12]

Criticism of the legislation and the hearing by environmental organizations focused on the impact of the bill on public accountability. Michael Francis, director of Forest Programs for The Wilderness Society, noted that "this bill won't protect people from fire. It will only protect the profits of the administration's friends in the commercial timber industry."[13]

Amendments to the McInnis bill, renamed the Healthy Forests and Wildfire Risk Reduction Act of 2002 and developed by a bipartisan group of House members led by Rep. George Miller (D-CA), gave the Forest Service flexibility to streamline some environmental analyses, required new spending on forest thinning to reduce risk near communities, and preserved rights of individuals to appeal and litigate controversial land management decisions. The five-year plan prohibited the Forest Service from using this flexibility to build roads in roadless forests.[14] Rep. Inslee offered a competing substitute that would have required 85 percent of the money made available in the bill to be used in the area within one-half mile of communities and watersheds, but it was voted down 25-12 in committee. Other amendments offered by Rep. Tom Udall (D-NM) and Rep. Mark Udall (D-CO) were rejected.

Leading environmental groups, including the Natural Resources Defense Council, Friends of the Earth, The Wilderness Society, the National Environmental Trust, and the American Lands Alliance, denounced Reps. Miller and DeFazio for trying to work out a deal with Republican leaders. A spokesperson for the American Lands Alliance said he was "shocked and disappointed that Representative Miller and Representative DeFazio would support legislation that steam rolls environmental safeguards for forests."[15] Supporters, including the Society of American Foresters, said that H.R. 5319 "provides workable processes that forest managers need."[16]

But as quickly as the compromise seemed to come together, it unraveled. Miller and DeFazio removed their names from the proposal before the vote. Although the bill was approved by the House Resources Committee on a 23-14 voice vote, last-minute negotiations did not allow the bill to be voted on by the full House before it adjourned for the election recess. And other bills to enhance the authority of the Secretaries of Agriculture and Interior to reduce the threat of catastrophic wildfire—H.R. 5341 (The National Forest Fire Fuels Reduction Act), sponsored by Rep. Charles Taylor (R-NC), and H.R. 5376, sponsored by Rep. Larry Combest (R-TX)—made little progress.

Like their House counterparts, members of the Senate started early in the fire season to seek support for reform. Sen. Jon Kyl (R-AZ) introduced S. 2670, the Wildfire Prevention Act of 2002, on June 24, 2002. The measure called for practical science-based forest restoration treatments to reduce the threat of severe wildfires and sought to establish three institutes—including one in his home state—

to promote the use of adaptive ecosystem management. Kyl's bill did not pass in the 107th Congress, but it was reintroduced and eventually passed in 2004. The Emergency Forests Rescue Act of 2002, S. 2811 (Sen. Mike Enzi, R-WY) was a short bill dealing with emergency mitigation areas and alternative NEPA arrangements from the Council on Environmental Quality.

After the Healthy Forests Initiative was unveiled, competing measures were introduced in the Senate calling for massive forest thinning that would be exempt from or subject to only limited NEPA review and the administrative appeals process. Sens. Larry Craig (R-ID) and Pete Domenici (R-NM) called for the logging of ten million acres of federal land considered at highest risk of catastrophic wildfire. The legislation would allow the logging to be exempt from NEPA review, the Forest Service's administrative appeals process, and any work stoppages during legal challenges. They asked that their measure be attached to the Interior Appropriations bill under consideration on the Senate floor, becoming S.A. 4518, The Emergency Hazardous Fuels Reduction Plan.

Sen. Max Baucus (D-MT) introduced a different measure (S. 2920) that reduced hazardous fuels logging to 3.75 million acres and excluded some projects from environmental review and formal public comment, but under more tightly controlled circumstances. It also required that at least 10 percent of hazardous fuels reduction funds be spent on projects benefiting businesses in small, economically disadvantaged communities "like Libby, Montana."[17]

The Republican-sponsored bill ran headlong into partisan debate. Several members tried to broker a bipartisan compromise that had backing from the Bush administration but failed to gain support for their measure. Two supporters of that legislation, Sens. Dianne Feinstein (D-CA) and Ron Wyden (D-OR), came under fierce attack by environmental groups, provoking an unprecedented rebuke of Feinstein by the Sierra Club. The group approved a resolution calling the senator's actions "unconscionable" after only fifteen minutes of debate. Sierra Club executive director Carl Pope warned about the gap developing between the organization and Feinstein. "This is a very big issue to us. Depending upon what happens down the road, this has the potential to be a very serious break [with Feinstein.] And I think she understands that."[18]

After two weeks of trying to come up with an agreement with Republican leaders, Feinstein said she was fed up. "I deeply regret that the issue has become so polarized that a compromise has not been possible and that groups such as the Sierra Club would condemn those who try to find a solution."[19] She later condemned the Sierra Club, saying the group made it impossible for her to gather the support she needed among Democrats to cut off debate and force a vote. Craig lent his support, noting "The Dianne Feinsteins of this world have every reason to be frustrated and angry. I think she felt herself a friend of that organization only to have them bite her as hard as they did."[20]

What the environmental groups failed to recognize was the power that the framing of the issue held, and the difficult position in which the Democratic members of Congress had been put. Although not wanting to emasculate appeals and litigation as techniques of public involvement and citizen protest, the successful castigation of environmental groups as a threat to forests, people's property, and fire fighters' lives made it difficult for the legislators to align their response totally with environmentalists' positions. Moreover, there was no denying the explosive situation in the national forests. Most environmentalists also acknowledged the "crisis" in the national forests and the need to do something. Publicly the nuanced differences between "logging versus small-diameter thinning" or "restoration versus fuels reduction" escaped the public. It was difficult for legislators committed to dealing with hazardous fuels build-up to kill legislation that grouped regulatory reform as part of a larger package labeled forest health and restoration.

Despite last minute attempts to reach agreement, the Senate refused on a 50-49 party-line vote to limit debate on wildfire-related amendments to the $19.3 billion Interior spending measure. Sixty votes were needed to overcome a filibuster, and no action was taken on the Craig-Domenici proposal by the end of session. An alternative proposal offered by Sens. Daschle and Jeff Bingaman (D-NM) that would have eased some logging restrictions on 2.5 million acres also failed to secure the sixty votes necessary to avoid further procedural delays.

After the November 2002 elections, the president and members of his cabinet began to reframe the forest thinning debate. The inflammatory rhetoric of the 2002 fire season was replaced by a more moderate-sounding appeal to "common sense" as a rationale behind new administrative actions to expedite the administrative rulemaking process. But the wildfires were also used to reinforce the notion that the nation faced a monumental crisis "of unprecedented proportions," according to CEQ chairman James L. Connaughton. "These common sense steps will allow federal agencies to spend millions of dollars a year on environmental restoration and conservation rather than needless paperwork."[21] The administration called for amendments that would "encourage early and more meaningful public participation," phrasing that identified the procedural changes with efficiency rather than blame.

CHANGES IN THE 108TH CONGRESS

The 2002 mid-term elections turned over control of the Senate to the Republicans and made some sort of forest reform legislation inevitable. Once the 108th Congress opened its first session in January 2003, members moved quickly to keep the momentum for NEPA change rolling. The House Natural Resources Committee selected a new chair, Richard Pombo (R-CA) to replace retired James Hansen (R-UT), and newly elected members picked up where the 107th had left off. The administration seemed to have toned down its rhetoric, but conservative members of Congress continued to frame the appeals process as a problem that could be blamed on environmental groups. Newly elected member Rick Renzi (R-AZ) called for an end to "obstructionist environmentalists" and declared that "not to thin [the forests] is a sin." Renzi repeated the "common sense" phrasing used by Bush in August 2002 and Connaughton in December 2002.[22] This phrasing was not accidental. One of nine principles in the Luntz memo emphasized using the "common sense solutions" theme. By implication, anyone who opposed the administration's proposals was *not* using common sense and was therefore unreasonable.

At the same time, timber industry representatives returned to the idea that existing administrative regulations were still the major cause of wildfires. "We have so many overlapping regulatory requirements that it's impossible for professional managers to do what's necessary to create forests that are resilient and resistant to catastrophic fire," said David Bischel of the California Forestry Association.[23]

By February 2003, the agenda setting process revved up again as a result of three other focusing events: concerns about North Korea's nuclear power capacity, U.S. buildup of troops and materiel in the Persian Gulf in preparation for war with Iraq, and explosion of the space shuttle Columbia. The high visibility of all three of these crises pushed forest reform off the governmental agenda, at least for the short term. But even during the first few months of 2003, officials warned that the 2003 fire season was likely to start earlier and be more intense because of a massive insect infestation that had killed or damaged trees, underscoring the belief that legislative action must be swift to deal with the inevitable catastrophic fires.

Reps. Mark Udall and Tom Udall were the first to introduce their measure on February 27, 2003 (H.R. 1042), followed by Reps. Miller and DeFazio on April 3 (H.R. 1621—The Federal Lands Hazardous Fuels Reduction Act of 2003). All four members had been active in the debates during the 107th Congress, so it was not unexpected that they would jump back into the fracas with the new Congress. The House Committee on Resources staff requested an analysis of the bills from the Congressional Research Service, comparing them to a bill that was soon to be introduced by Rep. McInnis. The report noted that the three bills were significantly different from one another, but they all focused on the same key issues, including priorities for fuel reduction activities, environmental considerations under NEPA and other statutes, and public involvement (especially appeals).[24]

THE 2003 GAO REPORT

Members of Congress may have postponed new action on legislation to implement the president's Healthy Forest Initiative while they waited for results of another GAO study on decisions involving fuels reduction activities. The study had been requested in summer 2002 by Rep. McInnis, chair of the Forests and Forest Health Subcommittee of the House Committee on Resources; Sen. Craig, now chair of the Subcommittee on Public Lands and Forests of the Senate Energy and Natural Resources Committee; and Sen. Bingaman, now ranking member of the Senate committee.[25]

Like previous GAO studies, the May 14, 2003, report to requestors explored dangerous forest conditions caused by decades of fire suppression policies, implementation of the National Fire Plan, and possible delays in implementing specific forest fuels reduction projects because of appeals and litigation. Acknowledging the limited nature of the August 31, 2001, report, the GAO also noted that the 2002 Forest Service study had resulted in different analytical results. The GAO had been instructed by the requestors to perform a more comprehensive analysis—still another attempt by congressional members to find statistical data to back up the reform rationale.

In the new study, the GAO looked at a much broader range of data than it had in 2001 and took almost a year to release its findings. The study examined the following items:

- number of decisions involving fuels reduction activities and the number of acres affected in fiscal years 2001 and 2002;

- number of decisions appealed and/or litigated and the number of acres affected in fiscal years 2001 and 2002;

- outcomes of the appealed and/or litigated decisions and names of appellants and plaintiffs;

- whether appeals were processed within prescribed time frames;

- number of acres treated or planned to be treated by each of the fuels reduction methods; and

- number of decisions involving fuels reduction activities in the wildland-urban interface and inventoried roadless areas.[26]

The survey's methodology included all 155 national forests, with a 100 percent response rate. The GAO worked with other parties to verify 10 percent of decisions for accuracy but in a congressional briefing on May 9, 2003, acknowledged that the verification process was not yet complete. The report further noted that information provided was self-reported and so the agency was not able to independently ensure that all decisions were reported. As had been the case with other studies, the GAO also said that lack of a common Forest Service definition of "fuels reduction activity" or "wildland-urban interface" may have resulted in inconsistent data. In a footnote, the GAO noted various types of activities that were considered to be "fuels reduction" methods, including prescribed burning, mechanical treatment (bulldozers, chainsaws, chippers, mulchers), chemical/ herbicide treatment, and grazing.[27]

A brief synopsis of the GAO study's findings identified 762 decisions involving fuels reduction activities covering 4.7 million acres. Of those decisions 180 were appealed affecting nine hundred thousand acres and representing 24 percent of all decisions or 59 percent of appealable decisions. The differentiation was the result of decisions on projects that were categorically excluded from the require-ment to prepare an EIS, which are not appealable, and represented 457 decisions covering three million acres. Of the 762 decisions, 23, or 3 percent, were litigated, affecting one hundred thousand acres. Of the 180 appealed decisions, 133 required no change before implementation (affirming the Forest Service's original decision); 16 were modified to some degree; 19 were reversed, and 12 were withdrawn by the Forest Service.

During the study period, eighty-four interest groups and thirty-nine private individuals appeared as appellants. Seven groups appeared as appellants twenty or more times: Alliance for the Wild Rockies, The Ecology Center, Forest Conservation Council, Lands Council, National Forest Protection Alliance, Oregon Natural Resources Council, and Sierra Club. Of the twenty-three litigated decisions, ten were still in the courts at the time the survey was conducted; five had been settled by agreement of the parties; three had been reversed, overturning the Forest Service's decision; one was upheld by the court; and the outcomes of four others were unknown. Plaintiffs consisted of twenty-seven interest groups and one private individual; five groups appeared as plaintiffs in four or more decisions: The Ecology Center, Sierra Club, Oregon Natural Resources Council, Hell's Canyon Preservation Council, and Native Ecosystems Council.

Regarding the time frame for appeals, 79 percent were processed during the prescribed 90-day time period. In those cases where the time frame was exceeded, staff members cited as reasons inadequate staffing, insufficient staff around the holiday season, and a backlog of appeals. For some appeals, settlement was imminent.[28]

The Forest Service was invited to review and comment on the GAO report and generally agreed with the information presented. One methodological point of contention involved a one-million-acre personal-use firewood program that the agency felt skewed the results, but GAO included it because the Forest Service had reported and documented it as a fuels reduction project.[29]

Although the GAO report had long been anticipated by stakeholders on all sides of the fire-appeals policy debate, its findings produced little response, perhaps because it corroborated information in previous research or because it failed to provide a rationale for reform as some lawmakers had hoped. The lack of commentary might also have been the result of caveats included in the GAO's commentary, which some observers felt made the findings less useful. In any case, reaction was as might have been expected, with Republican members of Congress spinning the findings one way and environmental groups using the same data to support their opposing contentions. Sen. Craig, one of the report's requestors, referred to the GAO study as peeling "back the bark of the tree to reveal the disease ridden underside of the appeals system. Actions speak louder than words, and the actions of these preservation organizations show a pattern of obstruction and false pretense when it comes to fuel reduction projects." The senator noted, too, that in Montana and Northern Idaho 90 percent of important hazardous fuels reduction projects had been appealed, and only 10 percent of the 180 wildfire mitigation projects were reversed, suggesting to Craig that many of the other 160 appeals were frivolous.[30]

In contrast, the Native Forest Network, based in Missoula, Montana, reported that the study showed 95 percent of the 762 Forest Service fuels reduction projects were ready for implementation within the standard 90-day review period.[31] One of the more moderate environmental groups, the Grand Canyon Trust, noted that the GAO's statistics "cast serious doubt on the assertion that environmentalists and environmental regulations are impeding the Forest Service's ability to implement hazardous fuels reduction projects."[32]

2003 CONGRESSIONAL LEGISLATION

Reps. Walden and McInnis did not wait for the GAO study to be released before introducing the Healthy Forests Restoration Act of 2003 (H.R. 1904). The measure focused on hazardous fuels reduction projects on twenty million acres in national forests and on Bureau of Land Management lands near municipal water sources and communities in the wildland-urban interface. The Walden/McInnis bill codified recommendations in the Western Governors' Association's Ten-Year Strategy, including prioritization for funding projects in the wildland-urban interface. It authorized $50 million to establish two biomass grant programs, along with $15 million to create the Watershed Forestry Assistance Cost-Share Program, which would provide financial and technical support to private landowners for protecting and improving municipal drinking water supplies. It also called for the creation of a habitat restoration program to restore forested habitats for rare and endangered species on private lands.

The most controversial elements dealt with NEPA, appeals, and judicial review of projects. Although agencies would have to perform a full environmental analysis of projects, the bill lifted the requirement that agencies analyze alternatives to proposed projects. It called for developing a new appeals process open only to those who submitted specific and substantive written comments during the preparation stage of the project, thereby limiting public participation. Judicial review would be expedited by establishing a 15-day filing deadline for lawsuits, a 45-day limit on preliminary injunctions, and encouraging completion of proceedings within 100 days. Mark Rey, undersecretary for natural resources and environment in the Department of Agriculture, said the exclusion from NEPA and judicial restrictions were needed to "balance the proposition that you cannot uncut a tree and you cannot unburn a forest."[33]

To obtain the necessary Democratic support for their bill, McInnis and Walden tried a new strategy to expand the issue beyond the West. In discussions with their colleagues, they discovered that a number of members represented districts with massive insect infestations that posed a threat to timber operations. The House bill was redrafted with the cooperation of Bush administration officials to include new sections calling for university research on forest pests that infiltrated areas from Florida to Minnesota and authorizing "such sums as may be necessary." The new language satisfied Rep. Charles Stenholm (D-TX), ranking member of the Agriculture Committee, and Rep. James Oberstar (D-MN), ranking member of the Transportation Committee. In Walden's words, "That's the section that really drives those guys. We built a different, successful coalition."[34]

H.R. 1904 moved through the House with amazing alacrity, while the two competing measures, H.R. 1042 and H.R. 1621, seemed to languish. The Walden/McInnis bill was introduced April 25 to the House Resources Committee and approved in draft form on April 30 by a vote of 32-17 after Reps. Miller, Mark Udall, and Steve Pearce (R-NM) failed in their attempts to amend the bill.[35] It was formally introduced on May 1 for referral to the House Agriculture Committee, then approved on May 9 on a voice vote and without amendment. It reached the House floor on May 20 and, after discussion of an unsuccessful amendment by Rep. Miller, was passed on a vote of 256-170 with the help of forty-two Democrats. It had been supported by the National Association of State

Foresters, the Society of American Foresters, and other forest and paper products organizations.

SENATE ACTION

The Senate's consideration of forest legislation in the 108th Congress was more protracted and contentious for several reasons. Changes in leadership resulting from the 2000 election put the fate of many environmental initiatives into the hands of Republicans with a more conservative agenda, as rated by the League of Conservation Voters scores. The chair of the Senate Energy and Natural Resources Committee, Sen. Bingaman, handed over the gavel to Sen. Domenici; Sen. Wyden gave up his chairmanship of the Public Lands and Forests Subcommittee to Sen. Craig.[36] Upon becoming chair of the committee, Domenici declared healthy forests legislation one of his top three priorities, and in May 2003 said he and Sen. Craig would introduce legislation reflecting the goals of the president's forest agenda and H.R. 1904.[37]

Another action that affected the progress of forest reform in the Senate was the referral process. The Walden/McInnis bill was referred initially to the Senate Committee on Agriculture, Nutrition, and Forestry, where southern and midwestern Democrats had already indicated their support for H.R. 1904. Complicating matters further, Sens. Daschle and Bingaman offered their own version of a forest reform measure, as did Sens. Wyden and Feinstein. Those two bills were referred to the Senate Committee on Energy and Natural Resources, rather than to Agriculture, Nutrition, and Forestry. This created a jurisdictional battle over forest health issues between two powerful committees and competing Senate measures significantly different from the House bill. Sen Craig, who had also announced his intention to sponsor a forest-thinning measure, said he was withdrawing his plan because of concerns it would be watered down or excluded altogether from the 2003 Interior spending bill.[38]

When the Senate Agriculture Committee held its first hearing on June 26, 2003, Sen. John McCain (R-AZ) acknowledged that although there were disagreements over the provisions of the House bill, the Senate needed to work aggressively to forge agreement on how to address the growing threat of wildfire. "We face a major crisis," McCain said. "I can not go back to Arizona, look those citizens in the eye and say, 'We have taken sufficient measures to prevent future occurrences of this nature.'"[39] Much of the hearing testimony centered around differing perspectives by researchers. One committee hearing witness, Dr. Norman Christensen of Duke University, said he supported the intent of the bill but thought it could be improved by more specifically identifying what types of hazardous fuels reduction projects should be the priority. Another scientist, Dr. Hal Salwasser of Oregon State University, noted that the science on how to manage lands afflicted by drought, fire suppression, and insect infestation is unclear. "Science tells us what the problems are but science does not have all the solutions yet."[40]

At its July 24 full committee business meeting, Chair Thad Cochran (R-MS) gathered sufficient support to pass the bill out of committee, with the chair's markup, on a voice vote. The chair acknowledged the committee's awareness that there was a desire to substantially amend H.R. 1904, but that it had chosen instead to allow further discussion in the full Senate.

The threat of continuing wildfires and necessity for rapid response, although traditionally persuasive, did not stop the Senate from taking time to consider legislation proposed by its own members. The Daschle/Bingaman proposal, S. 1314 (the Collaborative Forest Health Act), had been introduced June 23, 2003. The bill differed from the Walden/McInnis measure by attempting to define the wildland-urban interface as lands within one-half mile of an at-risk community and within municipal watersheds. It called for eliminating environmental documentation for relatively small projects within the wildland-urban interface or municipal watersheds and required that at least 70 percent of funds be spent within the one-half-mile boundary. This bill kept intact the existing appeals process and judicial review, except for categorical exclusions, and directed an annual appropriation of $25 million for research on damaging insects, best management practices for thinning and prescribed fire, and development of new technology and markets for valued-added products. It did not address the issues of habitat restoration, watershed assistance, or biomass projects.

A second Senate bill, S. 1352, was introduced as the Community and Forest Protection Act on June 26, 2003, by Sens. Wyden and Feinstein. The bill authorized up to $3.8 billion over five years to thin areas within the wildland-urban interface. It differed from the Daschle/Bingaman bill by widening the interface to an area between one-half mile and three-quarters mile from community boundaries. Within that area, forest thinning projects could be undertaken without extensive environmental analysis; outside the interface, a full NEPA review would be required. Although it added additional requirements for scoping and public notice prior to environmental review, once a decision on a project was rendered, the public would have only thirty days in which to appeal. Regarding judicial review, it required lawsuits to be filed in the federal court where the project is located and encouraged, but did not require, expeditious judicial review.

Like the Daschle/Bingaman proposal, S. 1352 required at least 70 percent of the funds to be spent within the interface area but also allowed a governor to petition for adjustment down to 50 percent. Insect infestation was addressed in the plan by proposing that a center be established in Prineville, Oregon (Wyden's home state), to evaluate current and future forest health conditions. Like S. 1314, it also made no provision for watershed assistance, habitat restoration, or biomass projects.

A third bill sponsored by Sen. Patrick Leahy (D-VT), S. 1453, was introduced on July 24, 2003. Called the Forestry and Community Assistance Act of 2003, S. 1453 focused on the wildland-urban interface (defined as within one-half mile of at-risk communities) by establishing a watershed forestry assistance program through state foresters, a healthy forests reserve program to promote the recovery of endangered species, and incentives to promote investment in community development and private enterprise, including small forest products businesses.

Even though the Senate bills had much in common, the Wyden/Feinstein measure appeared to have the most support within the Senate itself and among environmental organizations. But at the July 22 Senate Energy and Natural Resources Committee hearing on all three legislative proposals, testimony focused on the Walden/McInnis bill and the need for immediate attention to wildfire threats rather than support for either of the Senate measures.

Undersecretary Mark Rey spoke on behalf of both the Departments of Agriculture and Interior in supporting H.R. 1904 and opposing S. 1314 and S. 1352 because those proposals were considered too narrow. In a statement on behalf of the Western Governors' Association, witnesses called for Congress to work with them on the Ten-Year Comprehensive Strategy and Implementation Plan.

From the research and environmental communities, Dr. Wallace Covington of Northern Arizona University called for large-scale restoration-based fuel treatments instead of just thinning trees, while Tom Robinson of the Grand Canyon Trust spoke on NEPA planning, prioritization of projects, and ecological restoration. Laura McCarthy of the group Forest Trust cautioned the committee about the inconclusiveness of current studies on the role of thinning and supported the plans developed by the Western Governors' Association. She cited both the GAO study and our NAU study as indications that appeals were not causing significant delays in project implementation. One of the few to directly support the Walden/McInnis bill, Bruce Vincent, a logging company owner from Libby, Montana, called upon Senate members to use mechanical removal of forest fuels, along with prescribed fire. "It is physically possible to restore the health of the forests of our nation. The question before you is whether or not it is politically possible."[41]

Two former chiefs of the U.S. Forest Service entered the public debate in August with a simple prescription: "It is time to declare old growth off-limits to logging and move on." The comments, from Mike Dombeck and Jack Ward Thomas, noted that the forest policy debate "is draining time, money, energy and political capital needed to address more pressing problems. Forest management should focus on restoring forest health and reducing fire risk, initially in areas where risk to human life and property are greatest. Then, appropriate management practices should be strategically targeted in the right places and at the right scales across the landscape." The men called upon those who had fought to protect old growth in the past to now support forest management, including thinning, to address forest health problems.[42]

ATTEMPTS AT LEGISLATIVE COMPROMISE

President Bush and Forest Service officials attempted to keep the spotlight on the House bill, virtually ignoring the Senate proposals and public criticism. In visits to communities ravaged by the summer's wildfires and in public addresses, Bush repeatedly referred to the McInnis bill, urging Senate passage when senators returned from their August recess. An interesting twist developed in September when Rep. McInnis announced he would not seek re-election. As a six-term member and chair of the Forests and Forest Health Subcommittee, he had been the key steward of the president's legislative package and a spokesman for Colorado's interests on natural resources and public lands issues. The healthy forests bill would be a way for McInnis to leave the House with an important legacy, and there was speculation that he might run for governor or the Senate.[43]

In late September, a group of ten senators (six Republicans and four Democrats) announced that they had reached an initial agreement on changes to H.R. 1904. The compromise package, in the form of a substitute for the bill, called for half of funds earmarked for forest thinning to be spent in forested areas closest to population centers and for judges to consider long-term damage from wildfire against shorter-term damage from selective logging, prescribed burns, and overgrown forests. The bill authorized $760 million for each fiscal year to implement hazardous fuels reduction activities. The measure also removed a controversial section of the Bush administration plan that would require judges to defer to the expertise of the U.S. Forest Service and other land management agencies.[44]

Environmental groups criticized the substitute bill on several fronts. They noted that the 50 percent split of funds between the wildland-urban interface and land outside the interface was too discretionary, and that the Secretaries of Interior and Agriculture could allocate the funds as they wished because the requirements only applied at the national level. The concern was that this would allow federal agencies to further subsidize logging and logging road construction on remote forest lands. Criticism also was leveled at the definition of the wildland-urban interface, which was expanded to include not only the one-half mile area around an at-risk community but also "an area within or adjacent to" an at-risk community. Leaders feared this created a loophole that would allow logging projects in roadless areas and ancient forests where commercial timber sales would be most lucrative.[45] Other environmental leaders showed little enthusiasm for the compromise. Sean Cosgrove, national forest policy specialist with the Sierra Club, and Todd Schulke, forest policy director for the Center for Biological Diversity, characterized the measure as a "nothing burger" that was merely a "repackaging" of the Bush initiative.[46]

Critics also assailed proposed changes in public participation in hazardous fuels reduction projects. The measure gave the Secretary of Agriculture thirty days after enactment of the statute to promulgate interim final regulations establishing a pre-decisional administrative review process, which would begin after completing an environmental assessment or environmental impact statement and end not later than the date of issuing the final decision approving the project. The interim regulations would be replaced by final rules after "a reasonable time has been provided for public comment."[47]

The Forest Stewards Guild, a national organization of more than five hundred foresters, lobbied the Senate to reject H.R. 1904, noting "the end result will set back the course of excellent forestry for years to come." The group focused their criticisms on the bill's failure to provide a vision of public stewardship and reliance on intensive harvesting in the short-term without addressing the long-term maintenance of healthy forests to ensure control of new fuel accumulation.[48]

The compromise also limited the number of alternatives that could be considered in an EA or EIS. Those opposing the bill said that data did not indicate that limiting the number of alternatives would increase the effectiveness or efficiency of planning and implementing a project, and that it was "contrary to the basic concepts of the National Environmental Policy Act, which is to provide for meaningful public involvement and thorough analysis."[49]

Another important change required any person bringing a civil action challenging a hazardous fuels reduction project to first exhaust the administrative review process. But it eliminated more specific elements of the Bush proposal that required appellants to submit specific and substantive written comments during the notice and comment stage of the project. For those seeking injunctive relief and stays pending appeal, the compromise set a 60-day limit and allowed the court to issue renewals of any preliminary injunction if the parties presented updated information on the status of the project.

Although timber groups generally supported the compromise version, they suggested ways to strengthen the bill. The nation's oldest conservation group, American Forests, sought a multiparty monitoring process "to help build trust and understanding among diverse interests about the effects of these projects, as well as increase trust in the project and monitoring activities of the federal agencies." The organization also recommended ways to strengthen the link to rural forest communities.[50] Arizona governor Janet Napolitano and New Mexico governor Bill Richardson sent a joint letter urging the Senate to require removal of slash, clarify language on old-growth stands, and allocate 70 percent of funds for the interface.[51]

Virtually lost in the discussion was the October release of the final version of the GAO survey of appeals and litigation of fuels reduction activities that had originally been issued in May 2003 as preliminary information. The agency's report, which covered fiscal years 2001 and 2002, concluded that of the 818 decisions involving fuels reduction activities, about 24 percent were appealed. Of the 818 decisions, more than half could not be appealed because they involved activities with little or no environmental impact. The study also found that about 79 percent of the appeals were processed within the prescribed 90-day time frame, with the remainder processed within 91 to 241 days. Only 3 percent of decisions were litigated.[52]

The report's appendix on scope and methodology began by noting that the Forest Service does not maintain its own database and that an agency contact person provided responses to the survey, addressed follow-up questions, and provided requested documents. The GAO verified about 10 percent of the survey responses for accuracy (eighty-five decisions) and determined that the data submitted were generally reliable. As had been the case with its previous reports on administrative appeals, the GAO noted inconsistencies and lack of uniform definitions in the data reported to the agency by the Forest Service. "There are some limitations to the data we gathered. As with any survey, the information obtained from the national forests was self-reported, and we were not able to independently ensure that all decisions were reported."[53]

The lack of interest in the final GAO report can be attributed to several factors. First, the preliminary May report had already indicated overall trends in appeals and litigation, so the October final report simply reiterated already available information. Second, environmental organizations may have felt that the report's results were moot because the Healthy Forest Restoration Act had already been passed by the House and was close to passage in the Senate. Third, supporters of the administration's package probably did not want to focus on the fact that, once again, a government study had found that few fuel reduction projects had been appealed, contrary to the rhetoric heard for the previous two years. Finally, most of those interested in this issue were busy lobbying the Senate rather than attempting to analyze the nearly 100-page document.

In late October, Sen. Cochran, head of the Agriculture Committee, attempted to bring the substitute bill to the Senate floor for debate. But the compromise language did not satisfy Sen. Bingaman, ranking Democrat on the Energy and Natural Resources committee, or Sen. Tom Harkin (D-Iowa), the ranking Democrat on the Agriculture Committee, who put a hold on the measure until it could be heard by their respective committees. A Bingaman staffer said, "We're not putting a hold on it forever. We're not trying to be obstructionists. The truth of the matter is we're having a hard time making heads or tails out of this text."[54] McInnis saw it differently. "Exactly five months after a bipartisan majority acted in the House, the Senate itself has been crippled by a couple of Democratic Senators whose passion for appeals and lawsuits obviously trumps their alleged love of the forests."[55]

The last week of October 2003 saw a flurry of efforts to push the compromise measure to the Senate floor. Republicans agreed not to limit amendments to the bill; both Majority Leader Bill Frist (R-TN) and Minority Leader Daschle said action was urgent. "The risks of delay are simply too high."[56] The alacrity of the Senate was largely in response to the massive wildfires that were ravaging hundreds of thousands of acres in southern California.

Ironically, most devastation occurred in urban communities far from forests or on private land that would not be covered under the healthy forests bill. The multimillion-dollar homes of California's Scripps Ranch and the houses of blue-collar workers in Del Rosa would not likely have been saved had the legislation been enacted earlier. Neither area was part of the dense chaparral wildland-urban interface; much of the rest of the landscape that was burned had not been subject to the Forest Service administrative appeals process that was blamed for "analysis paralysis." In San Bernardino, fire whipped through canyons and washes with non-native eucalyptus trees, bamboo, oleander, and olive trees, and through backyards overgrown and filled with flammable debris.

The *Washington Post* made note of this fact in an editorial in which it urged Congress "to encourage the Forest Service to spend whatever money it does have on brush clearing projects closer to human communities."[57] The *Los Angeles Times* echoed those sentiments. "If we're going to be dumb enough to continue building in high-fire-danger areas, brush needs to be cleared to prevent the spread of killer blazes."[58] Another article noted that the burned acreage was in areas that get comparatively little funding to reduce the threat of fires and, even when money was available for brush clearning, "there is no blueprint for keeping it in check for long. Cut back, and it quickly regrows. Try to carefully burn it, and homeowners and air-quality officials often resist."[59]

In the resort community of Lake Arrowhead, fire suppression efforts had begun in the early 1900s, when a dam was built to create the lake. Thousands of vacation cabins began to spring up in the 1920s and 1930s, and any fires were quickly extinguished. By the 1970s and 1980s, homeowners' associations ringed the lake and required residents to obtain permits to cut down even a single tree on their property. Even Forest Service officials admit that thinning was not an option because of public opinion. "People didn't move there to be next to a logging operation," one spokesperson said.[60]

But the blazes were sufficient reason for the Senate to vote 97-1 in favor of Cochran's amendment to replace the original bill with the compromise agreement; the only dissenter was Sen. Jack Reed (D-RI), who an aide said thought the bill went too far in limiting public participation in decisions on forest policy. Other successful amendments allowed OSHA to monitor long-term health of fire fighters; authorized $8 million to provide EPA regional offices with equipment to monitor hazardous air pollutants and report information on Web sites on a daily basis; required best-value contracting criteria in awarding contracts and agreements; and required collaborative monitoring of forest management projects on public lands. The final amendment package was passed in the Senate by a vote of 80-14 and sent on to a conference committee to reconcile differences between the Senate and House versions of the bill.

"A LIGHT AT THE END OF THE TUNNEL"

The House responded by rejecting the Senate version and voted for a nonbinding motion asking conferees to approve a conference report by November 13 in order to get a bill to President Bush by the end of November. The deadline was proposed to allow the Forest Service to use the expedited measures for fuel reduction before the 2004 fire season.

Reaction to the amended bill's passage was as expected. President Bush issued a news release commending the Senate for their "bipartisan support for this commonsense legislation," and urged the House and Senate to quickly resolve the differences in their bills.[61] The unions of the Forest Products Industry National Labor Management Committee applauded the "active management of America's public forests based on science, not emotions and lawsuits. Passage of this legislation will lead to job security for forest-dependent communities and families."[62] Rep. Walden referred to the measure as *his* Healthy Forests Restoration Act and said he had received assurances from the Speaker of the House that they would move quickly on a final version of the bill.[63] One newspaper voiced its opposition to the bill when it praised Rep. Wyden for "answering the call" and risking "the wrath of his party's environmentalists and his Senate leadership" by voting against the proposed amendments to the bill.[64]

The House appointed its eighteen conferees on November 6, but procedural bickering delayed the naming of Senate conferees after the House formally rejected the Senate compromise bill. To break the stalemate, members agreed to begin informal discussions on outstanding issues outside of a formal conference. Sens. Feinstein and Wyden lashed out at "partisan skirmishing," warning that they and other Senate Democrats would vote against a conference report if it included House language they deemed unacceptable on environmental and funding issues.[65] On November 19, House Resources chair Pombo announced that a compromise had been reached in bicameral—but informal—negotiations, allowing the Senate to appoint its seven conferees. "We have a light at the end of the tunnel," Pombo said. "This bipartisan agreement puts the Healthy Forests legislation within reach of the White House."[66] Rep. Bob Goodlatte (R-VA), chair of the House Agriculture Committee and Chair of the House conferees, called the final agreement a "historic event. The last time House and Senate conferees reported a major forestry bill, today's large trees were saplings. This bill creates the first real relief from bureaucratic gridlock after over eight years of legislative effort."[67]

The House passed the conference committee compromise by a vote of 286-140 on November 21, and the Senate agreed to the conference report on a voice vote, paving the way for the president to sign the bill into law. Most lawmakers lauded the efforts of those who had worked on the bill and cited its importance in forest policy. Rep. Walden, one of the major players in the compromise negotiations, called the vote "a tremendous victory for our forests, watersheds, critical species habitats and rural communities. Considering the many years we have invested in this effort, today's action is truly a watershed moment." Other members said the agreement was "long overdue," "landmark lands legislation," and "the cure we need for the paralysis by analysis that plagues our nation's forests."[68]

In its final form, the Senate amendments struck out all of the text of H.R. 1904, which was then agreed to by the House. Much of the final negotiations on the conference report focused on provisions for hazardous fuels reduction and the definition of wildland-urban interface.

As passed, the Healthy Forests Restoration Act has six titles and includes the following major provisions.

TITLE I: HAZARDOUS FUEL REDUCTION ON FEDERAL LAND

Defines the wildland-urban interface (accepting the Senate definitions); limits the acreage available for hazardous fuel reduction projects to twenty million acres; emphasizes old-growth and large-tree retention except stands at risk of windthrow, insects, or disease; gives funding priority for hazardous fuels reduction projects to communities that have adopted wildfire protection plans; provides special expedited environmental analysis processes for projects within the 1.5 miles of at-risk communities; allows the respective departmental secretaries to utilize multiparty monitoring with diverse stakeholders; directs the Secretary of Agriculture to establish interim regulations within thirty days after enactment to establish a pre-decisional administrative review process to serve as the sole means by which a person can seek review of a project, with final regulations to be established after public comment; provides that a person can bring a civil action challenging a project if the issue was raised during the administrative process and the person has exhausted the administrative review process; requires lawsuits challenging a hazardous fuels reduction project to be filed only in the U.S. District Court in which the federal land to be treated is located; limits preliminary injunctions to sixty days (renewable with reporting requirements); directs the court to balance the impact to the ecosystem against the impacts of not undertaking the project; and authorizes $760 million annually for hazardous fuels reduction activities covered by the act.

TITLE II: BIOMASS

Establishes biomass commercial use and value-added grant programs to facility operators to produce energy from biomass; increases authorization levels for research in biomass/small-log utilization; establishes a program to create new small-scale businesses and community-based enterprises that use biomass and small-diameter materials; and authorizes funding at $5 million for fiscal years 2004–2008 to promote existing biomass utilization facilities.

TITLE III: WATERSHED FORESTRY ASSISTANCE

Establishes the Watershed Forestry Assistance Program to assist state foresters in expanding stewardship capacities to address watershed issues on non-industrial private forest lands and authorizes $15 million for this program for each of fiscal years 2004 through 2008; and directs the Secretary of Agriculture to provide assistance to Indian tribes for expanding forestry projects and authorizes $2.5 million for assistance to tribes for fiscal years 2004–2008.

TITLE IV: INSECT INFESTATIONS AND RELATED DISEASES

Establishes a program for gathering information on damaging insects and for assisting landowners with treatments and strategies for reducing pest/disease problems; allows for applied silvicultural assessments (including timber harvesting, thinning, prescribed fire, and pruning) for research and information gathering purposes on federal lands at risk for insect infestation and associated diseases; and excludes from NEPA analysis projects to treat infestations on up to one thousand acres.

TITLE V: HEALTHY FORESTS RESERVE PROGRAM
Directs the Secretary of Agriculture to establish a program to protect, restore, and enhance forest ecosystems to promote the recovery of endangered species, improve biodiversity, and enhance carbon sequestration; establishes a maximum enrollment of two million acres; protects and compensates landowners for any costs related to compliance with the ESA; provides landowners with technical assistance for restoration planning; and authorizes funding of $15 million per year through fiscal year 2008.

TITLE VI: MISCELLANEOUS PROVISIONS (FOREST MONITORING AND RISK ASSESSMENT)
Instructs the Secretary of Agriculture to carry out a program to inventory and monitor forest stands on national forests and private lands (with owner consent); and authorizes $5 million per year for fiscal years 2004 to 2008.

WINNERS AND LOSERS?

With the signing of the bill on December 3, 2003, the Bush administration was the biggest winner, because the president had placed his Healthy Forests Initiative on the top of his environmental agenda. Although the compromise language did not include all elements announced in his August 2002 proposal, the timing of the final measure was crucial, coming just weeks after the disastrous southern California wildfires and just before Congress ended the session for its holiday recess. Media headlines referred to the measure as "forest thinning" rather than focusing on the more controversial aspects of public participation and old growth and clearly linked the passage of the measure by Congress to the October/November wildfires in southern California. In a White House fact sheet released on the day the bill was signed, the president referred to the fact that "[i]n the past two years alone, 147,049 fires burned nearly eleven million acres."[69]

Bush could claim this as a major victory on the domestic front while his foreign policy and the ongoing struggle in Iraq were facing heavy criticism both at home and abroad. Although Democratic presidential hopefuls had been left out of the debate, western Senate Democrats like California's Dianne Feinstein could claim credit for brokering the compromise. The Democrats could also claim to have been successful in killing the more egregious public involvement limitations while furthering the goals of healthy forests and forest restoration.

Other winners included House Republicans who had jumped on the Healthy Forests bandwagon early on, including Arizona freshman Rick Renzi, who was facing a well-supported contender in his first re-election bid; outgoing Rep. Scott

McInnis, who could point to the measure as part of his political legacy as he pondered other political opportunities; and House Resources Committee chair Richard Pombo. Even though the compromise bill reflected many of the concessions demanded by Democrats in the Senate, House members could boast that they had been first up with a credible proposal supported by the administration.

Industry groups and professional associations congratulated themselves for their strong support of the president, hoping that implementation of the compromise would tilt future timber activities in their favor. Others welcomed the powers returned to forest managers. The executive director of the Society of American Foresters said the bill "is an important step in a long-term effort that is needed to allow forest managers to be able to address the forest health crisis on our nation's forests,"[70] while the president of the American Forest & Paper Association noted, "Federal land managers will now have the tools they need to address the forest health crisis that has resulted in the destruction of millions of acres of public and private forestland, not to mention the loss of homes and other property resulting from catastrophic wildfire."[71]

Another obvious winner was the Forest Service, which had finally found some relief from its historic appeals problem. The agency, whose management discretion had generally been circumscribed by legislation such as NEPA, NFMA, and the Endangered Species Act, had now regained part of that lost discretion and would have greater flexibility to push forward its plans and preferences. However, the price of greater managerial discretion and fewer constraints imposed by public participation may also have been lost opportunities for the agency to build upon the broad social consensus among major stakeholders that there is a problem and forge a meaningful and enduring social consensus with those stakeholders about what exactly should be done about it. Finally, HFRA gave both the Forest Service and the Bureau of Land Management additional program authorities and held out the promise of additional appropriations for much needed fuels reduction activities.

The major environmental organizations retained their strident opposition to the bill, although some privately admitted that the damage could have been much worse. Considered a giveaway to the logging industry, the Sierra Club's forest policy specialist said, "This isn't compromise, it's surrender to the Bush administration and timber companies, who apparently have no interest in protecting communities from forest fires."[72] Similar sentiments were expressed by the National Environmental Trust. "This bill provides a false sense of security for the American people. Congress has let politics and scare tactics drive a wildfire policy that only serves the needs of the timber industry while ignoring the needs of the community."[73]

Other smaller interests found that their concerns, attached as part of the Senate compromise language in Title VI, became "junk in the trunk" as the conferees struck provisions related to a public land corps that would enlist the help of disadvantaged young people to carry out rehabilitation projects; a rural community forestry enterprise program; a program to monitor the long-term medical health of fire fighters; a mobile air pollution monitoring network for disaster areas; financial assistance for conservation of lands and natural resources in the Highlands region; a program for emergency treatment and reduction of nonnative invasive plants; establishment of a national agroforestry center and a research center for uplands hardwood research; grants for an emergency fuels reduction program; grants to the Eastern Nevada Landscape Coalition; a "sense of Congress" reaffirmation of the importance of enhanced community fire protection programs; use of best-value contracting; establishment of a suburban and community forestry and open space program; requirements related to wildland fire fighter training for private entities; modifications of the Green Mountain National Forest boundaries; efforts to acquire and manage caves in the Karst Region of Puerto Rico; provisions related to the Farm Security and Rural Investment Act; enforcement of cockfighting prohibitions; and changes in fines for violations of public land regulations during a fire ban. These add-ons were estimated to cost an additional $630 million to $1 billion over the next five years.[74]

Unwilling to declare total defeat, a few organizations called for extensive monitoring of the act's implementation. "The Nature Conservancy calls on government agencies, local communities, industry and private conservation groups to work together to ensure that the law is implemented in a way that protects human life while also restoring the health of the nation's forest ecosystems," one press release noted.[75] Groups like the Native Forest Network and the Natural Resources Defense Council said they would "watch closely" and "do everything in our power to stop projects that don't protect communities or restore our public forests."[76] A Wilderness Society spokesperson said, "It is a less than perfect bill that leaves the Forest Service a huge responsibility to do the honorable thing. It's going to take vigilance as it's implemented."[77]

NOTES

1. Jerry F. Franklin and James K. Agree, "Forging a Science-Based National Forest Fire Policy," *Issues in Science and Technology Online* (2003), at www.issues.org/issues/20.1/franklin accessed October 1, 2004.

2. See, for example, Thomas Sterner, *Policy Instruments for Environmental and Natural Resource Management* (Washington, DC: Resources for the Future Press, 2003), 194.

3. An analysis of these measures can be found in Ross W. Gorte, *Report to Congress: Wildfire Protection: Current Issues and Legislation in the 107th Congress* (Washington, DC: Congressional Research Service, January 21, 2003).

4. Sierra Club, Letter to the Editor, "Protect National Forests" (July 26, 2002), at www.sierraclub.org/logging/fires_july accessed July 31, 2002.

5. "Politics Returns in Forest Fire Debate," *New York Times* (September 19, 2002), at www.nytimes.com/2002/09/19/politics accessed September 19, 2002.

6. "USDA and DOI Deliver Legislation to Implement President's Healthy Forests Initiative," News release (September 5, 2002), at www.doi.gov/news/020905 accessed September 7, 2002.

7. Sherry Devlin, "Forest Chief Says '93 Appeals Law Should Be Axed," *The Missoulian* (September 12, 2002), at www.missoulian.com/archives/index accessed February 8, 2003.

8. Office of the Governor, "Owens: Changes in U.S. Forest Policies Long Overdue," News Release (August 22, 2002), at www.state.co.us/owenspress accessed August 26, 2002.

9. Jennifer McKee, "Martz: Ban Logging Appeals," *Billings Gazette* (August 22, 2002), at www.billingsgazette.com/index accessed August 26, 2002.

10. Rep. Scott McInnis, Opening Statement, H.R. 5319, The Healthy Forests Reforms Act, U.S. Congress, House, Committee on Resources Hearing on Initiatives for Wildfire Prevention (September 5, 2002), at www.house.gov/search accessed January 24, 2003.

11. Prepared Statement for the Record of Charles H. Burley for the American Forest Resource Council, U.S. Congress, House, Committee on Resources Hearing on Initiatives for Wildfire Prevention (September 5, 2002), at www.resourcescommittee.house.gov accessed January 25, 2003.

12. Testimony of Timothy H. Creal, Forest Counties Payment Committee, U.S. Congress, House, Committee on Resources Hearing on Initiatives for Wildfire Prevention (September 5, 2002), at www.house.gov/search accessed January 24, 2003.

13. Billy House, "Bush's Forest Plan Lands in House," *Arizona Republic* (September 6, 2002): B7.

14. Rep. George Miller, "Bi-Partisan Forest Management Policy Announcement," News Release (October 2, 2002), at www.biologicaldiversity.org/swcbd/Programs/fire/miller-pr accessed October 4, 2002.

15. Eric Pianin and Juliet Eilperin, "At Loggerheads Over Forest Plan," *Washington Post* (October 9, 2002): A29.

16. David W. Smith, President, Society of American Foresters, Letter to Hon. James Hansen (October 17, 2002).

17. Sherry Devlin, "Western Senators Prepare Forest Management Legislation," *The Missoulian* (September 11, 2002), at www.missoulian.com/articles/2002 accessed January 15, 2004.

18. Zachary Coile, "Sierra Club Board Blasts Feinstein on Logging," *San Francisco Chronicle* (September 24, 2002): A3, at www.sfgate.com accessed September 24, 2002.

19. Ibid.

20. Scott Sonner, "Sen. Feinstein Blames Sierra Club for Blocking Wildfire Bill," *San Francisco Chronicle* (November 1, 2002).

21. "Bush Administration Proposes Steps to Restore Forest and Rangeland Health," Joint press release (December 11, 2002), at www.usda.gov/news/releases/2002 accessed December 12, 2002.

22. Renzi's remarks were made at a town hall meeting in Flagstaff, Arizona, on February 1, 2003.

23. Glen Martin, "Sierra Protection Plan Under Review," *San Francisco Chronicle* (February 4, 2003), at www.sfgate.com accessed February 5, 2003.

24. Ross W. Gorte, *Wildfire Protection Legislation*, Memorandum to House Committee on Resources, Subcommittee on Forests and Forest Health (April 29, 2003).

25. Senators Craig and Smith made their request in July 2002; a separate request was made by Senator Bingaman in August 2002.

26. U.S. General Accounting Office, *Forest Service: Information on Decisions Involving Fuels Reduction Activities*, GAO-03-689R (Washington, DC: GAO, May 14, 2003).

27. Ibid.

28. Ibid.

29. Although focusing more specifically on fuel reduction projects, data in the GAO report were consistent with data we had reported earlier in March. Our study had been publicized in a press release developed independently by the Native Forest Network, a press release distributed by our institution, Northern Arizona University, and covered by both print and radio media. Native Forest Network, "New Reports from Researchers at Northern Arizona University Put Appeals Myth to Rest," News release (April 24, 2003), at www.nativeforest.org accessed April 25, 2003. National press coverage included, for example, Michelle Rushlo, "Data on Forest Management Decisions Difficult to Track," *San Diego Union-Tribune* (April 22, 2003), at www.signonsandiego.com/news accessed April 25, 2003; Eve Byron, "Study: Individuals File Most USFS Appeals," *Independent Record* (April 24, 2003), at www.helenair.com accessed April 25, 2003; "Study Finds Drop in West Forestry Appeals," *Washington Times* (April 24, 2003); and National Public Radio during the week of April 22, 2003.

30. U.S. Senator Larry Craig, "Craig Reacts to GAO Report on Forest Fuels Reduction Activities," News release (May 14, 2003), at www.senate.gov/~craig/releases/pr051403a accessed July 16, 2003.

31. Native Forest Network, "New GAO Report Shows that 95% of Forest Service Fuels Reduction Projects Get Green Light within Standard Review Period," News release (May 15, 2003), at www.nativeforest.org/press_room accessed July 16, 2003.

32. Grand Canyon Trust, "Independent Reports Show Healthy Forests Restoration Act Premises Flawed," Fact Sheet (2003), at www.grandcanyontrust.org/pdfs/HF accessed July 16, 2003.

33. J. R. Pegg, "Senate Panel Juggles Wildfire, Forest Management," *Environment News Service* (June 26, 2003), at www.ens-news.com/ens/jun2003 accessed June 27, 2003.

34. Jim Barnett, "Congress May Be Close to Wildfire Law," *Oregonian Live* (July 21, 2003), at www.oregonlive.com/news accessed July 22, 2003.

35. See Gary Harmon, "Enviros Set to Attack Healthy-Forests Bill," *Grand Junction Sentinel* (April 30, 2003), at www.gjsentinel.com/news accessed May 2, 2003; and J. R.

Pegg, "Wildfire Debate Sweeps Through Congress," *Environment News Service* (April 30, 2003), at www.ens-news.com/apr2003 accessed May 2, 3003.

36. Natural Resources Defense Council, *Legislative Watch* (December 6, 2003), at www.nrdc.org/legislation/legwatch accessed December 10, 2002.

37. U.S. Senator Pete Domenici, "Domenici Praises Bush's Remarks Today, Affirms Plans to Introduce Healthy Forest Bill Next Month," News Release (May 20, 2003), at www.senate.gov accessed May 21, 2003.

38. Jim Barnett, "Senator Pulls Forest-Thinning Plan," *The Oregonian* (January 8, 2003), A-7.

39. Pegg, "Senate Panel Juggles Wildfire."

40. Ibid. See also the prepared statements of the witnesses.

41. Testimony of Bruce Vincent before the U.S. Senate Committee on Energy and Natural Resources, July 22, 2003.

42. Mike Dombeck and Jack Ward Thomas, "Declare Harvest of Old-Growth Forests Off-Limits and Move On," *Seattle Post-Intelligencer* (August 24, 2003), at www.seattlepi.nwsource.com/opinion accessed September 15, 2003.

43. Gary Harmon, "McInnis Out of Politics . . . For Now," *Grand Junction Daily Sentinel* (2003), at www.house.gov/mcinnis/ed031017 accessed October 27, 2003.

44. Billy House, "Key Senators Reach Initial Agreement on Bush's Forest Plan," *Arizona Republic* (September 25, 2003): A4.

45. Personal e-mail correspondence with author from Roxane George, Southwest Forest Alliance, October 3, 2003.

46. House, "Key Senators Reach Initial Agreement."

47. Senate Legislative Counsel, Comparison of substitute and original versions of H.R. 1904 (2003): 16.

48. Forest Stewards Guild, Letter to Senators on H.R. 1904 (October 20, 2003).

49. E-mail correspondence with Roxane George.

50. Gerald J. Gray, Letter to Senators on H.R. 1904 (October 28, 2003).

51. Governors Janet Napolitano and Bill Richardson, Letter to Senator Tom Daschle (October 20, 2003).

52. U.S. General Accounting Office, *Forest Service: Information on Appeals and Litigation Involving Fuels Reduction Activities* (Washington, DC: GAO, October, 4, 2003).

53. Ibid., 43.

54. M. E. Sprengelmeyer, "Senators Stall Forest Thinning Bill," Scripps Howard News Service (October 20, 2003), at www.knoxstudio.com/shns/story accessed October 27, 2003.

55. Rep. Scott McInnis, "McInnis Criticizes Senate Obstruction of Bipartisan Healthy Forests Bill," News release (October 20, 2003), at www.house.gov/mcinnis/pr031020 accessed October 27, 2003.

56. Helen Dewar, "Senators Reach Pact on Forest Thinning," *Washington Post* (October 30, 2003), at www.washingtonpost.com accessed October 30, 2003.

57. Editorial, "Fire Damage," *Washington Post* (October 29, 2003), at www.washingtonpost.com accessed October 29, 2003.

58. Steve Lopez, "Using Fires to Blow Political Smoke," *Los Angeles Times* (October 29, 2003), at www.latimes.com/news/local accessed October 29, 2003.

59. Bettina Boxall and Gary Polakovic, "Fires Roaring Mostly Where Prevention Funding Lagged," *Los Angeles Times* (October 30, 2003), at www.latimes.com/news/local accessed October 31, 2003.

60. Paul Rogers and Josh Susong, "Area Called Ripe for a Disaster," *San Jose Mercury News* (October 30, 2003), at www.bayarea.com/mld/mercurynews/2003 accessed October 31, 2003.

61. George W. Bush, "Statement of Healthy Forests Restoration Act," News release (October 30, 2003), at www.whitehouse.gov/news/releases/2003 accessed October 31, 2003.

62. Forest Products Industry National Labor Management Committee, "Labor Unions Applaud Senate's Bipartisan Passage of Healthy Forests Restoration Act," News release (October 30, 2003), at www.yahoo.com/prnews accessed October 31, 2003.

63. "Walden Praises Senate OK of Forest Measure" (October 30, 2003), at www.bend.com/grp1 accessed October 31, 2003.

64. David Reinhard, "Two Cheers for Ron 'Hot Seat' Wyden," *The Oregonian* (November 2, 2003), at www.oregonlive.com accessed November 2, 2003.

65. Dan Berman, "House Rejects Senate Compromise on 'Healthy Forests' Bill" (2003), at www.eenews.net/Greenwire accessed November 6, 2003. See also Dan Berman, "Members Look to Behind-the-Scenes Talks on Wildfire Bill As Leaders Bicker" (2003), at www.eenews.net accessed November 6, 2003.

66. House Committee on Resources, "Deal Struck on Healthy Forests, Senate to Appoint Conferees," News release (November 19, 2003), at www.resourcescommittee.house.gov accessed November 20, 2003.

67. House Committee on Agriculture, "Goodlatte Applauds Conference Agreement on Healthy Forests Legislation," News release (November 20, 2003), at www.agriculture.house.gov accessed November 20, 2003.

68. House Committee on Resources, "Healthy Forests Legislation Passes, Next Stop: White House," News release (November 21, 2003), at www.resourcescommittee.house.gov accessed November 21, 2003.

69. The White House, "President Bush Signs Healthy Forests Restoration Act Into Law," Fact Sheet (December 3, 2003), at www.whitehouse.gov/news/releases/2003/12 accessed December 4, 2003.

70. Society of American Foresters, "Healthy Forests Bill An Important First Step," News release (November 20, 2003), at www.safnet.org accessed November 21, 2003.

71. Society of American Foresters, "Bush Signs Healthy Forest Restoration Act Into Law," *The Forestry Source* (January 2004), 5.

72. Billy House, "Forest Thinning Bill OK'd," *Arizona Republic* (November 22, 2003): A1.

73. Ibid.

74. Society of American Foresters, "Healthy Forests Compromise Appears Headed for Rapid Approval," News release (November 21, 2003), at www.safnet.org accessed November 21, 2003.

75. The Nature Conservancy, "The Nature Conservancy Urges Cooperative, Science-based Approach to Implementing New 'Healthy Forests' Law," News release (December 3, 2003), at www.nature.org/press accessed December 4, 2003.

76. Sherry Devlin, "Bush Signs Forest Legislation," *The Missoulian* (December 4, 2003), at www.missoulian.com/articles/2003 accessed December 4, 2003.

77. Puanani Mench, "Forest Protection on the Honor System," *High Country News* (December 8, 2003), 5.

REFORM BY RULEMAKING

HISTORICALLY, FOREST POLICY HAS BEEN DOMINATED BY THE MANAGERIAL MODEL IN WHICH government administrators were responsible for identifying policy options and making choices in the public's interest. When the Forest Service was founded, Gifford Pinchot, the agency's first chief, sought to manage public lands and resources to produce the greatest good for the greatest number for the longest time—a concept of social welfare maximization that still exists in many agencies today. But Pinchot's emphasis on scientific forestry—management by experts with specific forest expertise—was somewhat counter to growing demands for government accountability in a pluralistic system.[1] This is a central paradox throughout government, not just in the Forest Service. "A fundamental challenge for administrative governance is reconciling the need for expertise in managing administrative programs with the transparency and participation demanded by a democratic system."[2]

Chapter 2 explored the development of public participation in administrative law, with special emphasis on the 1946 Administrative Procedure Act. Subsequent legislation, from the Freedom of Information Act of 1966 to the Government in the Sunshine Act of 1976, greatly expanded the public's access to government decision making, and most of the major environmental statutes of the 1970s were "pluralist-created and pluralist-driven"[3]—more groups, more voices. More recently, environmental policies have been formulated through a wide variety of public participation mechanisms, from facilitated mediation, regulatory negotiation, and formal scoping sessions to mass electronic mail and collaborative decision making. Although there are still concerns over the public's expectations of, and satisfaction with, existing participatory processes, there is little question that the managerial model is no longer appropriate.[4]

Rather than waiting for Congress to act on the Healthy Forests Initiative— the legislative process is time-consuming, partisan, and highly visible—the administration sought to use the administrative rulemaking process to affect change. In this way, the president could continue to seek support among members of Congress and the public for legislative reform while using agency staff members to push reform through administrative rules. This two-pronged approach to changing forest policy was strategically sound because it doubled the chances of policy success. It also forced opponents of the president's forest policies to use their resources on two fronts, potentially lessening the impact of their criticism.

Considerable expertise in administrative law, as well as political clout, are required to push and pull a proposal through the administrative rulemaking maze. Administrative procedural changes go through a netherworld of regulatory review that is part of the accountability mechanism built into the current rulemaking process. Rulemaking reviews are usually conducted by staff in the Office of Information and Regulatory Affairs (OIRA) under the Office of Management and Budget (OMB). Since the Carter administration, presidents have also used executive orders as a way of channeling or curtailing regulations.[5] For example, in the case of one new directive—the limited timber harvest rule (discussed later in this chapter)—agency officials shepherded the new rule through a series of reviews designed, for the most part, to determine any unintended consequences of rulemaking prior to implementation. In this case, in addition to deciding if the rule was subject to a NEPA analysis (it was not), the rule was reviewed according to provisions of Executive Order 12866 (significant regulatory actions), Executive Order 13132 (federalism), Executive Order 13175 (tribal implications), the Regulatory Flexibility Act (impact on small business), Executive Order 12630 (property rights), Executive Order 12988 (civil justice reform), the Unfunded Mandates Reform Act of 1995, Executive Order 13211 (energy effects), and the Paperwork Reduction Act of 1995. This process of regulatory oversight is not unique to this particular rule change, exemplifying the complexity of the rulemaking process and how arcane language and the procedural maze can make it difficult for citizens to find their way.

Proposed rules can be sidetracked by public opposition or the oversight process through which all rules must go before implementation, but it is generally difficult to generate widespread public interest in rules. Although regulations such as the recent roadless rule and the Forest Service's attempts to eliminate project-level appeal rules in 1992 did generate significant public involvement, rulemaking nonetheless most often occurs under the radar screen of the general public. Sweeping changes in legislation often capture major headlines or stories on the nightly news such as "President proposes repeal of . . ." or "Congress set to de-authorize the . . ." But many rule changes seldom merit such extensive coverage and, even when they do, there is often minimal follow-up; they have already had their fifteen seconds of fame. Many times the most significant changes are only apparent to "policy wonks" and interests likely to be affected. Businesses whose profits might be greatly affected by a "simple" change in definition, or interests who see a rule shifting the burden of proof onto them or power away from them, will certainly follow the process closely and be actively involved in trying to influence the rulemaking process. The significance of such changes is not likely to be readily apparent, however, to those not well-versed in the intricacies of that policy area. Most certainly they are not likely to raise widespread concern or spur involvement of average citizens.

Rules can give substance to vague congressional statutes, such as the rules developed by the Council on Environmental Quality to guide development of NEPA's environmental impact statements. Under the right circumstances it is also possible to essentially "rewrite" legislation by writing the rules that govern its interpretation and the scope of its implementation. Rather than risking public ire by seeking overt congressional repeal of popular statutes, rules can also whittle away at the heart of the legislation, in effect "gutting" the law. When the public's attention is deflected and when the executive's proposed changes are also consistent with the goals of the ruling party in Congress, such changes can occur without significant scrutiny.

From fall 2002 through 2004, the Bush administration focused on a series of regulatory proposals to implement the Healthy Forests Initiative, make forest planning and management processes more efficient, increase timber harvesting, and reduce fuel loads.[6] Not unexpectedly, reaction to the administration's December 11, 2002, announcement that it intended to move administratively on several regulatory fronts split along expected lines, with Republicans and industry generally supportive and Democrats and environmentalists generally critical. House Republicans praised the administration for freeing forest managers from the regulatory straightjacket so they could expeditiously remove hazardous fuels.[7] On the other hand, New Mexico senator Jeff Bingaman, the outgoing chair of the

Senate Energy and Natural Resources Committee, said the administration was ramming through proposals that the Congress had rejected. "I think most of us in Congress wanted to facilitate the thinning of these high-risk areas . . . but we felt the administration was pursuing too much exemption from existing law in order to accomplish that, and we were trying to get agreement to do something that seemed more reasonable."[8] Democratic representative George Miller of California, who had earlier tried to broker a compromise, noted, "Obviously, President Bush has interpreted the recent elections [2002 midterm that gave the Republicans control of the Senate as well as the House] as a mandate to pollute, cut and drill."[9]

In this chapter we examine more closely several of the administration's efforts on the regulatory front. Four major rulemaking activities relate to appeals and exemptions from NEPA, including revisions of the planning regulations governing national forest planning under the National Forest Management Act (NFMA); revisions in the regulations governing Forest Service project appeals covered under the Appeals Reform Act; addition of several new types of categorical exclusions for forestry projects conducted on both BLM and Forest Service lands; and changes to the appeals process of the BLM. In addition, the administration undertook other actions related to the Healthy Forests Initiative and wildfire issue by modifying consultation provisions of the Endangered Species Act for projects in support of the National Fire Plan and by proposing changes to two major regional plans that had been hammered out during the past decade—the Northwest Forest Plan and the Sierra Nevada Framework. These efforts, which would have been significant even without passage of the Healthy Forests Restoration Act, further illustrate the major redirection of forest policy consistent with the president's overall environmental agenda.

NATIONAL FOREST PLANNING

The rulemaking process has been used several times to restructure national forest planning conducted under NFMA and its implementing regulations. Under Section 6 of NFMA, the Secretary of Agriculture is required to promulgate regulations under the principles of the Multiple-Use Sustained-Yield Act of 1960 and set out the process for development and revision of LRMPs. The first planning rule (1979) was substantially amended in 1982 to guide LRMPs now in place in all national forests and grasslands. Several reviews of the planning process were undertaken in 1989. The agency itself undertook an extensive evaluation covering all aspects of planning in an eleven-volume critique that included among its topics organization and administration, analytical tools, public participation, planning coordination, and decision making. One volume in the critique was an ancillary report by the Conservation Foundation and Purdue University that relied on contributions from more than thirty-five hundred people. In addition, responding to a congressional request, a now-defunct congressional agency, the Office of Technology Assessment (OTA), reviewed both RPA and NFMA planning. All of these reviews found major deficiencies in the agency's public participation processes. A major conclusion of the OTA review was that the "Forest Service model of public participation impedes effective participation." It recommended that Congress direct the agency to improve its public involvement. The agency's critique found that the agency's attitude toward and conduct of public participation needed to be improved and that its planning procedures needed to be simplified and clarified.[10]

A proposed rule change was published in 1995, but the secretary did not proceed with the proposal. The Clinton administration's Committee of Scientists was convened in late 1997, but the controversial rule based on its recommendations was essentially dead in the water, having been adopted two days after an election that would bring in a new administration with decidedly different views. (In adopting rules, timing is a significant political consideration.) Agency planners would still be allowed to use the 1982 rules. Subsequently, a coalition of environmental groups and another representing the forest and paper industries filed suit challenging the rule.[11]

As the Bush administration began scrutinizing all Clinton-era rules, the Department of Agriculture initiated a review of the 2000 rule's "implementability." Completed in April 2001, the study, *The NFMA Planning Rule Review*, concluded that many of the implementability concerns were valid and required attention. In addition, the Forest Service developed a business analysis model of the 2000 rule and conducted a workshop with field-level planners to provide a systematic evaluation. When this evaluation indicated a lack of clarity, limitations on the availability of scientists, and unnecessarily detailed procedural requirements, the new administration asked the chief of the Forest Service to develop a revision of the 2000 rules.[12] No actions were taken at this time to formally suspend the 2000 rules before the new administration assumed office; there really was no need because there had been no time to institutionalize the rules.

The proposed 2002 changes published in the *Federal Register* on December 6, 2002, embraced the concept of sustainability and multiple use found in the 2000 rule but called for programmatic planning that allowed for plans to be permissive— that is, they allowed, but did not mandate, site-specific actions. Forest Service officials said the new rules were designed to make forest planning more efficient, reduce costs by eliminating procedural detail, and give more flexibility to local managers. "What we like most about this rule is it engages the public better than we have done in the past by promoting early involvement, making the plans easier to understand, and getting them done in less than seven years."[13]

As from the beginning, how rules should be developed to meet NFMA's requirement that forest plans provide for a diversity of plant and animal communities proved highly contentious. In the proposed rule, the agency presented two diversity options, both of which deleted mandatory protection of species viability and replaced it with more permissive language that would make it difficult for groups to find a legal basis for suing the agency. To discuss diversity options the agency convened a workshop in February 2003 that was organized through an official rule announcing the workshop and formally soliciting nominations of potential attendees.[14] At the workshop's conclusion the agency's director of planning expressed surprise about the degree of support many participants had shown for the 1982 rule (as opposed to both the 2000 and 2002 revisions), as well as surprise and frustration that the agency had not convinced many participants of the need for a less costly and time-consuming planning approach. At the meeting's outset, he had estimated that the 2002 rule would cost between $9 and $9.5 million per plan while the 2000 rule would cost $13 million per plan.[15]

There were also changes to the public participation and appeals provisions in the 2002 rules. One criticism of the 2000 rule was over a requirement that the Forest Service participate in the cooperative development of landscape goals. The 2002 proposed rule clarified that the agency should *consider* participating in existing groups to address resource management issues within the community but should not make this a requirement "because it will not always be useful and may often be unachievable with participating groups."[16] Citing time and expense, the 2002 rule eliminated a requirement for establishing advisory committees. It kept the 2000 rule's replacement of a post-decision administrative appeals process with a pre-decisional objection process but made several additional changes to make the Forest Service process more like the BLM's pre-decisional objection process, specifically by not requiring publication of the objections received and by eliminating any discussion about the possibility of an objector or interested party requesting a meeting with the reviewing officer. In filing an objection it included a specific requirement that an objector make "a concise statement explaining how the environmental disclosure documents, if any, and proposed plan, amendment, or revision are inconsistent with law, regulation, Executive Order, or policy and any recommendations for change."[17] Such changes in the rules governing public consultation, appeals, and monitoring and evaluation raised questions about the effect on democratic accountability, generally defined as the ways in which an agency or individual must be held responsible for implementation and compliance, fulfilling promises, and performance of duties and obligations.[18]

Public interest in the proposed rule was so extensive that the Forest Service extended the formal public comment period an additional thirty days, from March 6 to April 7, 2003. The agency received 195,787 comments to the planning rule.

One aspect of the proposed rule relating to public review and comment was controversial enough that the Forest Service abandoned it early on. Upon taking office in 2001, President Bush had initiated another set of government reform efforts, collectively known as the President's Management Agenda (PMA), "to make the Federal government more results-oriented, efficient, and citizen-oriented."[19] One element of the PMA was Expanding Electronic Government, composed of a suite of twenty-four cross-agency projects to modernize and integrate information technology. The initiatives were in response to studies reporting that forty-two million Americans viewed federal regulations through the Internet in 2001, with twenty-three million using the web to comment on proposed rules, regulations, and policies.[20] Congress followed up on the directives with passage of H.R. 2458, the E-Government Act of 2002, which Bush signed into law on December 17, 2002.

While the administration was encouraging use of the Internet as part of the regulatory process, the Forest Service attempted to move in the opposite direction. The agency was responding to an unprecedented 2000 campaign by environmental organizations and their members supporting the roadless rule. It is estimated that the Forest Service received 1.6 million comments on the policy, with 90 percent in support of the rule. Critics of the roadless rule noted that the majority of the comments were mass e-mails and pre-printed postcards.

The barrage was sufficient to convince the Forest Service to use e-mail filters that sometimes rejected thousands of citizen comments and to propose a provision banning form letters, check-off lists, pre-printed postcards, or similar duplicative materials from being considered as public objections to proposed plans, amendments, or revisions.[21] A Forest Service spokesman said, "A bunch of e-mails that say the same thing with no specific comments don't tell us anything," although the agency would still accept originally composed e-mail and letters from the public as long as they did not go through an outside service such as a business or environmental Web site.[22]

Advocacy groups have increasingly relied upon the Internet as a way of communicating their concerns to both their members and decision makers. Although Forest Service concerns were aimed principally at environmental organizations, "bundled" e-mail is commonly used by organizations ranging from the National Rifle Association and the National Right to Life Committee to the AFL-CIO and the American Cancer Society. Supporters of this measure, like the California Farm Bureau Federation, said that allowing the Forest Service to ignore mass e-mails was a good idea. "If we are relying upon e-mail and postcards to manage our national forests, that's a problem. You should have to invest the time to write an original letter."[23] Generally, however, the agency's proposal met with negative reaction from both environmental and timber industry groups. A spokesman for the American Forest and Paper Association, which has a Take Action! feature on its Web page for sending messages to congressional members, responded, "If they are blocking Viagra ads that's one thing. . . . If they are blocking public comments, that's not spam—that's thwarting democracy. It's an issue of public access."[24]

A coalition of public interest groups organized by the Electronic Frontier Foundation (EFF) sent a letter to the director of the OMB and the chief of the Forest Service opposing the proposed rule, noting that new technology "makes it easier and more convenient for average citizens to communicate with their government from the privacy of their homes. We believe that reducing the barriers to speaking to government is one of the greatest gifts of the Internet to citizens."[25] EFF also submitted formal comments on the proposed rule, noting that the organization could not detect why the agency felt such a rule was necessary and that it would "disadvantage members of the public in favor of lobbyists, large organizations and businesses that can afford to hire professionals to prepare unique, separate comments. This sort of favoritism is inconsistent with the policy goals of the Administrative Procedure Act."[26]

After months of comments and study, the Forest Service announced in December 2003 that it was abandoning the plan "as a show of good faith. We are concerned that people misconstrued it—that we didn't care about what they were saying when in fact that's not the reason why we put it in there."[27]

During fall 2004 it became clear that a final rule based on the 2002 proposed rule would not be adopted prior to the election. On September 29, 2004, the agency issued an interpretive rule exempting management activities from complying with both the 1982 and 2000 planning regulations, except for the provision of the 2000 rule that the agency use the best available science.[28] In essence, this exempted the agency from compliance with the 1982 requirements to monitor population trends of management indicator species. The agency claimed that the 1982 provision prevented it from using the best available science, because tools other than population data can be more useful and appropriate for examining effects of proposed projects on species habitat.[29]

On December 22, 2004, the Forest Service announced the final rule, again emphasizing that the changes would make planning more timely, cost effective, and adaptive. The final rule (now called the 2004 Planning Rule) became effective on January 5, 2005. The new regulations maintained the emphasis on strategic planning, specifying that generally plans will not include specific project-level management decisions. Similar to both the 2000 rule and the 2002 proposed rule, the final rule contained a pre-decisional objection process. In response to the ongoing controversy over how to meet NFMA's diversity requirement, the new rule deleted the 1982 and 2000 rules' requirement to maintain viable populations of plant and animal species. Instead, the 2004 rule required that plan components establish a framework for sustaining native ecological systems and moved many of the previous rules' detailed procedural requirements concerning species protection to the less stringent agency directive system. Another new feature of the 2004 rule adopted the ISO 14001 Environmental Management System model, an adaptive management approach that requires independent audits to monitor plan accountability. At the same time the administration announced the final planning rule, it also served notice through another proposed rulemaking process that it intended to allow forest plans to be excluded from NEPA procedures.[30] On February 17, 2005, a coalition of environmental groups sued.

FOREST SERVICE PROJECT APPEAL PROCEDURES

A second major initiative targeted Section 322 of the Interior and Related Agencies Appropriation Act of Fiscal 1994, or the Appeals Reform Act (ARA), which was discussed in Chapter 2.[31] On December 18, 2002, the agency proposed changes to the rule implementing that act "to clarify certain provisions and reduce complexity in the current rule; improve efficiency of processing appeals; encourage early and effective public participation in the environmental analysis of projects and activities; and ensure consistency with the provisions of the statutory authority."[32] The proposed rule limited the administrative appeals process to those who submit "substantive" oral or written comments during the thirty-calendar-day public comment period on an environmental assessment for a specific project or activity (or forty-five days for a draft environmental impact statement) with the Forest Service Responsible Official given discretion for identifying which comments were "substantive." The rule would not allow the comment period to be extended and allowed the agency to respond to electronically mailed comments using an automated electronic acknowledgment. Oral comments could be made via telephone or in person to the Responsible Official's office or, if during non-business hours, at an official agency function designed to elicit public comment. In cases with multiple appellants, the Appeal Deciding Officer could appoint the first name listed as the lead appellant to act on behalf of all parties to that appeal when the appeal does not specify a lead appellant. The previous designation of "interested party" to the appeal was eliminated. The rule also required the

Responsible Official to contact the appellant as soon as practicable and offer to meet and discuss resolution of the issues raised in the appeal. The date of the meeting must be within fifteen days after the closing date for the appeal and located in the vicinity of the lands affected by the decision. Projects that are categorically excluded from further documentation under NEPA would be exempted from the regulations. (As will be discussed later in this chapter, at the same time this rule was moving forward, new rules expanding the types of projects that would qualify for categorical exclusion status were also moving forward.)

Notice of the proposed rule was sent to more than 150 national organizations and federal agencies, with approximately twenty-five thousand comment letters received during the sixty-day comment period. The opinions of those who generally supported the proposed rule changes stated that the changes would improve procedural effectiveness and efficiency, reduce the abuse of the appeals process, and improve forest health. Not surprisingly, those opposing the rule contended that the changes would reduce a citizen's right to participate in the project planning process, might result in increased litigation, and would decrease forest health.[33]

In its five-page comment letter, the Society of American Foresters noted its long-term support for proposed changes to the appeal process and, in particular, those related to substantive comments. "This amendment would improve the public participation process by ensuring pre-decisional, constructive involvement. It would help restore the fundamental purpose of public participation to inform agency decision making and ensure that all reasonable values and methods are considered prior to making decisions." However, the letter also pointed out that there was limited documentation demonstrating that the appeals process is the ultimate cause of the current gridlock in forest management and urged thorough study and monitoring of the proposed process.[34]

In contrast, the Gifford Pinchot Task Force (with concurrence by the Blue Mountains Diversity Project and the Klamath-Siskiyou Wildland Center) submitted a twenty-three-page comment letter opposing virtually every section of the proposed rule changes. Their comments cited the failure of the Forest Service to provide any information demonstrating that the process of public involvement is flawed, arguing that, rather than increasing efficiency, the new system "will simply force otherwise cooperative members of the public to take their grievances directly to court. It is our experience that the public comment and appeal process frequently results in changes to projects that make them more environmentally acceptable, which circumvents the need to litigate issues. However, the proposed regulations would remove this incentive to cooperate."[35]

The Forest Service singled out comments submitted by Native American tribes, who expressed a general concern that the proposed rule failed to recognize particular rights granted under various statutes, treaties, and other legal instruments. Tribal representatives wrote that they believed that tribal participation in many Forest Service decisions would be greatly reduced by the proposed changes and that consultation is required to negotiate a process for harmonizing the proposed rule with their concerns. Although acknowledging the sovereignty of tribal governments, the Forest Service responded that the concerns expressed were primarily general in nature, and the government "does not believe it is appropriate to include special provisions relating to tribes in the final rule."[36]

As a result of the public comments and analysis, several changes were made before the final rule was published in the *Federal Register*. There was some reorganization resulting in sections having new titles or new designations, and clarification was added to proposed sections. Definitions of terms such as "emergency situation" and "principal newspaper" were refined. Much of the controversy appeared to be over the term "substantive comments," with the majority of those commenting on the rule opposing the terminology. Some found the term too vague, others felt it would limit public participation, and some questioned who would have the discretion to determine if a comment was "substantive" or not. The final rule revised the definition somewhat, giving the Responsible Official the responsibility for determining if comments received met the definition. One significant change was that the final rule (published June 4, 2003) dropped the proposal to limit appeals to issues raised during the comment period.[37] These rules would complement the pre-decisional rules for hazardous fuels authorized under the Healthy Forest Restoration Act.[38]

CATEGORICAL EXCLUSIONS

The third major initiative involved categorical exclusions (CEs). The 215 rule changes excluded projects covered under categorical exclusions from appeals. In two separate rulemaking activities related to CEs initiated at approximately the same time and directly in response to the Healthy Forests Initiative, the Forest Service added a total of five new categories of categorical exclusions.

In compliance with CEQ regulations, agencies are authorized to identify those types of projects—called categorical exclusions—that tend to have no individual or cumulatively significant effect on the human environment and that warrant no further analysis and documentation under NEPA.[39] Projects defined as CEs do not require preparation of an EA or an EIS. Categorical exclusions are described in the *Forest Service Handbook* and the *Department of the Interior Manual*; the latter is applicable to lands managed by Interior agencies, including BLM, National Park Service, Fish and Wildlife Service, Bureau of Indian Affairs, and Bureau of

Reclamation. Consequently, the proposed exemptions outlined in the text of the rules would be incorporated into the departments' respective handbooks.

The first set of CE rulemaking related to NEPA documentation for fire management activities. Notice of the proposed action was published in the *Federal Register* on December 16, 2002, and sought public comment on two new proposed categorical exclusions for Forest Service and Department of the Interior projects. The first related to hazardous fuels reduction activities to reduce risk to communities and ecosystems, while the second covered post-fire rehabilitation activities. Almost thirty-nine thousand responses were received during the comment period, of which nineteen hundred were individual letters and more than thirty-seven thousand were form letters. The controversy over the proposed categorical exclusion rule centered around four issues.

1. Categorical exclusions would be used for fuel reduction projects that result in sales of commercial timber.
2. Categorical exclusions would be used to treat large wildland forest areas.
3. The public would not be able to appeal categorical exclusions.
4. The proposal did not address the size of the treatment areas.[40]

The final rule became effective June 5, 2003.[41] Activities eligible for categorical exclusion under the hazardous fuels category applied only to projects identified under the Ten-Year Comprehensive Strategy Implementation Plan, could not be conducted in wilderness areas, were limited to one thousand acres for mechanical treatments and forty-five hundred acres for prescribed burning activities, could not include the use of herbicides or pesticides, may not involve construction of new roads or other infrastructure, must be conducted only in interface areas or in areas in high fire risk areas outside of the interface, and cannot involve the sale of materials that do not have hazardous fuels reduction as their primary purpose. Projects categorically excluded under the post-fire rehabilitation category are limited to forty-two hundred acres, must not involve the use of herbicides or pesticides, must not involve new roads or infrastructure, and must be completed within three years after a fire.

The second set of CE rulemaking was officially proposed January 8, 2003, almost a month after the first. The proposal outlined three new categories of exclusions related to limited timber harvesting on Forest Service lands. The first covered live tree harvest, the second salvage of dead and dying trees, and the third tree removal for preventing the spread of insects and disease. In a news release announcing the proposals, Forest Service chief Dale Bosworth argued that "[c]ategorical exclusions like those we are proposing will assist the agency in meeting its mission of caring for the land. The proposed categories are about how we document our decisions regarding activities that are environmentally safe. Through these proposed categories, the agency hopes to reduce the bureaucratic red tape and save time, energy, and money in preparing small, routine projects that are supported by local communities."[42]

The first of the three proposed categories would allow the harvest of live trees not to exceed an area of fifty acres. The second would allow salvage of dead or dying trees in 250 acres or less, and the third would allow removal of any trees necessary to control the spread of insects and disease on not more than 250 acres. None of the proposed CEs would allow more than one-half mile of temporary road construction or be subject to administrative appeal.[43]

During the sixty-day public comment period, approximately 16,700 comment letters were received in response to the initial proposal, some as form letters and others from individuals and organizations. Some groups and individuals voiced general agreement with the proposal, indicating that they found the current analysis and documentation requirements too burdensome and that the proposal would provide for more efficient management. "Others believed that the proposal had appropriate limitations on the use of the categorical exclusions and that the agencies had done sufficient analysis to conclude that the categories of limited tree harvest do not have significant environmental effects."[44]

As a result of the public comments it analyzed, the Forest Service made five revisions to the original proposal, which became effective July 29, 2003. The final directive changed the acreage limitation for harvesting live trees from fifty to seventy acres and dropped an example that it felt was better covered in the hazardous fuels reduction category, which had been adopted the previous month. Three changes were made in language related to tree length, live, uninfested/uninfected trees, and noncommercial activities related to tree removal for insect and disease control.[45]

The Forest Service estimated that the new provisions would save up to four months of planning on each project. Chief Bosworth said, "These new categorical exclusions will save the Forest Service time, energy, and money in preparing small, routine timber harvest projects that contribute to healthy forests and economies. Many of these projects are time sensitive and only have small windows of time in the year to conduct the work."[46] Not all, however, saw the net result in terms of decision efficiency. Reflecting upon the regulatory changes that had been made to forest planning, categorical exclusions, and the Appeals Reform Act, Rep. Tom Udall (D-NM), a member of the House Committee on Resources and the Subcommittee on Forests and Forest Health, said, "The synergistic effects of these radical rollbacks are breathtaking. I predict that the assault will only foment more controversy and stimulate more distrust of the Forest Service for years to come. . . . Add to the mix a congressional rider that allows the agency to pay for restoration work with the logging of large trees, as well as the Healthy Forests Restoration Act that Congress stands poised to pass, and a revolution has occurred."[47]

BUREAU OF LAND MANAGEMENT APPEAL PROCEDURES

While considerable attention was being focused on Forest Service appeals, the Bush administration sought similar changes to the less controversial issue of BLM hearings and appeals. Unlike the relatively recent congressional mandate for the Forest Service's administrative appeals process, the BLM has had a review procedure for public land cases since 1946, and the concept was reaffirmed in 1976 with the passage of the Federal Land Policy and Management Act. The Department of the Interior created the Office of Hearings and Appeals (OHA), and the Interior Board of Land Appeals (IBLA) was given responsibility for considering appeals to BLM decisions.[48] The IBLA is made up of a chief administrative judge, a deputy chief administrative judge, and eleven administrative law judges. Grazing appeals do not go initially to the IBLA but to administrative law judges in the Hearings Division of the Office of Hearings and Appeals in Salt Lake City. Decisions made by these judges can then be appealed to the IBLA.

The administrative appeals process for the BLM begins with the requirement that the agency must notify those with permits and leases, and other members of the interested public, of a proposed decision. Under the APA, persons adversely affected or aggrieved by an agency action can seek redress in a federal court only when a decision is "final," which requires a party to first exhaust administrative remedies. A BLM grazing decision does not go into effect until a thirty-day appeal period expires. If a petition for a stay is filed within the appeal period, the decision is not in effect for forty-five days after the expiration of the appeal period or until OHA acts on the stay petition, whichever occurs first. If the stay is not granted, the party has exhausted administrative remedies and may then seek review in federal court.

On December 16, 2002, the BLM and the Office of Hearings and Appeals jointly proposed rules that would make BLM decisions on wildfire management effective immediately and would expedite OHA decisions on appeals of such BLM decisions. OHA also proposed to amend its existing rules governing the right to appeal and proof of service that documents have been filed.[49]

The June 5, 2003, summary of the final rule noted that the great majority of the approximately nine thousand comments received on the proposed rule were form letters generally supporting or generally opposing the proposal. The remaining specific and substantive comments came from trade and governmental organizations, commercial public land users, environmental groups, local and tribal government entities, and individuals. Those comments focused on four topics: standing to appeal, point at which BLM wildfire management decisions became effective, timeliness and expedited OHA review of appeals from those decisions, and proof of service.

The first topic involved existing regulations that limited standing and participation to those who were "party to a case" and those who were "adversely affected." In the proposed rule, the OHA defined those terms more specifically so that party to a case meant "one who has taken action that is the subject of the decision on appeal, is the object of that decision, or has otherwise participated in the process leading to the decision under appeal, e.g., by filing a mining claim or application for use of public lands, by commenting on an environmental document, or by filing a protest to a proposed action." Adversely affected was defined to mean "a party has a legally cognizable interest, and the decision on appeal has caused, or will cause, injury to that interest." The comments submitted on who should have standing to appeal represented a wide spectrum of opinions. Some contended that appeals should be limited to only those persons who could show direct economic damage, while others sought to broaden the scope of a "legally cognizable interest" in some way and cited prior court cases on the issue. Several mentioned concerns that the proposals would do away with or limit public participation in BLM decision making or restrict access to the appeals process— views almost identical to those expressed in public comments on changes to the Forest Service appeals procedures.[50]

The second issue raised dealt with the addition of two provisions to existing regulations that would make the agency's wildfire management decisions effective immediately. The proposed rule defined "wildfire management" as including but not limited to (1) fuel reduction or fuel treatment such as prescribed burns and mechanical, chemical, and biological thinning methods; and (2) projects to stabilize and rehabilitate lands affected by wildfires. Many comments stressed the urgency of dealing with current wildfire threats and supported the idea that if the BLM could act more quickly to reduce the threat of wildfire, it could better safeguard public and fire fighter safety, protect property, and improve conditions in the wildland-urban interface.

Those opposing the proposed rule noted that it would allow action to begin prior to sufficient public input and that this would discourage potential participation from those who felt they could have no real or immediate effect on a proposed project. Making decisions effective immediately, another said, would reduce the opportunity for a project to be modified on the basis of citizen concerns. Others wrote that the proposed rule change would undermine public trust in public land management agency decisions.

Questions were also raised about the fire condition class of the tract of range or forest land in question, and at what point the BLM wildfire management decisions would go into effect. Some observed that the proposed rule was overly broad or vague because it did not require any determination that the proposed BLM action would accomplish the goals of protecting safety, property, or interface conditions. One timber company noted the differences between thinning and removal; the final rule amended the language to allow thinning with or without removal. Timber sales, which are not considered wildfire management projects, would not be covered by the proposed rule, although sales of small amounts of timber might be incidental to fire management thinning projects. In the final rule, however, the BLM rejected recommendations that restoration treatment of unburned acres be added to the definition of wildfire management, saying that it would be too far beyond the scope of the proposed rule. Some had also criticized the rule because, as had been the case in the debate over the Healthy Forests Restoration Act, the term "wildland-urban interface" was not defined, nor was "priority area." In response, the BLM said that it had discretion to choose those areas based on its strategies for implementation of the National Fire Plan but that it would be unduly narrowing to limit the effect of the rule to forest land near developed areas and, therefore, no priorities would be stated in the final rule.

The third issue identified in public comments dealt with the timeliness of appeal decisions. As had been the case with the HFRA, supporters contended that placing limitations on administrative appeals would expedite fuel management treatment and reduce wildfire threats. Similarly, this proposed rule added a new section to the Office of Hearings and Appeals procedures requiring the Interior Board of Land Appeals to decide appeals from BLM wildfire management decisions within sixty days after all pleadings were filed. After receiving comments that the 60-day time limit was unreasonable, the final rule was changed to require that decisions be made within 180 days after the appeal is filed, extending the deadline.

The fourth issue related to three proposed amendments that would bring the IBLA's practice requiring proof of service of documents into line with current rules in federal and state courts. Some comments said that it was not unreasonable to require an appellant to provide hard proof that an appeal had been filed in a timely manner, but others approved the proposed rule. The final rule remained unchanged from the proposed rule.

The final rule, as amended, became effective July 7, 2003, less than eight months after it had been proposed and just five months before President Bush would sign the Healthy Forests Restoration Act. The rulemaking process was notable because these changes in the BLM and OHA appeals process were designed to affect public participation and appeals processing in ways similar to the regulations that were proposed in the wake of the administration's August 2002 Healthy Forests Initiative. The final rule also became effective in the same time frame as the new Forest Service rules, between June 5, 2003, and July 29, 2003. These "first generation" regulations provided a mechanism for rapid implementation of the administration's forest and wildfire policies. In this case, administrative rulemaking significantly altered procedures in the two primary federal agencies with jurisdiction over public lands at virtually the same time and at minimal political cost.

CONSULTATION UNDER THE ENDANGERED SPECIES ACT

A somewhat less visible round of policy change during the president's first term involved the Endangered Species Act, which had been passed thirty years before in a flurry of environmental lawmaking. Like the appeals and wildfire issues discussed previously, calls for reform were based on undocumented commentary and finger-pointing. Rep. Richard Pombo (R-CA) criticized the Southern Appalachia Biodiversity Project for using lawsuits to manipulate the ESA to protect endangered mussels. "These frivolous, politically motivated lawsuits have already bankrupted the critical habitat program. I have never seen a law so abused in the name of a good cause. It's egregious."[51]

The issue that garnered the most attention was a provision under the ESA's Section 7 that required federal agencies to consult with the Fish and Wildlife Service to insure that any action they authorize, fund, or carry out would not jeopardize a listed species or result in the destruction of adverse effects on designated critical habitat. In January 2003 the Department of the Interior announced "the availability of guidance in evaluating the net benefit of projects that reduce hazardous fuels," which would ensure consistency. "It is essential that these consultations be carried out as quickly and efficiently as possible to promote the timely implementation of preventative actions that will help to ensure public safety."[52]

In the proposed rule, issued June 5, 2003, the Bush administration argued in favor of streamlining consultation on proposed projects that support the National Fire Plan. The alternative consultation process in the proposed counterpart regulations "will eliminate the need to conduct informal consultation and eliminate the requirement to obtain written concurrence from the Service for those NFP actions that the Action Agency determines are 'not likely to adversely affect' (NLAA) any listed species or designated critical habitat."[53] The regulations would affect the U.S. Department of Agriculture's Forest Service; the Department of the Interior's Bureau of Indian Affairs, Bureau of Land Management, and National Park Service; and the Department of Commerce's National Marine Fisheries Service and National Oceanic and Atmospheric Administration.

In its *Federal Register* notice, the government said that under the existing consultation process, thousands of proposed actions that ultimately received written concurrence were found to have only insignificant or beneficial effects on listed species, or posed a discountable risk of adverse effects.

> The concurrence process for such projects has diverted some of the consultation resources of the Service from projects in greater need of consultation and caused delays. The proposed counterpart regulations will effectively reduce these delays by increasing the Service's capability to focus on Federal actions requiring formal consultation by eliminating the requirement to provide written concurrence for actions within the scope of the proposed counterpart regulations.[54]

One of the strategies critical in building support for the change was the administration's framing of the issue as part of the Healthy Forests Initiative, rather than as a tactic designed to reduce environmental review or limit protection for endangered species. The proposed rule was released just as the wildfire season began and made numerous references to fuels treatment activities, the implementation of the National Fire Plan, and the need to protect habitat from catastrophic wildfire. In this way, it could easily be perceived as a technical change to an existing policy rather than as a new initiative, although the announcement did include language noting that, in accordance with Executive Order 12866, it was a significant proposed rule "because it may raise novel or legal policy issues."[55]

While the rulemaking process moved forward, members of Congress commented on the Section 7 consultation process during public hearings. Using the same strategies as had been used by critics of the Forest Service administrative appeals process, they relied upon anecdotal information and rhetoric rather than data. Sen. Lisa Murkowski (R-AK) said the consultation process needed "major surgery," arguing that it is a mass of red tape that needlessly delays federal projects and permits, bogs down agencies with paperwork, and costs private citizens and companies considerable money. Sen. Michael Crapo (R-ID), chair of the Senate Subcommittee on Fisheries, Wildlife and Water, noted, "The services are expending colossal resources on a process that produces a lot of paperwork without a lot of positive impacts on recovery."[56] There was virtually no mention that the proposed rule would potentially reduce the level of protection afforded endangered species.

But a General Accounting Office official countered that they were having trouble tacking down a paper trail in order to draw conclusions about the overall impact of Section 7. "No one really has any good information about how long this entire process actually takes. There is not a lot of data out. You hear some horror stories, but we do not really know how prevalent those are."[57]

A National Wildlife Federation official said that the consultation process resulted in "great conservation gains at modest resource outlays. We hear about delays and that is a legitimate concern, but the heart of the problem is inadequate funding and staffing at the agencies. Funding increases do not match the increased workload."[58] The GAO noted, too, that there was not a lot of information on the benefits of the process and its overall effectiveness.

The initial public comment period closed on August 4, 2003, with the EA for the counterpart regulations issued on September 30. The Fish and Wildlife Service re-opened the comment period on October 9 and extended it until November 10 so that parties could comment on both the proposed rule and the EA. The EA referred back to the need to streamline ESA consultations and to accelerate the process of approving National Fire Plan projects to reduce "unnecessary regulatory obstacles that have at times delayed and frustrated active land management activities."[59]

Although the EA provided a narrative that included some statistics on how many consultations had been conducted in recent fiscal years, no evidence was provided indicating that any delays had occurred, the length of the delay, or how delays had affected the implementation of the NFP. As had been the case with the Healthy Forests Initiative, these changes appear to have been proposed without any solid data to support the need for the rule. The tradeoff between the costs of conducting training programs and increased diligence in keeping current on new information regarding species biology would be offset, the EA noted, by the benefits of procedural change. The Action Agency, which would generally be the Forest Service, would not expend its resources on the informal consultation process or lose time waiting for a concurrence letter. "The time saved ultimately equates to a financial savings in staffing expenses and can ultimately move the projects that support the NFP faster, potentially decreasing the number and severity of wildland fires, which would be a long term biological and economic benefit."[60]

More than fifty thousand comments were received during the two public comment periods, although none spoke to the environmental effects of the rule itself. The Fish and Wildlife Service said that many of the comments focused on effects that might occur as a result of actions taken during implementation of the NFP. Because the rule was considered only a procedural change in the consultation process, the agency determined that the majority of comments were beyond the narrow scope of the proposed rulemaking. The final rule, issued December 8,

2003, just five days after President Bush signed the Healthy Forests Restoration Act, became effective January 7, 2004. The regulations eliminated the need to conduct informal consultation and also eliminated the requirement to obtain written concurrence for National Fire Plan activities determined not likely to adversely affect any listed species or designated critical habitat.[61] Environmental groups said the new rule removed a key check and balance. "The conflict of interest is that the agency whose top job is to do the logging will make this decision, rather than the agency whose top job is protecting threatened or endangered species," said a spokesperson for Earthjustice.[62]

THE NORTHWEST FOREST PLAN

The president's Healthy Forests Initiative also reopened the issue of the Northwest Forest Plan, a plan that covers twenty-four million acres of federal forest lands in Oregon, Washington, and northern California. During the 1980s, the old-growth forests in the Pacific Northwest were the principal battleground upon which the future of national forest policy centered. Scientists presented studies that detailed the loss of old-growth habitat for the northern spotted owl, a shy, threatened bird. Radical organizations like Earth First! drew attention to the issue of clear-cutting, using tactics like tree-sits and what critics called "ecoterrorism" to bring the problem to the policy agenda. Other groups, like the Oregon Natural Resources Council, threatened to file administrative appeals against 220 Forest Service timber sales in a single month. Confrontation between the agency, timber companies, and environmental protesters became common as attempts were made to galvanize public opinion.[63]

The decision space narrowed as timber harvesting continued and owl habitat declined. Unsatisfied with both legislative and executive branch responses, environmentalists sued the agencies. Eleven judges found the federal land management agencies to be in violation of one or more federal laws or regulations affecting federal forest management and endangered species protection or compliance with NEPA procedures.[64] The agencies appeared to be in denial, believing that they would ultimately win in court and be cutting timber just as before. In 1991, a ruling by U.S. District Judge William Dwyer, however, was the flashpoint in the ongoing controversy.[65] The judge banned new timber sales to protect the habitat of the owl. The decision shut down about 80 percent of proposed timber sales west of the Cascade Mountains, stopping logging on sixty-six thousand acres until the Forest Service completed a long-delayed management plan for the owl. The issue was highly volatile, nationally visible, and emotionally charged. Neither Congress nor the federal agencies were able to adequately resolve the issue.

During the 1992 presidential election, both George H.W. Bush and Bill Clinton spoke publicly about the region's forest controversy. Candidate Clinton made a campaign pledge in a timber worker's backyard to hold a timber "summit" to find a solution. Clinton was described as "the great green hope" and pledged to use "the presidential pen to make government the greenest in history."[66] In a largely urbanized West—even in the face of strong opposition from rural, resource-dependent communities—Clinton, the more environmentally friendly candidate, was able to carry Washington, Oregon, and California. Clinton followed through on his campaign pledge and the forest summit was held in April 1993 in Portland, Oregon. At the conclusion of the summit Clinton committed to developing a plan—released three months later—that embraced three themes: forest management, economic development, and agency coordination.[67]

The Northwest Forest Plan (NWFP) appeased some activists who wanted to end all logging in the Pacific Northwest to preserve the threatened bird's habitat. One of the major stakeholders in the development of the NWFP said that Clinton's actions "changed a hot war into a cold war."[68] But the plan did not satisfy timber interests, who were permitted to harvest over one billion board feet of timber annually—about one-quarter of what was logged on federal lands in the Northwest during the late 1980s. The battles shifted from the forests to the courtroom as parties on both sides filed lawsuits over the interpretation and implementation of the Clinton agreement. In 1994 the American Forest Resource Council unsuccessfully filed suit challenging the plan's provisions placing old-growth and riparian lands in reserves. Fishing and conservation organizations filed three suits to protect threatened and endangered salmon from harmful logging practices and, after the Clinton administration settled the last case, the timber industry vowed to override the decision of the courts.[69] Additional lawsuits were filed by timber companies and trade associations to delist the marbled murrelet and withdraw its critical habitat designation as well as that of the northern spotted owl.[70] The agencies maintained that the plan's requiring the Forest Service and Bureau of Land Management to foot the bills for surveys of little-known species (the Survey and Manage Mitigation Measure Standards and Guidelines) and other procedural requirements created paperwork delays. Despite NWFP's promise that companies would have access to substantial amounts of timber, over the years lawsuits, protests, and delays led to dwindling harvests. "We've met the protection pieces of the Northwest Forest Plan, but the production piece we've never been able to meet," declared a regional Forest Service spokesperson.[71]

After the election of George W. Bush in 2000, the potential for addressing the plan's shortcomings in terms of timber harvesting substantially improved. An internal Forest Service memo surfaced in summer 2002 that was purported to be the Bush administration's three-year schedule for increasing timber production in the region and easing regulations that created "process gridlock." Undersecretary of Agriculture Mark Rey said he hoped to find "common ground" with both environmentalists and the forest products industry in developing the memo's proposed changes.[72] Fulfilling the timber production promises of the Northwest Forest Plan was a component of the Healthy Forests Initiative, and when President Bush went to Oregon to announce the initiative he also discussed his intention to implement the plan as intended, citing the jobs it would provide. By linking discussion of the prospect of increased timber harvesting in the old-growth forests of the Northwest with his discussion of fires and forest thinning, the president made a tie-in that convinced environmentalists the Healthy Forests Initiative was more about increased timber production than it was about forest restoration and protection of communities from wildfires.

One of the actions that triggered major changes in the Northwest Forest Plan derives from a September 2002 agreement between the Bush administration and logging interests that settled a lawsuit filed by the Douglas Timber Operators.[73] As part of the settlement, the administration agreed to revise the NWFP and drop the plan's controversial Survey and Manage guidelines. Groups like The Wilderness Society accused the president of attempting to further weaken protection for forest lands in order to appease logging interests. "The proposal to eliminate the Survey Standards is the result of a deal made behind closed doors between the Bush Administration and the timber industry that will result in increased logging of old growth forests across the Northwest. The Survey Standards are an essential measuring stick for the Northwest Forest Plan that helps ensure the continued protection of our mature forests and rare wildlife," a spokesman said.[74] "This is the latest example of the Administration's outrageous and unethical strategy to use industry lawsuits as cover to undermine important and broadly supported policies."[75] On the other hand, prominent forest scientists— including Jack Ward Thomas, former Forest Service chief and principal architect of the forest plan—supported the decision to drop the Survey and Manage guidelines.[76]

In records of decisions announced in March 2004, the BLM and Forest Service amended the Northwest Forest Plan. These decisions removed the Survey and Manage guidelines and modified provisions related to the plan's Aquatic Conservation Strategy.[77] Several months earlier in settlement agreements related to industry suits the administration had also agreed to industry demands to review the status of the northern spotted owl and marbled murrelet and to redesignate critical habitat based on economic effects analysis.

THE SIERRA NEVADA FRAMEWORK

In a similar move, the administration also reversed course on the Sierra Nevada Framework, another Clinton-era plan that covered eleven national forests in California. The plan, which had taken ten years to develop, had involved extensive collaboration and public involvement. Even then the agency received 276 appeals on the plan, including appeals by environmentalists, timber organizations, ranchers, local chambers of commerce, utilities, farm bureaus, and county boards of supervisors.[78] The chief of the Forest Service basically affirmed the plan although he expressed some reservations and directed the regional forester for the Pacific Southwest Region to review specific areas of the plan. One year after approving the plan the Forest Service announced on January 1, 2002, that it would be revising the framework. Agency officials in the region maintained that under the plan as approved it would be impossible to protect the region's forests from catastrophic wildfire.

Two years later, in January 2004, the regional forester announced that the agency would triple the amount of logging allowed under the original plan and abandon restrictions on the harvesting of the old-growth that had been set aside in the original plan. The agency labeled its new plan "Forests With a Future: A Campaign to Protect Against Catastrophic Wildfire."[79] This new moniker was the product of a public relations firm the agency had hired to help it sell the new plan. The firm had urged the agency to link its controversial new plan to one clear message: wildfire hazard around small communities.[80] The revised plan reduced the amount of fuels treatment that would take place in the interface from 75 to 50 percent and allowed the cutting of larger trees (raising the diameter limit from twenty to thirty inches) deeper in the forest to offset the costs of hazardous fuels reductions. In announcing the new plan the regional forester cited the impact of the 2003 California wildfires on his decision. Under the policy, he projected, during the next fifty years the total acres burned by severe wildfire would be reduced by 30 percent and the amount of old-growth forests and habitat for the spotted owl would be doubled; during the next twenty years, thinning would reduce fuels on seven hundred thousand acres near communities.[81]

Appeals and subsequent litigation were almost certain. Environmentalists were outraged and industry groups wanted more.[82] Several critics complained that the revision process had been anything but collaborative.[83]

NOTES

1. Samuel Hays provides the most cogent description of the origins and role of scientific efficiency in the Forest Service. Samuel P. Hays, *Conservation and the Gospel of Efficiency: The Progressive Conservation Movement, 1890–1920* (New York, NY: Atheneum, 1959).

For a description of how this ideology has affected the agency's institutional culture over time, see Paul Hirt, *A Conspiracy of Optimism: Management of the National Forests Since World War II* (Lincoln, NE: University of Nebraska Press, 1994).

2. Thomas C. Beierle and Jerry Cayford, *Democracy in Practice: Public Participation in Environmental Decisions* (Washington, DC: Resources for the Future Press, 2002), 3.

3. Ibid., 4.

4. See, for example, Thomas C. Beierle, "Using Social Goals to Evaluate Public Participation in Environmental Decisions," *Policy Studies Review* 16:3–4 (1999): 75–103; Sandra Davis, "Does Public Participation Really Matter in Public Lands Management? Some Evidence from a National Forest," *Southeastern Political Review* 25 (1997): 253–279; Daniel Mazmanian and Jeanne Nienaber, *Can Organizations Change? Environmental Protection, Citizen Participation, and the Army Corps of Engineers* (Washington, DC: Brookings Institution, 1979); and Hanna J. Cortner and Margaret A. Moote, *The Politics of Ecosystem Management* (Washington, DC: Island Press, 1999).

5. Cornelius M. Kerwin, *Rulemaking: How Government Agencies Write Law and Make Policy*, Third edition (Washington, DC: CQ Press, 2003), 224–225.

6. USDA Forest Service, White House Council on Environmental Quality, and U.S. Department of the Interior, "Administrative Actions to Implement the President's Healthy Forests Initiative," News release (December 11, 2002), at www.usda/gov/news/releases/2002/12/fs–0504.htm accessed December 12, 2002.

7. U.S. Congress, Republicans of the House Resources Committee, "Resources Chairman, Forest Subcommittee Chairman and Members Laud White House Forest Management Reforms," News release, December 12, 2002.

8. Mike Allen and Eric Pianin, "Bush Sets Rules to Speed Logging in U.S. Forests," *Washington Post* (December 12, 2002), A-1.

9. Katherine Q. Seelye, "Bush Proposes Change to Allow More Thinning of Forests," *New York Times* (December 12, 2002), at www.nytimes/com/2002/12/12/politics accessed December 12, 2002.

10. USDA Forest Service, *Forest Planning in the Future: Planning Critique Recommendations* (Washington, DC: USDA Forest Service Policy Analysis Staff, 1990). A summary of the 11-volume document in the critique is contained in Gary Larsen et al., *Synthesis of the Critique of Land Management Planning, Vol. 1* (Washington, DC: USDA Forest Service Policy Analysis Staff, 1990).

11. *Citizens for Better Forestry v. USDA*, No. C-01-0728-BZ (N.D.Calif), filed February 16, 2001; and *American Forest and Paper Ass'n v. Veneman*, No. 01-CV-00871-TP (D.D.C.), filed February 23, 2001.

12. 67 *Federal Register* 235, *National Forest System Land and Resource Management Planning*, Proposed Rule (December 6, 2002), 727–772.

13. Matthew Daly, "Bush Plan to Streamline Forest Rules Nears Completion" (2003), at www.enn.com/news/2003–09–10/s_8273.asp accessed September 10, 2003.

14. 67 *Federal Register* 235, *National Forest System Land and Resource Management Planning; Diversity Options Workshop*, Proposed Rule, Notice of Workshop (December 6, 2002), 72816.

15. Meridian Institute, *Summary Report, Workshop on Options to Provide for Diversity of Plant and Animal Communities in Land and Resource Management Planning* (Conducted by the U.S. Department of Agriculture, Forest Service, and facilitated by the Meridian Institute, 2003), at www.fs.fed.us/emc/includes/summary/diversityoptionsworkshopsummary030317.pff accessed April 5, 2004.

16. 67 FR 235 at 72783.

17. Ibid., at 72804.

18. There is an extensive literature in public administration and public policy related to the concept of accountability. See, for example, Robert D. Behn, *Rethinking Democratic Accountability* (Washington, DC: Brookings Institution Press, 2001); Nancy C. Roberts, "Keeping Public Officials Accountable Through Dialogue: Resolving the Accountability Paradox," *Public Administration Review* 62:6 (2002): 658–669; Barbara S. Romzek and M. J. Dobnick, "Accountability in the Public Sector," *Public Administration Review* 47 (1987):227–238. Nancy Manring questions the wisdom of replacing appeals as an instrument of accountability before a more thorough assessment of how collaborative forest planning will actually evolve. Nancy Manring, "From Postdecisional Appeals to Predecisional Objections: Democratic Accountability in National Forest Planning," *Journal of Forestry* 102:2 (2004): 43–47.

19. Executive Office of the President, *Implementing the President's Management Agenda for E-Government* (Washington, DC: U.S. Government Printing Office, April 2003), 2–4.

20. Executive Office of the President, "OMB Accelerates Efforts to Open Federal Regulatory Process to Citizens and Small Businesses," News release (May 6, 2002), at www.omb.gov accessed December 19, 2003.

21. 67 FR 235 at 72803.

22. Matthew Daly, "Forest Service Rejecting Some E-Mail Comments About Rule Changes," *San Francisco Chronicle* (April 25, 2003), at www.sfgate.com accessed April 28, 2003.

23. Paul Rogers, "Forest Service Wants to Ignore Mass E-Mails," *San Jose Mercury News* (April 23, 2003), at www.siliconvalley.com/mld/siliconvalley accessed April 23, 2003.

24. Daly, "Forest Service Rejecting Some E-Mail Comments."

25. Electronic Frontier Foundation, Coalition Letter to the Office of Management and Budget and USDA Forest Service (September 30, 2003), at www.eff.org/Activism/Rules accessed December 19, 2003.

26. Electronic Frontier Foundation, Comment Letter to the USDA Forest Service on Proposed Rule (April 7, 2003), at www.eff.org accessed December 19, 2003.

27. Matthew Daly, "Forest Service Won't Block E-Mail" (2003), at www.newsday.com/news/politics accessed December 19, 2003.

28. 69 FR 55055, *National Forest System Land and Resource Management Planning; Use of Best Available Science in Implementing Land Management Plans,* Final Rule, Interpretation (September 29, 2004).

29. Ibid.

30. USDA Forest Service, "Forest Service Publishes Planning Rules for Better Management of National Forests and Grasslands," News Release (December 22, 2004), www.fs.fed.us/news/2004/releases/12/planning-rule.shtml accessed December 23, 2004. The final planning rules were published on January 5, 2005. 70 FR 3, *National Forest System Land and Resource Management Planning: Removal of 2000 Planning Rule,* Final Rule (January 5, 2005), 1022–1061. The proposed NEPA exclusion was published at the same time: 70 FR 3, *National Environmental Policy Act Documentation Needed for Developing, Revising, or Amending Land Management Plans: Categorical Exclusion,* Notice of Proposed National Environmental Policy Act Implementing Procedures, Request for Comment (January 5, 2005), 1062–1066.

31. Public Law 102-381, 106 Stat. 1419.

32. 67 FR 2430, *Notice, Comment, and Appeal Procedures for Projects and Activities on National Forest System Lands,* Proposed Rule (December 18, 2002).

33. 68 FR 107, *Notice, Comment, and Appeal Procedures for National Forest System Projects and Activities,* Final Rule (June 4, 2003), 33581–33602.

34. Jason N. Kutak, Society of American Foresters letter to USDA Forest Service Appeal Rule Content Analysis Team (February 18, 2003).

35. Susan Jane M. Brown, Gifford Pinchot Task Force letter to USDA Forest Service Appeal Rule Content Analysis Team (February 18, 2003).

36. 68 FR 107 at 33582.

37. Ibid., at 33583–33595.

38. 69 FR 6, *Predecisional Administrative Review Process for Hazardous Fuel Reduction Projects Authorized Under the Healthy Forests Restoration Act of 2003* (January 9, 2004).

39. 40 CFR 1507.3, 1508.4.

40. "Agencies Propose to Streamline Environmental Review for Hazardous Fuel Reduction Treatments," *Fire Chronicle* 15 (January 19, 2003).

41. 68 FR 108, *National Environmental Policy Act Determination Needed for Fire Management Activities; Categorical Exclusions;* Notice (June 5, 2003).

42. USDA Forest Service, "Forest Service Proposes Simpler Process for Small, Environmentally Safe Timber Sales," News Release (January 3, 2003).

43. 68 FR 5, *National Environmental Policy Act; Documentation Needed for Limited Timber Harvest;* Interim Directive (January 8, 2003), 1026–1030.

44. 68 FR 145, *National Environmental Policy Act Documentation Needed for Limited Timber Harvest,* Notice of Final Interim Directive (July 29, 2003), 44597–44608.

45. Ibid.

46. USDA Forest Service, "Forest Service Finalizes New Policy for Small, Low-Impact Timber Sales," News release (July 29, 2003), at www.fs.fed.us/news/2003/releases/07 accessed August 4, 2003.

47. Tom Udall, "Our Publicly Owned Forests Are Being Subverted," *High Country News* (November 24, 2003), 17.

48. 43 CFR 4.470 and 43 CFR 4160.

49. 67 FR 77011 (December 16, 2002).

50. The summary of comments, synopsis, and text of the rule are at 68 FR 33793–33804 (June 5, 2003).

51. David Whitney, "In a Barrage of Press Releases, He Attacks Conservation Groups," *Sacramento Bee* (June 29, 2003), at www.libertymatters.org/newsservice/2003 accessed April 4, 2004.

52. 68 FR 1629, *Endangered and Threatened Wildlife and Plants; Guidance on Evaluating the Net Benefit of Hazardous Fuels Treatment Projects* (January 13, 2003), 1629–1630.

53. 68 FR 33806, *Joint Counterpart Endangered Species Act Section 7 Consultation Regulations;* Proposed Rule (June 5, 2003), 33806–33812.

54. Ibid., 33808.

55. Ibid., 33810.

56. J. R. Pegg, "Senators Keen to Reform Endangered Species Act," *Environmental News Service* (June 25, 2003), at www.ens-news.com/ens/jun2003 accessed June 27, 2003.

57. Ibid.

58. Ibid.

59. U.S. Fish and Wildlife Service, *Environmental Assessment for the Healthy Forests Initiative Counterpart Regulations* (September 30, 2003), 3.

60. Ibid., 6.

61. 68 FR 236, *Joint Counterpart Endangered Species Act Section 7 Consultation Regulations;* Final Rule (December 8, 2003), 68254–68265. On March 23, 2004, the Departments of Agriculture, Commerce, and Interior announced they had signed agreements to implement the December 2003 regulations. The agreements outlined mechanisms for training USDA biologists to meet ESA requirements and for the Fish and Wildlife Service to monitor implementation of the new regulations. U.S. Department of Agriculture, U.S. Department of Commerce, and U.S. Department of the Interior, "Federal Agencies Sign Agreements to Continue Species Protection, Implement Forest Health Projects," News release (March 23, 2004).

62. Elizabeth Shogren and Richard Simon, "New Forest-Thinning Policy Drops Safeguard for Wildlife," *Los Angeles Times* (December 4, 2003), at www.latimes.com/news/nationworld accessed December 4, 2003.

63. For an exceptionally readable narrative describing the old growth issue, see William Dietrich, *The Final Forest: The Battle for the Last Great Trees of the Pacific Northwest* (New York: Simon and Schuster, 1992). For a comprehensive policy analysis, see Steven Lewis Yaffee, *The Wisdom of the Spotted Owl: Policy Lessons for a New Century* (Washington, DC: Island Press, 1994).

64. Thomas E. Tuchmann, Kent P. Connaughton, Lisa E. Freedman, and Clarence B. Moriwaki, *The Northwest Forest Plan: A Report to the President and Congress* (Portland, OR: Office of Forestry and Economic Assistance, 1996), 26.

65. U.S. District Court, Western District of Washington, "Memorandum Decision and Injunction," *Seattle Audubon Society et al. v. John L. Evans et al.,* No C89-160WD (May 23, 1991), 771 F. Supp. 1081.

66. Byron Daynes, "Bill Clinton: Environmental President," in *The Environmental Presidency,* ed. Dennis L. Soden (Albany: State University of New York Press, 1999), 259.

67. President William J. Clinton and Vice-President Albert Gore Jr., *Forest Plan for a Sustainable Economy and Sustainable Environment* (Washington, DC: White House, 1993).

For assessment of the NWFP, see K. Norman Johnson, Richard Holthausen, Margaret A. Shannon, and James Sedell, "Case Study," 85–116; Logan A. Norris, "Science Review," 117–120; Judy E. Nelson, "Management Review," 121–126; Paula Burgess and Kristen Aldred Cheek, "Policy Review," 127–132, all in K. Norman Johnson, Frederick Swanson, Margaret Herring, and Sarah Greene, *Bioregional Assessments: Science at the Crossroads of Management and Policy* (Washington, DC: Island Press, 1999). The NWFP also included a package of economic measures to help mitigate the socioeconomic impacts associated with the decline in federal timber harvest levels. For an assessment of the Northwest Economic Adjustment Initiative, see Forest Community Research, *Assessment of the Northwest Economic Adjustment Initiative* (Taylorsville, CA: Forest Community Research, 2002).

68. Andy Kerr, "Who Won the Owl War?" *Forest Magazine* (Winter 2003), 27.

69. *Pacific Coast Federation of Fishermen's Associations v. National Marine Fisheries Service,* 71 F. Supp.2d 1063 (W.D. Wash. 1999).

70. *American Forest Resources Council v. Secretary of Interior,* Civ. No. 02-6087-AA (D. Or), Filed March 2002; and *Western Council of Industrial Workers v. Secretary of Interior,* Civ. No. 02-6100-AA (D. OR), Filed April 2002.

71. Robert McClure, "Conflict Looms Over Timber," *Seattle Post-Intelligencer* (January 3, 2004), at http://seattlepi.nwsource.com/local/155179_enviroyrahead03.html accessed January 2, 2004.

72. "Internal Forest Service Memo Suggests Changes to Northwest Forest Plan," *The Forestry Source* 7:8 (August 2002), 1, 7.

73. *Douglas Timber Operators v. Secretaries of Agriculture & Interior,* Civ. No. 01-6378-AA (D. OR.), Filed December 2001.

74. The Wilderness Society, "Bush Administration Proposal Would Eliminate Northwest Forest Plan Safeguards to Protect Old Growth and Rare Species," News release (May 23, 2003), at www.wilderness.org/NewsRoom/Release accessed December 17, 2003.

75. Ibid.

76. Jack Ward Thomas, K. Norman Johnson, and Jerry F. Franklin, "In My Opinion: Dropping the Species Requirement from the Northwest Forest Plan" (July 2, 2004), at www.oregonlive.com accessed July 5, 2004.

77. USDA Forest Service and USDI Bureau of Land Management, "Agencies Amend the Northwest Forest Plan," News release (March 23, 2004), at www.fs.fed.us/ACSSMpressrelease.doc accessed April 4, 2004.

78. Dale N. Bosworth, *Decision for Appeals of the Record of Decision for the Sierra Nevada Forest Plan Amendment and Its Final Environmental Impact Statement* (Washington DC: USDA Forest Service, November 16, 2004), at www.fs.fed.us/emc/applit/includes/woappdec/sierranevada.pdf accessed April 4, 2004.

79. USDA Forest Service, *Forests with a Future: Protecting Old-Growth Trees, Wildlife and Communities in the Sierra Nevada* (2004), at www.forestsfuture.fs.fed.us. USDA Forest Service Pacific Southwest Region, "Forest Service Launches Action Campaign to Protect Old Growth Forests, Wildlife, and Communities With New Decision," News release (January 22, 2004), at www.fs.fed.us/r5/snfpa/final-seis/news012204.html accessed April 4, 2003.

80. Glen Martin, "Sierra Nevada: Forest Service Hired PR Firm to Sell Log Plan, Memo Urged Keeping Details Under Wraps," *San Francisco Chronicle* (March 10, 2004), at www.sfgate.com accessed March 11, 2004.

81. USDA Forest Service Pacific Southwest Region, *Record of Decision, Sierra Nevada Forest Plan Amendment Supplemental Environmental Impact Statement* (January 2004), at www.fs.fed.us/r5/snfpa/final-seis/rod accessed April 4, 2004.

82. California Forestry Association, "Sierra Nevada Review Established Need for a New and Effective Decision for the Sierra Nevada Forest Plan," News release (January 22, 2004) at www.foresthealth.org/Jan22PR.htm accessed April 4, 2004.

83. Cosmo Garvin, "Old-Growth Trees to Fall in the Sierra: The Forest Service Ditches a Collaborative Forest Plan in Favor of Getting Out the Cut," *High Country News* (March 1, 2004), 4.

THE SPILLOVER EFFECT

ONE OF THE REASONS WHY THIS ANALYSIS OF THE BUSH ADMINISTRATION'S FOREST POLICY agenda is valuable is that it is indicative of the major strategies used by the president to affect broader environmental policy change. The term often used to explain this political phenomenon is *spillover*, a chain of events establishing a principle that guides future policy decisions.[1] Although most policy change occurs incrementally, the passage of landmark legislation or a precedent-setting presidential decision may establish a new way of doing things that makes it difficult to reverse the new direction. Spillover may occur as a result, opening one policy window that then opens windows for change in other areas. Spillover also occurs because coalitions change and because policy entrepreneurs are encouraged to rush to a new issue once they have tasted success.

Part of the importance of establishing a new principle lies in its logic. "A precedent is set, so future arguments surrounding the policy are couched in different terms. But part of it is political: an old coalition that was blocking change is defeated, and life is never quite the same. . . . Establishing a principle is so important because people become accustomed to the new way of doing things and build the new policies into their standard operating procedures."[2]

Such is the case with President Bush's forest policy initiatives. Appeals to "common sense" and "streamlining" gained favor by framing problems and solutions in terms of process change. Having established precedent through success in one area, the administration is also using it to further change in similar policy areas involving natural resources. This process is called "appropriate category construction," when one issue, such as transportation safety, is combined with another similar problem, such as coal mine safety. "People easily move from one safety issue to the next, for instance, because they are all defined as belonging to the category 'safety.' But if coal mine safety were defined as belonging to the category of labor-management relations, then it would be much more difficult to carry over the safety reasoning."[3] House Resources Committee chair Richard Pombo (R-CA), for example, has linked the high unemployment rate in the forest products industry to government regulations and policies, an impenetrable web of red tape and lawsuits, and sensational campaigns by environmentalists, rather than to a loss of competitiveness or improved (and less-labor intensive) harvesting and manufacturing technology.[4] As this chapter will show, the Bush administration is now relying upon concerns about disputes and delays, frivolous lawsuits, and environmental extremists to construct other policy categories that also call for process change.

Many environmental policy changes are being debated as this book goes to press, but it seems clear that "old" principles and precedents, like enhancing public participation in natural resource decision making, are in the process of being replaced by "new" principles related to streamlining administrative procedures. The "environmental extremism" and "paralysis by analysis" rhetoric used to gain support for the president's Healthy Forests Initiative is also being used, for instance, to characterize the need for change in policies related to natural gas production, mining, grazing, endangered species, and a host of other actions. When issues such as grazing on public lands or reform of the Endangered Species Act are couched in similar phraseology, change is more palatable than framing the topics as opening more sensitive public lands to ranchers and miners or reducing protection for popular animals.

A RETURN TO RHETORIC

In Chapters 1 and 4, we explored the ways in which language and rhetoric could be used successfully not only to frame the forest policy debate over administrative appeals but also to show how stakeholders could do so without providing credible data to corroborate their claims. The strategy has been so successful that it is being used repeatedly in other natural resource policy debates. Two areas where this is exemplified are in energy and mining policy and grazing management.

ENERGY AND MINING POLICY

During the 107th Congress, members of the House Committee on Resources pushed energy legislation through the House and Senate, which included provisions related to the need for energy security, the potential collapse of the airline industry because of high fuel prices, and more than thirty other topics. The measure failed to gain support in conference and subsequently died at the end of the session. But the importance of energy as an issue flourished as prices for gasoline and natural gas skyrocketed. Instead of focusing on national security and oil importation from the Middle East, the administration and Republican members of Congress began to use the same terminology and carefully crafted rhetoric that they used in the healthy forests debate—terminology and rhetoric that emphasized process. As Rep. Pombo noted, "It is imperative that we act now to fix a system that has been broken for many years. We need to pass a common sense energy bill and deliver it to the President this year so that we can begin to address the energy security concerns we have neglected for so long."[5]

Rep. Pombo seemed to take seriously his role as rhetorical leader when he became chair of the House Resources Committee in January 2003. He gained a reputation for using inflammatory language in what the legislative director of the group Earthjustice terms "Pomblastes." Starting in June 2003, Pombo used the House Resources Committee as a platform for a series of press releases attacking the League of Conservation Voters and the Sierra Club. He called the Pew Oceans Commission's $5.5 million report on the health of the nation's coasts "a coffee table picture book."[6]

One of the more creative press releases was an account of what Pombo termed "radical environmental lawsuits," parodying a MasterCard advertising campaign that toted up various charges for items. Pombo listed—without documentation— where taxpayers had paid attorneys' fees, the average award per case, and "the most obscene taxpayer award for radical environmental lawyers' fees." Instead of ending the account with the MasterCard tagline, "priceless," Pombo wrote, "Filing frivolous lawsuits against the United States and getting rich off the American taxpayer: SHAMELESS."[7]

In July 2003, while congressional hearings over the Healthy Forests Initiative were still underway, Rep. Pombo announced that he had asked the General Accounting Office to conduct an inventory and report of all administrative appeals and judicial litigation that delayed critical energy exploration and production projects in the United States. As had been the case with appeals and litigation of Forest Service projects, Pombo clearly sought to use data and media coverage of government studies to bolster the case for change. The language Pombo used in warning about "the current natural gas crisis" was strikingly similar to accusations made against environmental groups accused of holding up projects dealing with hazardous fuel reduction.

> Expert testimony at several Congressional oversight hearings confirms that critical energy projects are often delayed by unnecessary appeals and litigation. The GAO study will identify the litigants, the number of cases, and the federal laws at issue in these cases. This data will help Congress assess the economic impact of these suits, both on the energy market and on the consumer, as we continue to examine the roadblocks in getting our energy supplies to market in America.[8]

Pombo's news release went on to state that Congress and federal agencies had failed to update old regulations. "This has led to unnecessary, perhaps even frivolous, legal challenges and appeals that negatively impact supply. . . . This study will help us identify part of the problem."[9]

Other members of Congress joined the rhetorical bandwagon as part of the House Task Force for Affordable Natural Gas (TFANG). In its September 2003 report on causes of the natural gas shortage, impact of natural gas prices on the U.S. economy, and ideas to encourage a stable supply of natural gas to ease prices, TFANG focused on process and familiar rhetorical phrases. The report referred to "numerous overlapping environmental regulations," "administrative land use decisions," and "numerous lawsuits filed by opposition groups from the environmental community" that tied up projects "for months or years and significantly increase the cost of natural gas to the consumer."[10]

Without citing any data to support the report's claims, TFANG noted, "Despite mountains of evidence to the contrary, radical environmentalists continue to bang the same old drum that we can't produce energy and still protect our environment. . . . There is also a shortage of common sense that is preventing us from developing rational government policies that will enable us to get access to our natural gas resources and deliver them to the American people and our economy."[11] The verbiage was straight out of the Frank Luntz playbook described in Chapter 1. When asked about the Luntz recommendation that Republicans carefully choose the words they use in an effort to portray environmentalists as extreme and Republican proposals as "common sense," Pombo agreed. "Language is important," he said. "That's one of the things I tell my staff. We have to distinguish between those who care about the environment—and most people consider themselves environmentalists—and fund-raising organizations that portray themselves as environmentalist groups. Their job is to scare people into giving them money."[12]

In a March 2004 oversight hearing of the House Subcommittee on Energy and Mineral Resources, the chair, Rep. Barbara Cubin (R-WY), accused "organizations whose goal is to thwart economic development in our country" of working with the Environmental Protection Agency to stop projects that would bring jobs to local communities. She stretched the connection to contend that "[t]wo politically driven factors stand out as the principal drivers behind the loss of these domestic jobs to foreign countries, they are—restricted access to areas prospective [sic] for energy and mineral development, and delays built into the permitting process. . . . Important sectors of our economy are forced overseas because of long lead times needed to acquire the appropriate operating permits, permitting delays, and frivolous lawsuits."[13] In effect, she was accusing environmental groups of contributing to the outsourcing of American jobs overseas.

Subcommittee witnesses echoed the same phrases that had been used in describing the problems with existing forest policy. One testified that Montana had lost thousands of blue collar jobs in mining, logging, sawmills, and energy production because "the U.S. Forest Service had been unable to manage the forest due to appeals, litigation, and analysis paralysis." One mine that had spent more than $100 million and almost fifteen years in the permitting process could not move ahead because "they still face a litany of lawsuits brought by extremist groups before they can begin operating."[14] Another witness, a former BLM official, spoke of problems with NEPA analysis requirements, which led to "additional extensive delays and uncertainties for development projects."[15] A mining consultant added that there were good mining projects left in the country, but investors have avoided the United States to explore and develop elsewhere.

> It is predominantly a function of the unconscionable lead time required to get a project up and running so that it can generate a return for its investors. The bureaucratic process and the mechanisms currently in place to catalogue environmental influences and to recognize public opinion have evolved as horrendously inertial influences. . . . Until the permitting process and the attendant regulatory protocols have been streamlined and made more time sensitive, the mining industry will continue to lose investors and the attendant jobs and revenues that the business creates.[16]

The rhetorical battle eventually found its way to the 2004 presidential campaign after Democratic candidate John Kerry was quoted as saying, "That black stuff is hurting us," referring to oil. Rep. Cubin, in a House Resources Committee press release, stated that "[t]he American people deserve a president who isn't a hostage to the radical environmental community and who knows that what's hurting us is red tape and frivolous environmental litigation—not American oil."[17]

Grazing Management

In the western United States, conflicts over grazing management on the 160 million acres of public lands deemed suitable for livestock attract as much debate as timber battles in the Pacific Northwest. Three major statutes—the 1934 Taylor Grazing Act, the 1976 Federal Land Policy and Management Act, and the Public Rangelands Improvement Act of 1978—are responsible for the myriad of rules that regulate public lands grazing. The last major change to regulations occurred in 1995. When the policy window opened for major changes to grazing policy in 2003, the administration worked quickly to develop reforms using many of the same tactics that were concurrently being used in the healthy forests debate.

On March 3, 2003, the Bureau of Land Management published an Advance Notice of Proposed Rulemaking and Notice of Intent to Prepare an Environmental Impact Statement, announcing its intention to revise rules governing the administration of livestock grazing.[18] The proposal would amend the Rangeland 1994 and 1995 rules changes adopted under the Clinton administration and included a wide range of regulatory changes. Among them were provisions considering ways to streamline the grazing decision appeal process and limit public participation. No evidence was provided, however, to explain what problems the BLM had encountered and why change in the process was needed. There were no data on the number of appeals or analysis of how they affected the overall decision-making process. The proposal also contained dozens of other issues that were sure to gather significant attention, including performance requirements for permit renewal, definitions of who is qualified for public lands grazing use, and criteria covering range improvements like fencing, livestock ponds, and pipelines.

Under the Administrative Procedure Act, persons adversely affected or aggrieved by agency action must exhaust all administrative remedies before resorting to litigation and may seek relief in a federal court only when a decision is "final." Under the Bush administration's rules, grazing would be allowed to continue even though an appeal had been filed by the permittee or another party and a stay of the decision had been granted. The BLM argued this provision does not present a conflict with the "finality" requirement of the APA. "BLM believes it is necessary to allow grazing even if a stay is granted. . . . To do otherwise would potentially eliminate grazing and deny a user the ability to graze the lands for years awaiting an administrative decision."[19]

Environmental groups immediately criticized the reform proposal, especially the sections related to the public's role. A Forest Guardians' press release noted, "This is yet another blatant attempt by the Bush Administration to curtail the ability of the public to participate in decisions affecting our public lands."[20]

Earthjustice officials commented, "The administration continues to use misleading language to try to make the public believe that weakening environmental protections is somehow beneficial. As usual, the details of the proposed rule tell a different story."[21] Defenders of Wildlife responded by arguing, "These rules take the public out of the management process, in complete contradiction to the Secretary of the Interior's commitment to the four Cs—Communication, Consultation, Cooperation in the service of Conservation."[22]

Four public scoping meetings were held in March 2003 in Albuquerque, Billings, Reno, and Washington, D.C., and by July 2003 the BLM had received more than eighty-three hundred comments. The agency said that most were form letters, with only about thirty-five containing "substantive comments." Among those who responded, the Oregon Natural Desert Association stated that "the present grazing decision appeal process takes an inordinate amount of time, is largely ineffective, and does not actually stop an action from going forward."[23] The group supported streamlining times and process. The Matador Cattle Company not only supported streamlining but also recommended that the BLM require an appellant to post a bond when they appeal a decision. Environmental groups tended to recommend broader public involvement rather than limiting participation, and several noted that the regulations would restrict their right to participate in the appeals process.[24]

Based on the scoping period comments and hearings, Interior Secretary Gale Norton announced the proposed grazing rule on Friday, December 5, 2003, before the Joint Stockmen's Convention of livestock owners in Albuquerque. Norton said that the new rules "will help public lands ranchers stay on the lands," noting that the proposal "recognizes that ranching is crucial not only to the economies of Western rural communities, but also to the history, social fabric, and cultural identity of these communities." The director of the BLM called the proposal "a major step forward" that would "improve the agency's working relationships" with grazing permit–holders.[25]

In the proposed rule, the sections related to public participation sounded similar to those found in the Healthy Forests Initiative. For example, the BLM sought to remove the term "interested public" from the current regulations and replace it with "affected interests," as it had appeared prior to the changes made in 1995 under Clinton. BLM officials argued that although involving the "interested public" might be more appropriate for broader land use planning processes, increased participation from the interested public in day-to-day grazing management "created more work for the BLM and resulted in substantial program-related backlogs."[26] From a practical perspective, the rule change would limit participation just as had been proposed in healthy forests regulations, and thus limit legal standing in cases where there was opposition to the agency's actions.

The draft EIS on the rule, released January 2, 2004 (a Friday), opened up a sixty-day public comment period. The document referred to the need for rule changes as reflecting issues the BLM had encountered, and little more.[27] In its proposed action alternative, the draft EIS focused on three categories.

- *Improving working relations with grazing permittees and lessees.* In this category actions would require the BLM to analyze and document social, economic, and cultural effects of proposed changes in grazing preference and incorporate them into NEPA documents; phase in changes in grazing use; provide for joint ownership of range improvements; cooperate with established grazing boards; and clarify the opportunity to provide input on biological assessments prepared under the Endangered Species Act.

- *Protecting the health of rangelands.* These changes would remove the three consecutive year limit on temporary nonuse of a grazing permit; require assessments and monitoring of resource conditions to determine how existing practices are affecting rangeland health; and provide as long as twenty-four months for BLM to propose actions after a determination that grazing practices are failing to achieve standards.

- *Increasing administrative efficiency and effectiveness.* Actions in this category would eliminate the "conservation use" permit regulatory provisions to comply with federal court rulings; expand the definition of grazing preference; modify the definition of "interested public" to ensure that only those who actually participate in the process are involved; provide flexibility to the federal government in decisions related to livestock water rights; clarify satisfactory performance determinations and the meaning of changes in grazing uses; increase certain service charges; clarify actions if a livestock owner is convicted of violating a law; and clarify that an ESA biological assessment is not a decision and therefore not subject to protest or appeal.[28]

Six public hearings on the proposed rule were held in late January and early February 2004 in Salt Lake City, Phoenix, Boise, Billings, Cheyenne, and Washington, D.C. During the meetings, agency officials noted that the proposed changes would result in administrative efficiency through more focused communications with interested persons, more timely decisions, improved cost recovery for processing actions, and improved clarity of regulations. Again, little information was provided about the problems that required these process reforms. There was virtually no evidence to support changes that environmental group representatives testified would severely restrict the public's ability to participate in decisions about how rangelands were managed.

At one hearing, a representative from the American Farm Bureau Federation explained the group's support for the rule, noting, "We support BLM's efforts to cut red tape so that more time and effort are devoted to on-the-ground improvements." The comments from a representative for the Public Lands Council and the National Cattlemen's Beef Association mentioned how removing from regulations the need to involve the interested public in many day-to-day planning and management actions would facilitate a "more rapid and efficient way to perform the management obligations of the land managers and the ranchers." One of the few who spoke in opposition to the changes in public participation, a representative from the National Wildlife Federation, warned that "[t]he result of all this will be that decisions about how our public lands will be grazed will be made in private deals between ranchers and the agency, while the public is not notified or allowed to participate in making those decisions."[29]

Because the draft EIS on the proposed rule was not published until January 6, 2004, the BLM filed a notice in the *Federal Register* on January 16 that it was extending the public comment from February 6 to March 2, 2004.[30] In addition to allowing more time for public comment, the BLM noted that it was correcting the proposed rule to conform to a provision in a new final rule published by the Office of Hearings and Appeals on December 10, 2003. That rule, discussed in Chapter 6, referred to the authority of an administrative law judge to make a grazing decision effective immediately. Corrections to the 2004 proposal were made to cross-reference the OHA rule.

A FORTUNE OF REVERSALS

One simplistic way of explaining why the Bush administration has attempted to change the direction of U.S. environmental policy is that "this is what presidents do." The legacy of Ronald Reagan, who was credited as being one of the worst presidents in terms of his record on environmental protection, contrasts with that of Bill Clinton, who had a modest, but nonetheless "green" environmental agenda. George H.W. Bush was able to claim credit for passage of the Clean Air Act Amendments of 1990; his administration was moderate in comparison to Reagan on environmental issues. Is it surprising, then, for George W. Bush, to return to the more conservative Reaganesque approach when his turn came to mold the policy agenda? Based on historical perspective, when administrations change, policies are likely to follow, becoming more conservative or more liberal depending upon which political party occupies the White House.

Although it is generally true that citizens do not vote based solely on environmental issues, it is also true that the environment has been important to people, a lesson Republicans learned in 1992 when, after taking control of the House from the Democrats, they pushed too far in easing up on environmental protection and encountered stiff opposition. Bush has gone even further and without significant political repercussions.[31] Bush's actions on cabinet appointments, judicial appointments, legislative initiatives, and administrative rulemaking are clearly aligned with the interests of business and industry and his supporters in the ranching, logging, mining, and resource extractive communities.[32]

The changes in forest policy that have accompanied the Healthy Forests Initiative are significant by themselves. But seen in the broader context of the allied changes in other areas of environmental policy, the changes are profound. George W. Bush has succeeded in what the wise use groups in Ronald Reagan's heyday failed to do. Not only has he redirected forest policy by strategically redefining processes, participants, problems, and products, but he also has reframed the entire environmental debate. This reframing is affecting the scope of public involvement in decision making as well as reestablishing the primacy of traditional resource management values.

Significant changes have taken place in the processes by which the public can challenge agency decisions. The assumptions that public participation provides opportunities for better decision making, makes decision making democratic, and results in better environmental decisions have been seriously challenged. Lawsuits and appeals challenging agency action are portrayed as largely frivolous. Delays in moving an agency's preferred alternative forward are assumed to serve no useful purpose. Lawsuits and appeals are viewed as obstacles to common sense environmental decisions and, in the case of fire, responsible for catastrophic results. Opportunities afforded by these particular participatory and oversight processes have been redefined as obstacles and problems.

Related to reducing access points for groups challenging agency decisions is increasing agency discretion. Rather than focusing on shrinking government, the conservatives of the Bush administration have concentrated on controlling the bureaucracy. They have done a superb job of ensuring that the myriad of appointees within agencies who exercise decision-making discretion share the administration's conservative pro-business/pro-industry philosophy.[33]

The appeals-fire interface enabled the Bush administration and the Forest Service to regain control of the appeals process. In the 1980s the problem was that appeals made it difficult to meet timber production targets (a result many might argue had some environmentally beneficial outcomes). The agency's attempts to remove appeals in 1992 to solve that problem were so controversial the agency ended up with a legislatively mandated appeals process, which added new problems and frustrations. Attaching appeals to the fire problem provided the opportunity for the Forest Service to gain control over something the agency, as well as other stakeholders, felt had gotten out of hand. As to whether fixing appeals will "fix" the forest is another matter, because solutions on the policy agenda that get attached to problems often are only tangentially related to a problem's root causes.

At one level, there is considerable consensus by agencies, scientists, industry, and environmental groups that something needs to be done to restore the nation's forests. Removal of dense, small-diameter trees, which are low in commercial value, is often not a contested point (although if there should be any commercial profit from such removal is a flash point for some groups). As the debate over the healthy forests legislation showed, a principal fly in the ointment is the fear that agencies will resort to industrial timber programs of the past for solving the fire problem—that is, go after the old-growth and the commercially valuable larger trees, open more roads, and use fire salvage sales as an excuse for undertaking timber harvests and road construction in roadless areas. The Bush administration has exacerbated these fears rather than alleviated them, partly because of its insistence that some timber sales will need to occur to offset the costs of fuels reduction and partly because of changes it has made to the Sierra Nevada Framework, the Northwest Forest Plan, ESA consultations, the roadless rule, and a host of other plans and regulations.

Framing wildfire issues as a problem worsened by appeals and environmentalist obstructionism may have eclipsed opportunities to develop more comprehensive policies on forest restoration as well as fire management.[34] This framing also prevented building upon the broad social consensus that exists about the need to restore forests by forcing protagonists into corners. It raised fears that whether it is forests, wetlands, or fisheries, restoration rhetoric can easily be used to greenwash a decidedly anti-environmental agenda, "rekindling the old warnings that ecological restoration would only serve to justify the destruction of what the powerful desired."[35]

As an alternative to appeals, President Bush, members of Congress, and the Forest Service desire to focus public input in pre-decisional forums. Consequently, the proposed new planning regulations replace appeals with a pre-decisional objection process. How these new processes as implemented will differ from the way the agency has traditionally sought pre-decision input is unknown. Having circumscribed appeals—which some groups believe is their best option for public involvement—what innovations will be introduced in pre-decisional processes to account for deficiencies in existing participatory and collaboration processes? Much more than restricting appeals, reducing environmental analysis and expediting projects must be done to fix the agency's long-standing problems of not being able to work effectively with the public.

The conjoining of fires, forest health, and administrative appeals on the political agenda provided a superb venue for changing the scope of public oversight, and it was consistent with the larger goal of the Bush administration of restoring the power that traditional resource users—miners, ranchers, loggers—had before the rise of the environmental movement. The administration effectively mobilized these groups, and by strategic use of rhetoric was also able to expand the issue, convincing an even larger pool of people that they and the forests would be positively affected by new policy direction. Environmentalists were unable to mobilize the broader, more diffuse, environmentally concerned public to support their positions. Thus, they lost ownership of fire and forest restoration issues.

Successfully painted as the chief culprits in delaying projects that could have saved peoples' homes, environmentalists retreated. Recognizing the need for restoration but in favor of more passive approaches and less active timber management approaches, environmentalists were left with little maneuvering ground by the Bush approach. Moreover, they saw results of their forest work totally redefined—creating ecosystem sickness rather than ecosystem health. Environmentalists were socially constructed as the culprits. In this redefinition of participants, the good guys became the bad guys. Environmentalists were "nut cases" and "evil"; loggers, the "physicians of the forest."[36] To avoid totally being painted as defenders of the status quo—that is, unhealthy forests—they moved to the interface.

The Healthy Forests Restoration Act is testimony to the partial success of the environmentalists' interface strategy in that 50 percent of HFRA-eligible projects must be in the interface. But this success might be a Pyrrhic victory. The interface has become an environmental sacrifice zone, where fuels reduction projects to "fire proof" the forest can be tolerated. In a sense, this strategy can be viewed as akin to environmentalists arguing for structural flood control projects to make the flood plain acceptable to further development.

HFRA no doubt will spur additional fuels reduction projects in the interface, not just because of the law, but because the interface is where the political problem is. In September 2004 Agriculture Undersecretary Mark Rey predicted that even if John Kerry defeated Bush in the November election, fuels reduction efforts would need to continue. The reason, he said, is that since the mid-1980s about 8.4 million homes had been added to the interface. "We've moved the equivalent of the population of California into wildland-urban interface areas . . . that raises the stakes."[37] It is also significant that although fires during the 2004 fire year burned the second largest acreage in a half-century (behind 2000), most of the fires occurred in Alaskan backcountry (burning a record for Alaska of 6.5 million acres). Without the highly visible and media-worthy interface fires, the 2004 fire year was thus considered relatively quiet.[38]

During 2004 the land management agencies treated 2.3 million acres in the wildland-urban interface. This was out of a total of four million acres treated, exceeding the goal of 3.7 million acres. Attributing the increase to the president's Healthy Forest Initiative, the Council on Environmental Quality and Departments of Agriculture and Interior noted in an October 2004 press release that the number of acres treated in 2004 tripled the number of acres treated in 2000, "with more acres than ever being treated near homes and communities."[39]

Fuels reduction targets (acres treated) have become figuratively, and perhaps even literally, the new timber targets. It remains, however, to be seen how much restoration will occur in the interface. Fuels reduction is not the same thing as restoration. Viewed in the holistic sense, restoration entails repair of entire forests; that is, the understory, the seeps and springs, the wildlife habitat, as well as the tree cover. As a result of the interface strategy, important resources (time, money, personnel) could be directed to rather conventional projects in the interface, while other legislative and administrative rule changes will make it easier for mining, grazing, and water development projects to continue to degrade backcountry ecosystems and harder for endangered species protection and wilderness values to be advanced. In this scenario, environmentalists who might be expected to argue for holistic restoration projects and protection of biodiversity in the backcountry could be politically boxed into supporting significant subsidies for the built environment. The core elements of biodiversity protection and holistic forest restoration could be pushed off to the 50 percent of HFRA projects outside the interface or to restoration activities taken outside the purview of the legal and financial framework of HFRA—if the money can be found.

Even for HFRA projects, money has already become an issue. Although the act authorizes an additional $760 million, not all dollars budgeted by the administration for fuels reduction is "new" money; it includes dollars taken from existing agency programs. The "new" money versus "old" money issue has increased concerns that watershed, wildlife, and fisheries projects as well as rural revitalization programs may be raided for fuels reduction dollars. As noted above, a shortage of money will also invariably provide justification for cutting larger trees to help offset costs.

At least one observer has dubbed HFRA a twenty-million-acre experiment.[40] The fate of the experiment and its on-the-ground ecological results will depend largely on how it is funded and implemented, and how other rule changes made, or yet to be proposed, under the auspices of the Healthy Forests Initiative are exercised in relation to HFRA. Most importantly, it will depend greatly on the tone and direction of political leadership exerted by the president and his administration in the next four years.

HFRA implementation also will be affected by spillover events. While the administration and environmental organizations were engaged in the fight over the healthy forests legislation and rules, numerous other rules and regulations in the environmental arena were moving forward. The fact that so many proposed regulations and legislative initiatives were under consideration made it difficult for both supporters and critics to keep up with the barrage of *Federal Register* notices, public hearings, and comment periods. Several environmental organizations complained that as soon as they finished submitting comments on one rule or EIS, they were already behind on several others due at almost the same time. The administration, on the other hand, had the advantage of relying upon different members of Congress and agency officials to shepherd legislation through dozens of hearings that were often held simultaneously or in different regions of the country. Some environmental groups were able to piggyback their comments on one another to leverage their coverage and clout. Others admitted they simply were using a triage approach, taking on the most time-sensitive issues and hoping that other organizations would pick up the slack. Organizations siding with the administration could be confident that there would be a place at the table for them, literally and figuratively.

The Bush administration's emphasis on process and streamlining decision making has enabled the administration to make a sweeping set of substantive changes across the board in the environmental policy arena. The first term of George W. Bush was anything but environmentally friendly. There has been a rollback of environmental standards and regulations. Not only has there been a reversal of fortunes, but there has also been a fortune of reversals.

NOTES

1. Ernst B. Haas, *The Uniting of Europe* (Palo Alto, CA: Stanford University Press, 1968), 291–299.

2. John W. Kingdon, *Agendas, Alternatives, and Public Policies,* Second edition (New York: Longman, 2003), 191.

3. Ibid., 193.

4. Jenny Hawkins, "Resources Committee Examines Issues Affecting Jobs in Forest Industry," *The Forestry Source* (March 2004), 7.

5. Opening Statement of Hon. Richard Pombo, House, Committee on Resources, Oversight Hearing on Enhancing America's Energy Security (March 19, 2002), at www.resourcescommittee.house.gov/archives accessed April 4, 2004.

6. David Whitney, "In a Barrage of Press Releases, He Attacks Conservation Groups," *Sacramento Bee* (June 29, 2003), at www.libertymatters.org accessed April 4, 2003.

7. House Resources Committee, "A Priceless Look At Radical Environmental Lawsuits During the 1990s," News release (June 4, 2003), at www.resourcescommittee.house.gov/Press/releases/2003 accessed April 4, 2004.

8. Rep. Richard Pombo, "Natural Gas Task Force Co-Chair Pombo Requests GAO Study on Roadblocks to Energy Production," News release (July 21, 2003), at www.house.gov/resources/press/2003 accessed July 22, 2003.

9. Ibid.

10. U.S. House, Task Force for Affordable Natural Gas, Report (Washington, DC: U.S. House of Representatives, September 2003).

11. Ibid.

12. Whitney, "In a Barrage of Press Releases, He Attacks Conservation Groups."

13. Opening Statement of Rep. Barbara Cubin, House, Subcommittee on Energy and Mineral Resources, Oversight Hearing on Minerals and Energy: Outsourcing American Jobs Overseas (March 3, 2004), at www.resourcescommittee.house.gov/archives accessed March 18, 2004.

14. Testimony of Terry L. Andreessen, House, Subcommittee on Energy and Mineral Resources, Oversight Hearing on Minerals and Energy: Outsourcing American Jobs Overseas (March 3, 2004), at www.resourcescommittee.house.gov/archives accessed March 18, 2004.

15. Testimony of Carson W. Culp Jr., House, Subcommittee on Energy and Mineral Resources, Oversight Hearing on Minerals and Energy: Outsourcing American Jobs Overseas (March 3, 2004), at www.resourcescommittee,house.gov/archives accessed March 18, 2004.

16. Testimony of Donald K. Cooper, House, Subcommittee on Energy and Mineral Resources, Oversight Hearing on Minerals and Energy: Outsourcing American Jobs Overseas (March 3, 2004), at www.resourcescommittee.house.gov/archives accessed March 18, 2004.

17. Critics contended that members of the House Resources Committee were using the newly revised committee Web site as a platform for campaign politics. House Committee on Resources, "That Black Stuff Is Hurting Us," News release (2004), at www.resourcescommittee.house/gov/Press/releases/2004 accessed April 4, 2004.

18. 68 FR 9964–66 and 10030–10032 (March 3, 2003).

19. Ibid.

20. Forest Guardians, "Interior Department Proposes Weakening Environmental Standards for Grazing on Public Lands," News release (March 3, 2003), at www.fguardians.org/news accessed December 9, 2003.

21. Earthjustice, "Bush Administration Proposes Weakening Grazing Rules," News release (December 5, 2003), at www.earthjustice.org/news accessed December 9, 2003.

22. Ibid.

23. Bureau of Land Management, "Appendix C: Summary of Scoping Comments" (2003), at www.eplanning.blm.gov/us accessed April 6, 2003.

24. Earthjustice, "Bush Administration Proposes Weakening Grazing Rules."

25. U.S. Department of Agriculture, Bureau of Land Management, "Interior Secretary Announces Proposed Grazing Rule That Would Improve Grazing Management, Help Continue Public Lands Ranching," News release (December 5, 2003), at www.blm.gov/nhp/news/releases accessed December 9, 2003.

26. Ibid.

27. U.S. Department of Agriculture, Bureau of Land Management, Public Hearing to Receive Comments on the Draft Environmental Impact Statement on the Proposed Grazing Rule (February 5, 2004), at www.blm.gov/grazing/transcripts accessed April 5, 2004.

28. U.S. Department of Agriculture, Bureau of Land Management, Executive Summary, *Proposed Revisions to the Grazing Regulations for the Public Lands/Draft Environmental Assessmen.* (January 2, 2004), at www.eplanning.blm/gov/us_grazing accessed April 5, 2004.

29. Public Hearing to Receive Comments.

30. 69 *Federal Register* 11, 2559–2560 (January 16, 2004).

31. For a discussion of Bush's anti-environmental actions during his first two years in office in the areas of air pollution, climate change, and toxics remediation and the lack of political impact, see Maurie J. Cohen, "George W. Bush and the Environmental Protection Agency: A Midterm Appraisal," *Society and Natural Resources* 17 (2004): 69–88.

32. Tom Brune, "Staffing from the Right," *Newsday.com* (2004), at ww.newsday.com/nes/politics accessed October 15, 2004. According to one public administration scholar quoted in the story, "The Bush people have vetted every candidate for every agency, down to the least important appointee to the least important agency. . . . They ask the hard questions. . . . If a candidate does not believe in their agenda, he is not going to be appointed." Another analyst commented that the president has appointed one of the most conservative and business-friendly administrations since the administration of Calvin Coolidge. See also Tom Brune, "Many Agencies Headed by Industry Veterans Who Are Watering Down Regulations," *Newsday.com* (October 10, 2004), at www.newsday.com/nes/politics accessed October 15, 2004.

33. Ibid.

34. Jerry F. Franklin and James K. Agree, "Forging a Science-Based National Forest Fire Policy," *Issues in Science and Technology Online* (Fall 2003), at www.issues.org/issues/20.1/franklin.html accessed February 26, 2004.

35. Dave Egan, "Wake Up, We're Being Green-Washed," *Ecological Restoration* 22:3 (2004):165–166, at 166. This editorial expressed concerns about the use of restoration rhetoric to greenwash an anti-environmental agenda that disregards important oversight and public participation processes. For the importance of public participation in restoration specifically, see Eric Higgs, "What Is Good Ecological Restoration?" *Conservation Biology* 11:2 (1997): 338–348; and R. Bruce Hull and David P. Robertson, "The Language of Nature Matters: We Need a More Public Ecology," in Paul H. Gobster and R. Bruce Hull, eds., *Restoring Nature: Perspectives from the Social Sciences and Humanities* (Washington, DC: Island Press, 2000), 97–118.

36. Comments on environmentalists by Rep. John Shaddegg (R-AZ) at an Arizona forest health rally. "Forest Health Is Focus of Rally, *Arizona Republic* (March 25, 2003). Comments on loggers attributed to Governor Judy Martz (R-MT) at the Montana Wood Products Association annual meeting. Sherry Devlin, "Logging Talk Alarms Conservationist," *Missoulian* (August 30, 2002), at www.missoulian.com accessed September 1, 2002.

37. Tim Heardon, "Forest-thinning Plan Lauded," *Record Searchlight News* (September 22, 2004), at www.redding.com/redd/nw_local/article/0,2232, REDD_17533_3200621,00/html accessed September 22, 2004.

38. Patrick O'Driscoll, "Wildfires: All Quiet on the Western Front; Rain, Low Temps Reduce Fire Danger," *USA Today* (September 13, 2004), A.03; "Alaska on Fire: Record 6.5 Million Acres Burned," *Forestry Source* (October, 2004), 1, 4.

39. U.S. Department of Agriculture, White House Council on Environmental Quality, and United States Department of Interior, "Bush Administration Officials: Federal Land Managers Set Record-Level Accomplishments of President's Healthy Forests Initiative," News release (October 12, 2004). An interagency web site at www.healthyforests.gov contains the agencies' reporting system for hazardous fuels reduction projects.

40. Michael Goergen, Executive Director, Society of American Foresters, personal communication.

INDEX